SLEEPING AROUND

CHALLENGING MY COMFORT ZONE

Mary L. Peachin

Palmetto Publishing Group
Charleston, SC

Sleeping Around
Copyright © 2020 Peachin Adventure
All rights reserved

Cover photo: Phares K. Weis III
Editor: Judy Carlock
Photo credits: Mary L. Peachin, Bill Kimball, Dave Jaskey, Rocky LaRose, Patricia Gordon, Suzanne Peachin, Jeffrey Peachin, Todd Martin, Matty Smith, Patagonia River Ranch, Pochy Rosario, Baja Charters, David F. Peachin, Joyce Follman, David Lovitt, Patricia Gordon

First Edition
Printed in the United States

ISBN-13: 978-0-9911981-3-9
ISBN-10: 0-9911981-3-1

Credit for this fabulous life has to be shared with my parents, brother, and especially my husband David, and children, Suzie, and Jeffrey. Not only did David get me involved in flying, diving, fishing, his support as well as that of my children allowed me to travel the world (mostly during tax season.)

Contents

Introduction

Sleeping Around is an inspirational biography of Mary's global, all seven continents, adventures. Her frequent exclamation "Defying death, once again" describes her close or dangerous encounters. Other times, Mary is happy to have experienced a challenging adventure with simply a happy ending. The intent of this book is to intrigue the reader either through armchair enjoyment or creating an inspiration or motivation to those who may feel encouraged to follow in her footsteps.

The cover photo, taken during a dive trip by Photo Editor of the late *Tucson Citizen* Phares K. Weis III, captures Mary awakening from a night's sleep on a cot outside a beachfront palapa in San Francisquito, Baja. *Sleeping Around* is not a chronicle of cruising nor is it a travelogue. While Mary has enjoyed luxurious accommodations, she has also has experienced coed bunks on dive boats, yurts in Mongolia, a filthy mosquito-infested room, during a West Nile epidemic, while being detained and then deported in Hanoi, a "penthouse" apartment in Istanbul, thatched-roof cabins in Costa Rica, sleeping bags, tents, luxurious safari-type glamps, and lodges, ranging from basic to upscale, and more.

The reader should know that Mary's learning to fly, dive, and travel solo to developing countries was not a natural inclination. It was not until she was in her 30s that she evolved into an "adrenaline junkie," when she had to overcome fear and anxiety to find the motivation spurring her adventures.

There is no pressure for the reader to follow Mary's plunging into the oceans of the world to dive with sharks, mantas, saltwater crocs, snakes, and other underwater critters. Nor is there pressure to fly or jump out of an airplane, soar, fly an ultralight, or bungee jump. If you are ambivalent about throwing a fly rod, jumping a tarpon, explore distant countries on a bicycle, or any of her other adventures, perhaps you'll feel like making an effort to learn by allowing Mary's experiences to encourage you, or perhaps, you'll simply enjoy reading about them.

Fear, concern and various levels of anxiety are common to all of us. The answer is to accept, face, and deal with it appropriately. As you become aware of your limitations or anxieties, you can climb that "wall" to overcome that challenging experience. There is always the option to pass.

If you come away from this book feeling inspired or entertained, then Mary has done a good job of sharing her adventures and a lifetime of fun. Let's hope so.

Part I.

Shark Encounters

1. Charged by an Oceanic Whitetip in the Banda Sea

White tip, Photo: Dave Jaskey

Teeth bared, the twelve-foot oceanic whitetip shark was charging at what seemed like a speed of a 100 mph. I didn't have time to panic, pray, or react. At a depth of about 60 feet, my buddy was looking at a tiny (grain of rice-size) pygmy seahorse whose tail was hooked around a reef sea fan. When seemingly inches away, my buddy looked up and clutched me as we watched the shark veer away sharply then disappeared into blue water at the same speed

We would later surmise that we were diving in such a remote area of Indonesia's Banda Sea that the shark had never seen a scuba diver. When it realized that we weren't his kind of food, he abruptly departed.

With more than 30 years of scuba diving under my weight belt, that was the worse scare I have experienced. Over the years, there was a time or two when I felt a shark was too curious and, as calmly as possibly, and with quivering thighs, I got out of the ocean.

2. Overcoming my Fear of Shark Diving

On one occasion, a Galapagos shark circled my buddy and I as we surfaced. We faced him, our backs pinned together, wondering what would happen when we reached fifteen feet to make our three-minute safety stop requirement to off-gas nitrogen. We exhaled a breath of relief into our regulators when he swam away.

Another time, in Papua New Guinea, I followed about fifty feet behind two spearfishing divers. I was confident that when they speared a fish, its struggling would attract a shark. My conclusion was correct, but I had the wrong target. The shark headed in my direction. I was alone, and I must have looked larger and tastier. Trying to remain calm, I got out of the water.

Great white shark in Guadalupe Mexico, Photo: Mary L Peachin

When I learned to dive, I was deathly afraid of sharks. During my first hundred dives or so, I kept my eyes glued to the reef rather than the open water arena where pelagics swim. Once I saw my first shark, it was a different story. I was awed by their grace. I wanted to see more, and I wanted to see the largest … a whale shark. Little did I know it would take a twenty-year global search to find them.

Learning to dive was a major challenge. After spending a weekend in San Carlos, Mexico snorkeling, I was so enthralled with the underwater world that my husband David bought me scuba certification lessons for the holidays. When it came time to learn buoyancy by jumping into the swimming pool with my tank, I was afraid. After sharing my fear with my instructor, he made arrangements for me to meet him at the pool for some "one on one" time.

A few of my concerns included a fear that the weight of the tank would prevent me from surfacing. While I was underwater, I felt claustrophobic. I would soon learn that the amount of air in my buoyancy compensator controlled my ascent. Thinking back, snorkeling was actually more claustrophobic. The snorkel mask allowed me to only view downward. I couldn't see anything to the side or behind me, nor could I view jellyfish and their floating, stinging tentacles. In shallow water, it was difficult to avoid sharp or stinging coral. Once I learned the technique of diving, I realized that it was easier than snorkeling.

Without that private lesson, I probably would never have become a scuba diver, much less travel the world visiting exotic destinations. It was two decades before I saw a whale shark. That was long after my first experience shark diving with blue and mako sharks in San Diego.

Twenty miles west of San Diego, I stood on the scuba platform of the sixty-three-foot *Bottom Scratcher*. I could see blue and mako sharks circling the boat. I signaled the chain-suited dive master that I was ready to take that giant stride into the 3,500-foot depth of the Pacific Ocean.

My "adrenaline junkie" persona superseded my role as a wife, mother, businesswoman and community volunteer. I had signed a witnessed liability release saying, "Scuba diving is dangerous, the open sea is a dangerous environment. The primary intent of the expedition is to attract dangerous and unpredictable sharks by baiting them. There may also be other animals and water conditions that are dangerous." I've signed a few releases in my time, but this one certainly got my attention. None of my family knew that I was taking this adventure. My adventure pal, Jeanie witnessed my signing the release.

Mashing tuna by hand in a milk carton, the divemaster released the chum (bait) overboard to drift with the current. When the sharks arrived, 17 minutes later (I won the time arrival betting pool), the crew lowered two steel cages into the water.

The moment of truth had arrived. Fully wet-suited with a hood, I wore an additional 25 pounds on my weight belt. The extra weight was to create negative buoyancy to make it easier to stand in the cage. Other dive gauges had been removed to prevent any tangling during entry or exit from the shark cage.

As I stood with regulator in my mouth on the dive platform, I could hear my own breathing. I knew the shark masters were monitoring my breathing as a safety precaution. During the trip to the dive site, twelve of us had made a checkout dive to practice entering and exiting the cage. Although none of us had experience with caged shark diving, we were experienced divers. No one else should attempt it.

Mark Thurlow, one of the two shark masters, did a 360 degree turn in the water to check for any sharks between the dive platform and the shark cage. I gave the OK circle hand signal, and when Mark beckoned to me, I jumped into the frigid water.

I swam twenty-five yards, descending a mere fifteen feet, to enter the shark cage. In the cold 60-degree water, I would have the opportunity to photograph sharks during two forty-five-minute dives. Most of us had previously dived with reef and nurse sharks, but not with these frenetic pelagics attracted to the cage by floating tuna chum plus dive masters holding fresh mackerel to entice sharks even closer to the cage for better close up photography.

Guadalupe, Mexico Great white shark diving, Photo: Mary L Peachin

It's difficult to explain the attraction of shark diving to non-divers. I planned this San Diego shark diving trip because I thought it would be a good opportunity to become aware of my comfort level diving with sharks – with the added safety of the cage. I was planning a trip to the Pacific Ocean's Cocos Islands, 200 miles south of Costa Rica, where I would spend a week diving with hammerhead sharks and other pelagics in open water.

As I would later discover, I was more comfortable in open water with elusive hammerheads. I preferred the freedom of swimming rather than the confinement of a cage. I didn't like that feeling or swaying in the current while I was motionless in frigid water with frenzy-baited sharks surrounding me.

Through my camera lens I observed two shark masters, wearing twenty-pound stainless steel shark suits, feed the sharks. Putting their hands and arms in the shark's mouth, they said that they felt light pressure from the gnawing teeth. When razor-sharp teeth accidentally caught on their steel-mesh-covered hands, they pushed up on the nose of the shark to release their hand.

Exiting the cage was the most frightening part of the experience. The sharks had been in a feeding frenzy for more than two hours. Headed upward, we could not see the sharks behind us. We were quickly guided by the shark master back to the dive ladder of the *Bottom Scratcher*.

I was "outed" the next day when a *San Diego Union* writer had our coincidentally shared adventure published, "A smiley grandmotherly gray-haired Tucsonan named Mary…" My friends and family knew that it had to be me.

Sharks have a horrific reputation. Many anglers have observed bloody water from a hooked fish being eaten after attracting a shark during the fighting frenzy. The tell-tale spread of blood drifts as the fishing line goes slack. The fin of the shark slithers like a snake as it cuts through the swells of the ocean.

Scuba diving with sharks is not for everyone. After their first experience, the divers typically begin scanning from the reef into the deep, blue water. The diver is searching for a glimpse of the "big stuff," open water pelagics like sharks, whales, and mantas. The shark cage diving with blue and mako sharks was a heart-thumping, frigid-water, cage-sharing memory of anxious moments spent while being transfixed by the graceful beauty of the sharks.

3. Whale Sharks Migrations off Isla Holbox, Mexico and La Paz, Baja

Mary Swimming with Holbox whale shark, Photo: Dave Jaskey

Having experienced the more dangerous shark diving requiring cages, I was ready to pursue my dream of seeing a whale shark. It was an unsatisfactory twenty-year search, one of those "you should have been here last week experiences."

Many dive operators knew to call me when a pod was heading in their direction. Marc Bernardi, then owner of *Aquatic Adventures*, remembered. After hearing his dive groups had encountered whale sharks, I was on his next dive trip to the Galapagos. Near Darwin's Arch, my first whale shark experience simply whetted my appetite. In strong current, wishing I had a reef hook attached, I clung to a 60-foot reef as barnacle bit through my gloves. Like a shadow, a whale shark momentarily appeared before swimming out of sight. It was an exhilarating, but brief sighting.

Then my *Chicken Divers* group got wind of a migration off the Yucatán.

My friends Bill, David, Jan and I visited Isla Holbox during the summer heat of August. Snorkeling, no scuba diving, is the requirement to being in the water with whale sharks as well as humpback and other whales. They are frightened by the sound of regulator bubbles.

We went to Isla Holbox simply for the thrill of observing and taking photographs. Whenever several sharks approached, two of us, the limit required by Mexican law, took turns quietly sliding into the 79-degree water. Visibility ranged from 25-30 feet, enough to give us a great view, but not enough to capture the shark's entire image on our digital and video equipment. We each made at least half a dozen entries, lasting up to fifteen minutes each.

Giant manta Holbox, Photo: Bill Kimball

Entering directly in front of whale shark's path, I peered into its approaching mouth. A few feet away, its eyes appeared to still be checking me out. The surface boiled with bait fish.

As many as sixty whale sharks moved slowly, mouths agape, in these plankton rich waters. Some fed in circles, giving us a second or even a third encounter. We had close up views of attached remoras dining on their skin parasites. Schools of sardines, a frenetic bait ball breaking the surface, gobbled anything escaping the shark's gaping mouth. Cobia, playing the role of pilot fish, kept pace with the shark's strong strokes. We never had to wait to find the next whale shark.

Viewing whale sharks from the boat was almost as exciting. It was thrilling to watch my buddies share this incredible experience. The higher vantage view from the boat allowed us to shout, whenever we spotted a shark heading their direction, or one coming a direction that they could intercept, "swim to your left or right."

Comfortable as the polka-dotted creatures—the locals call them dominoes—appeared (they appeared to be barely moving), their strong bodies swept through the water faster than we could fin. The current from their sweeping tails often pushing us forcefully through the water. After a tail hit Jan's leg, she wore her bruise like a badge of honor.

One whale shark snuggled along the side of the boat like it wanted to be petted—could I resist giving it a gentle pat? Did I?

Sometimes we heard excited whoops and hollers echoing across the water from passengers on other boats. When the afternoon wind picked up, the plankton descended deeper with the sharks following their food source. We returned to shore.

Publishing the story anonymously in *Undercurrent*, I never anticipated the story would be reprinted all over the world. The Mexican government agency *SEMARNAT* made their rules even more strict. When we returned the following year, we were rewarded by giant mantas co-mingling with the whale sharks — and unfortunately, a mass of other people. The *Undercurrent* article had brought thousands of divers, Mexican pangas from Isla Mujeres, and stricter government regulations.

Whale Sharks in La Paz

Baja Charters owner Terry Neal sent me a message about a juvenile whale shark migration in La Paz, Baja. Stating that his company offered the premier Baja whale shark expedition, I signed up for five days. A personable American expat, Terry cautioned me about the chilly, windy conditions in December.

Tucson is not an easy flight departure point so I flew to San Diego then *Ubered* to Tijuana's CBX bridge, one that crosses the US-Mexico border into Tijuana's relatively new airport. Mexican airlines offer non-stop flights at cheaper fares.

Scooping plankton, the juvenile whale sharks of La Paz seemed to be swimming vertically in circles. The 25-foot-long polka-dotted wonder was even more memorable because he had a row of remoras on his tail. I pinched myself, forgot about being chilled, and wondered if I was dreaming. Everywhere I looked there were whale sharks, appearing suspended in the water. This was a dream of every diver, would I be lucky enough to have five days of this experience?

Between the Mexican government agency *SEMARNAT* and high wind closure of the Bay, I had to be satisfied obeying their restrictive 30 minutes in the water. All I needed to do was stay out of the shark's path. Not because I might get injured, but because rules about not touching the whale sharks are strictly enforced by patrolling boats. It was a rude awakening to my incredible dream, but that agency rules the Bay of La Paz.

For divers, snorkeling with whale sharks can be equivalent to summiting Mount Everest for climbers. When skies are sunny, wind calm, and waves flat, plankton levels rise, and the first 17 (only) boats, ready and loaded with snorkelers, are hoping for the opportunity to swim with these gentle giants for a mere half-hour.

La Paz juvenile whale shark, Photo: Baja Charters

Staying in the zone, but without snorkelers in the water, is permitted for two hours, but that's not quite the same.

The Bay's whale shark population, estimated at plus-or-minus 125, are primarily juveniles. La Paz's weather conditions can be as unreliable as those on the peak of Everest — you can win big, but you can also lose. And that huge differential will either put you on top of the world or leave you incredibly disappointed.

The *Island Cat* is a 54-foot-long by 30-foot-wide Northwest catamaran that cruises between La Paz and Cabo San Lucas. The cabin has a nice-sized kitchen and dining table, plus toilets and two hot showers.

The Bay motor from the dock to zone 1 is about 30 minutes. That area is the only one where 4 people are allowed in the water for the limited 30 minutes. They can stay in zone 2 and 3 for two hours, without being in the water.

The zones are clearly marked to licensees, but not to visitors. We transferred from the luxurious catamaran to a panga to search 15 minutes before finding the whale sharks. There were so many!

In the 50-foot visibility, I could see huge open mouths approaching me as they scooped plankton through their baleen. Trevally pilot fish escorted them, while massive schools of anchovies huddled along their sides, seeking protection from jacks that darted in and out to feast on them.

La Paz, home to a cluster of low-lying hotels and a growing number of snowbird and ex-pat retirees, sits on perpetually-tanned flatlands along the Sea of Cortez. A land spit known as El Mogote, covered entirely by housing developments, parallels La Paz' shore, with a drop-off reaching 30 feet. Currents sweep plankton from the bottom of the Sea of Cortez, meaning the whale sharks have a great source of food in this protected harbor. Females also seek these shallow waters to give birth. This event has yet to be observed by humans.

The whale sharks we saw were estimated to be about 20 years old. After our exciting encounter, Chef Scott blended margaritas for everyone, plus chips with salsa and guacamole. A full open bar was also an option. I wish I hadn't chowed down when I found out later there was also going to be a buffet lunch of chicken and beef tacos, fresh fruit soaked in rum, more margaritas, and a chocolate cake from *Walmart* (La Paz' finest bakery.)

As the seven of us relaxed on the sundeck, we reminisced about our incredible encounter, not knowing we had experienced a record-breaking day. Captain Chris Miller reported that we snorkeled with 20 whale sharks. While we were snorkeling, the panga driver watched a humpback breech. Mariana Padilla, a University of La Paz marine biologist on board with us, shared a dorado sighting. She told us La Paz-tagged whale sharks have been found as far away as Thailand's Andaman Sea.

SEMARNAT, the Mexican government agency devoted to promoting the protection, restoration and conservation of the country's ecosystems, monitors and controls the whale sharks. It continues to tightened its grip. While there are 120 licensed boats, only the first 17 that call each morning is assigned a 30-minute time slots. If a boat is late, its departure time is delayed by three hours. The fine for not having a license in the whale shark zones is $10,000. This "iron grip" agency claims to have stopped long-lining and shark finning in the Sea of Cortez. That claim is strongly disputed by everyone I talked to in La Paz.

Returning again in 2019 with David in tow, we had a less satisfying experience. The weather was unseasonably cold and SEMARNAT closed the Bay three of the five days that we were there. While we were thrilled to see seven juvenile whale sharks or the same one seven times, this time they were cruising rather than vertically upright scooping plankton. We were in and out of the panga multiple times, and so cold, in spite of wearing wetsuits with hoods, that they gave us the tin-foil type blankets used in migrant camps.

The second trip required that the panga with snorkelers appear at the SEMARNAT dock with operator's license, donned in life jackets, and there were boats patrolling the area. No more early time slots by telephone. I realized that this incredible adventure is for those who live in the area rather than traveling long distance for an experience that is likely to be disappointing due to situations like weather and rules that are beyond control.

Part II.

Arizona Pioneer Third Generation
Granddaughter

Being a third generation Arizonan gives me a sense of great pride. The family's Arizona history began when my great Uncle Ben Levy, a healthy, strapping young man, was railroad foreman of a bull gang. He heard that Phelps Dodge was building a smelter in Douglas. Focused on his crew laying wooden ties and pounding nails to build the El Paso and Southwestern Railroad track between Cananea, Sonora and Douglas, Arizona, he thought about his brother Jacob, who owned a dry goods store in Texas.

Toiling in the heat of the day, his thoughts turned to the future. He was sure that Douglas would become a boom town. He telegraphed Jacob to pack up his dry goods business. "Come west with Mamie, it will be a great opportunity for you."

In 1903, after arduous weeks in a covered wagon on the trail from Victoria, Texas, the Levy's unloaded their worldly goods on a dusty street in the fledgling town of Douglas. Almost a decade later, on Valentine's Day, 1912, Jacob and Mamie Levy would celebrate Arizona's proclamation as the 48th state.

The Levy's had been attracted to Douglas by visions of a better life. And, Ben had been right. Copper miners needed a mercantile store. Jake and Mamie set up shop in a tent on Main Street, a prime location between the saloon and gambling hall. The store, which they named *The Red Star General Store*, offered everything from hardware to clothes. Their living quarters were in the back of the store.

After the railroad was completed in 1903, Jake persuaded Ben to join him in the business. Together, they built a masonry store front and changed the Red Star name to Levy Bros. Mamie and Jake continued to live in the back of the store following the birth of their son, Aaron, later that year.

Douglas was bustling and as mining prospered, so did the town. My cousin Jackie Levy Rosenfeld, Aaron's daughter, remembers stories her dad told her. "On payday, after time spent in the saloon or gambling hall, workers might brawl or face off with a quick draw gunfight on the dusty street. Whenever a shot was fired, Mamie would protect my dad by stashing him in the hand-operated washing tub."

During the Mexican revolution, my father Leon, born in 1913, would spend childhood evenings with Aaron watching bullets fly through the skies over the border town of Aqua Prieta. It was like kids watching fireworks on the 4th of July.

But life was not calm along the border. Francisco "Pancho" Villa was a well-known Mexican revolutionary. According to Jackie, Villa trusted the Levy brothers. "During his reign, he frequently used their safe to hide his gold."

One day in 1923, Villa asked Jacob to buy uniforms for him. Jake took the El Paso and Northeastern Railway as far as Chicago where he received a telegram stating the revolutionary had been assassinated. Returning to Arizona, he was surprised to find that Villa's men had made arrangements for him to receive, for his efforts, full payment in gold bullion.

Walter P. Douglas, son of Dr. James Douglas, developer of Bisbee's Copper Queen Mine, was one of the most powerful men in Arizona. His son and Aaron were best friends. He arranged for both boys to attend the posh Mount Clair Academy in New Jersey. After Aaron's graduation, he met and married Esther Farber. An El Paso gal, her family owned the Ciudad de Mexico department store.

Aaron and Esther, who briefly lived in a small Douglas house behind Jake and Mamie, decided to expand the business by opening a store in Tucson. A few years later, my father, Leon, would follow them to Tucson to attend the University of Arizona.

Leon became an All-American center and member of the Hall of Fame for the Arizona Wildcats. A concussion ended his football career, and college education. He had planned to go to law school.

In 1931, Aaron and Leon convinced Jacob to open a department store in Tucson. They purchased Myers and Bloom on the corner of Congress and Scott and named the store Levy's of Tucson. Little did they know that Levy's would become a Tucson retailing icon.

After Aaron died in the late 1950s, Leon saw the writing on the wall for small retailers. He sold Levy's to Federated Department Stores. The department store moved from downtown to El Con in 1960, and later added a store in Foothills Mall.

My father would not go to El Con without another anchor. Steinfeld's Department store join him, but they owned Jacome's lease. Steinfeld's would not break it to permit Jacome's to join them with a store in El Con.

The stores retained the name Levy's until my father died in 1984. The store then became "velcro a name" going from Sanger-Harris, Foley's, Robinsons-May and finally Macy's.

I worshipped my father. He was 6'4" tall, good looking and was rarely seen without being dressed in an Oxford suit and tie. Any teenager in Tucson looking for a job, who could speak English, would be hired including me who started working in the stock room at 14. My father had a scratch handicap, but old-fashioned, he didn't think women belonged on the golf course. It took me many years to change his attitude.

He also felt that the days of being an independent retailer were short lived, and that neither my brother Mike, 3 years younger (a retired stock broker living in Santa Fe), or I were capable of operating the store. At the time, I didn't agree with him, but was later grateful after owning an art gallery for 15 years. I would not have enjoyed, especially with my wanderlust, being tied down to a large retail store especially the demands of meeting his established criteria for excellent customer service. He dressed every client from Yuma, Arizona into the state of Sonora, Mexico, and he took Mexican silver as payment.

My mother, Marjorie, arrived in Tucson from South Bend, Indiana to escape asthmatic problems. Beautiful and petite, she met my father when he sold her a pair of size 4 shoes. She dressed so elegantly that the Arizona Daily Star retired their annual "best dressed" woman award after she won it multiple years. Sadly, around the age of 40, she was given a drug for an eye disease. The side effect, she became blind. She spent her remaining years requiring a driver and caregiver. When my father died in 1984, she moved permanently to their condo in La Jolla. She would die in the late 80s from Alzheimer's.

We were the first family in the Sam Hughes neighborhood to own a TV and have a swimming pool. At the same time, my father always stressed, "If your friends can't afford to go to a movie, then neither can you." I didn't realize at the time that this wisdom had been passed down from his father.

Both Jacob and Mamie died when I was a child. My time was spent participating in athletics, primarily swimming and tennis. I remember winning my first gold medal at the age of 6. My parents were having a dinner party when I snuck out to swim at nearby Himmel Park. A neighbor, who was officiating, told me, "Mary, just pretend that I'm holding a hot dog for you at the other end." Guess I enjoyed eating at a young age.

My father was also a strong believe in giving back to the community. He was a founder of many organizations: Chamber of Commerce, Tucson Airport Authority, United Way, the Conquistadors, Arizona-Sonora Desert Museum, and so much more.

He and I were the first father-daughter team on the Tucson Airport Authority. I led the way for the United Way achieving success during a 1980 $4 million campaign, and three years later, a $10 million campaign. This was a huge amount of money in Tucson. I recall being $90,000 short the next to last day of the first campaign. I was being congratulated for having such success, but to me it was a Win or Loss issue. I called in the community leaders the day before and told them that we weren't going home until we reached goal. We did!

That was in 1980 and I was named Tucson's Woman of the Year, followed by the Alexis de Tocqueville award presented by President Gerald Ford at the Kennedy Center in Washington.

During the late '70s, my father was on the Arizona Board of Regents. He hired a consultant to determine whether a medical school should be located in Tucson or Phoenix. Tucson was selected for the medical school. He knew well that the quality of education was ranked higher at the University of Arizona in Tucson than Arizona State in Tempe. I take pride in seeing my father's name on the placards of so many university buildings.

One day he met Dr. Sydney Salmon, an esteemed oncologist, working in a trailer next to the University of Arizona hospital. He told Sydney that he was going to build him a real building. I joined him with other community leaders to raise $10 million and build what they named the Leon Levy building. My father passed soon after its opening. I served as Chairman of the Board for twenty-five years until recently being named Founding Honorary Chair Emeritus.

Towards the end of dad's life, I had the opportunity to have him follow in my footsteps. I nominated him for Tucson's Man of the Year. When asked for additional references, I explained that he was a humble man. If he didn't deserve it, that would have to be the way it was. He won and acknowledged "now I am following in Mary's footsteps."

Mary Peachin with Warrior's Coach Steve Kerr at Tucson United Way Campaign

I'm proud to be the first father-daughter members of Bobcats, a University of Arizona senior, formerly men's only, honor society. My Uncle, great cousin Al Levy and husband David, (who I nominated) were also members—a five Bobcat family. I took a lot of woman-type verbal abuse those first years, but later served as its first woman president followed by first woman winner of its prestigious A.L. Slonaker award.

Following his tenure at Levy's, my dad became Honorary Chair of the Southern Arizona Bank. I would later break that glass ceiling when I became the first woman board member at Pima Savings. Then the RTC years brought some misery. We were sued for more millons that

I could imagine. Fortunately, we always operated professionally, the law suit was dropped, and was I ever relieved?

After I married David, we continued our giving back to the city with each of us serving on numerous boards. He was Chair of Tucson Medical Center at the same time I was Chair at the Arizona Cancer Center, we had our own private "town and gown" relationship.

Part III.

Loving the Sonoran Desert

4. Rattlesnake and Scorpion Critter Hunting

Diamondback rattlesnake Sonoran Desert, Photo: Rocky LaRose

When authors write biographies, they typically start from the beginning of their life to an ending point. In my case, the chapters are listed spontaneously not unlike the way I live. Some adventures have been inspired by a particular fascination with critters, others address the more interesting of my global adventures or a particular, maybe peculiar to the reader, interest.

I grew up loving the Sonoran Desert, and a lot of my time was spent admiring its fauna and critters, those that were venomous and any other type of critter. Equally interesting to me were relics left behind by the Hohokam, a prehistoric people that inhabited the area between A.D. 300 to 1400.

One of my friends, Rick, had a four-wheel jeep, packed a pistol, and he make sure I wore his extra pair of snake chaps to protect my legs. He spent every weekend searching different areas, and I benefitted from his geographical knowledge.

Every spring, when rattlesnakes were coming out of hibernation, he would take me to an *Indiana Jones*-type snake den. An event rarely observed by humans, we would watch dozens of rattlesnakes, lethargic as they woke from a winter's sleep.

Rick had a great collection of pottery shards, arrowheads, axes, metate grinding stones and other partial artifacts, very worn by time, that he was able to identify. My collection was smaller, with much of it coming from the area around my home where a major settlement had existed (it is still listed as an active archeological dig under government protection especially from vandals). I treasured pottery that still had remnants of paint on them, several metates, and a simple stone used for grinding.

Scorpion, Sonoran Desert, Photo: Rocky LaRose

While most of my hikes with Rick were on the northwest side of Tucson, my friend Jeanie and I regularly headed closer into the east side's Saguaro National Park. Exploring many unnamed game or cattle trails, an hour hike past a lesser-known entrance, we discovered a small waterfall cascading into a pool. It even had a sandy beach.

Stripping off our clothes, we skinny dipped in the cool water, then lay on the beach (where one day I adorned my crotch with a bright desert flower). We enjoyed the picnic lunch we had carried, and the unnamed waterfall became a regular destination.

At the time, I freelanced for the late *Tucson Citizen's* Outdoor Page whenever its Editor was away. And it was a page: the entire back cover of the Sports section. I never mentioned specific directions to our special swimming hole. I learned from my article about the whale sharks of Isla Holbox, that publicity could overwhelm a place with visitors.

On another trail, our cairn or marking spot was an old cattle water tank. One day, I spotted a naked man bathing. Approaching him while respecting his privacy, I learned that his name was Tom, and that he lived in a tent high in the Rincon Mountains. He came down to bathe and ride his bike one day a week to work somewhere in the city.

He was cute and Jeanie was single. She lived on a small ranch near the Park. I'm not sure if or how that relationship evolved, but shortly thereafter, we asked "Tom the Mountain Man" to take us on nighttime "critter hunts."

During the summer, especially after monsoon rains, critters come out for food and water. Some of the best places were in the wet restrooms in Sabino Canyon and along the trail up into the Catalina Mountains behind Jeanie's ranch.

We found scorpions, bugs, creatures of all kinds, and snakes. One night I stepped on a rattlesnake. Yikes! Fortunately, I was wearing boots and while rattling away, he struck. He missed me as I jumped away. That scare, however, put an end to our evening forays.

The isolation of Jeanie's ranch was great fun. There was a single road into the city. In the only memory I have of more than an inch of snow in the city, we grabbed some cross-country skis and used her road as a ski run. My thighs quivered with fear, but I couldn't miss the opportunity, so unique in our desert city.

5. Julia Squeezer the Boa Constrictor

If my gallery staff objected to my "acts of critter kindness" or other adventures, little did they imagine what would soon become a new addition to the company. (see Part XII.)

Lance, a regular client had a collection of snakes including pit vipers and venomous snakes. The latter are illegal, but he seemed to not care and was cautious. I asked if I could see his collection.

During my visit, I "bonded" with a Solomon boa constrictor. About six feet long, when my husband David came home and found me playing in the bed with the snake, he said, "Mary, it's the snake or me." Like a good wife, I chose him.

My team had no choice when Julia Squeezer came to work with me. Her aquarium tank was behind my desk. No one quit their job. I thought Julia would be easy to care for other than having to feed her live mice. There was even a snake vet near the office.

On my way to visit the vet, I stopped at my breakfast club. The women were eager to meet Julia who I had left in my car trunk. One of them asked if she could pick her up, that she was comfortable with snakes.

Julia quickly crawled through her bangle bracelet and got stuck. Scared, she turned her head and bite the woman on the hand. Snakes have an anti-coagulant so blood spilled over the parking lot. The other women became hysterical, and ran for the maintenance man hoping that he could cut off the bracelet. He was also afraid.

In the meantime, I was able to get Julia's head backed out of the bangle and put her back in her tank. That is not the end of the story.

Julia became a "man-eater." She would no longer eat her mice. They would nibble at her tail until I released them. We had mice in the office for months. I was torn, I liked seeing the mice live another day, but I didn't want the infections they could pass on to Julia. Taking her back to the vet, he planned to wait awhile before force feeding her. She was no longer an easy pet to care for.

David and I were scheduled to go on a bicycle tour, and I hate to see my now anorexic snake left behind. One of my staff volunteered to buy and feed her mice.

Sadly, Julia passed while I was away. I didn't ask what they did with her body.

6. Beady the Gila Monster

I was riding my bicycle between my home and Sabino Canyon, one of Tucson's great tourist attractions. At the time, regulations didn't allow riders after 9 a.m. and never on weekends. It was a hilly ride, with the last half-mile a steep 10 percent grade.

Gila monster, Photo: Rocky LaRose

During my childhood, after the Civilian Conservation Corps had put in seven bridges over streams, its riparian pools were my swimming destination, a place to get wet rather than do laps. As an adult, early one morning as I was grunting up that last grade, I recall a kid yelling from behind, "Hold your line, lady." Yes, he was running faster than I was pedaling.

I knew that my speed on that steep downhill would be faster than his pace on the way down. As I passed by, I asked him, "What is your mother doing today." I think he got my message.

But I have digressed. This story is about Beady.

Stout, beaded-body, red and black Gila monsters escape the heat of the day by sheltering in burrows. During the spring, I was told, they come out of their dens to mate.

As I was returning from Sabino Canyon one Sunday, a wonderful 10-mile downhill ride, I saw a small Gila monster lying in the road. Setting down my bike, I walked over for a better look at the pudgy lizard. A juvenile, it was dead, but it wasn't squished like a car had run over it. I thought, it is so rare a sight, maybe I could take it to a taxidermist and donate it to a school.

At home, I made a few calls, which led me to Arizona Game and Fish. They barked, "Don't you know what you have done is illegal? Bring it in right now!" I explained that their downtown office wasn't exactly 'geographically desirable,' and asked if they could pick it up from my midtown office the next day. My husband shook his head as I placed the critter in my freezer, my plan for the schoolchildren defeated.

The next day, several officers arrived flashing badges, scaring my clients. At the time, I owned an art and framing gallery. My office was in the building next door, the one with the lunchroom freezer.

As they left the gallery, one of my framers asked what they were going to do with the Gila monster. One of them replied, "DUMP him in the garbage."

7. Spring Flowers in the Sonoran Desert

Spring Flowers in the Sonoran Desert, Photo: Rocky LaRose

A dirt road curves from one scenic vista covered by majestic stands of saguaro to another bordering the east side of Saguaro National Park West. Signs along El Camino Del Cerro guide the hiker or horseback rider to Sweetwater trailhead. Depending on the winter's weather, this trail is just one place to admire a brilliant flower-covered desert.

Spring flowers, and the dates of their bloom, are contingent on winter temperatures combined with just the right amount of rain. For the hiker, biker, or horseback rider, timing is everything. Blooms are not consistent in different areas of the desert.

Whether you're hiking, soaring, or flying (Chapter 45) above it in an ultralight, the desert landscape is beautiful, a surprise to those who think of it as drab and dusty. What makes it so special is that this is not an annual experience. The bloom varies each year.

Even without blooming flowers, the hiking on Sweetwater Trail would be exceptional. The terrain is interesting, and one can become consumed by the beauty of its saguaros.

But when conditions are prime, hiking Sweetwater Trail can easily satisfy the wildflower nature lover. During a spring flower bloom, this area of the Sonoran Desert offers views of an incredible diversity of flowers joined by varied sizes of saguaros.

Elevation and southern sunlight exposure also deserve credit for the magnificence of this lush desert garden. The abundance of brilliant yellow brittlebush mixed with blue lupine and fuchsia penstemon line much of the trail.

After following a gently rolling ridge for about a mile, the trail crosses a wash, then begins to climb. Stone steps have been placed or carved into the hillside. Packrats nest along these stair steps, leaving signs of dried branches and the cholla spines they use to protect their nests.

As the trail rises, the Tucson Valley can be seen below along with views of the Santa Catalina Mountains. The scar of the trail on the ridge leading to King Canyon and Wasson Peak becomes visible.

Each elevation gain brings new desert flowers and cacti to enjoy. Blooming ocotillo, new pads on prickly pear, scatterings of Mexican gold poppy, more lupine, blue phacelia, fiddleneck, and paper daisy are everywhere. Apricot mallow appears to be rooted among trailside boulders.

A single yellow bloom of a prickly pear is paled by the brilliant orange color of half a dozen rare mariposa lilies. What a treat to discover this magnificent desert lily!

White stakes saying "road closed" distract from the view along the trail. Prickly pear and cholla have been planted as a warning to hikers to stay away from the less obvious "roads" that lead to open mine shafts. During the early 1900s, copper mines were excavated in this area of the Tucson mountains. The remaining shafts are a serious hazard and should not be explored.

The landscape and the terrain make Sweetwater trail very special, but it is only one of many options to enjoy Tucson's desert flowers. They can be viewed from Picacho Peak, almost halfway to Phoenix, to Saguaro National Park East and West, Sabino and Ventana canyons and many other destinations. When it's a banner year for spring flowers, hurry into the Sonoran Desert. Sadly, they are short-lived, and there next showing is unpredictable.

Saguaro National Park

"The saguaro has been described as the monarch of the Sonoran Desert, a supreme symbol of the American Southwest, a plant with personality. It is renowned for its variety of odd, all-too-human shapes, shapes that inspire wild and fanciful imaginings."

OFFICIAL MAP AND GUIDE OF SAGUARO NATIONAL PARK

Tucson is fortunate that since 1933, this extraordinary cactus has been protected within the boundaries of the east and west units of Saguaro National Park. The life of a saguaro is a struggle for survival.

According to the National Park Service, the saguaro begins its life as a shiny black seed no larger than a pinhead. One mature saguaro may produce tens of thousands of seeds in a year, as many as 40 million in its 200-year lifetime. Few of these seeds survive.

Seedlings growing under "nurse trees" like the palo verde or mesquite are the best. Nurse trees protect the seeds from intense sunlight, winter cold and being eaten by rodents, birds, and other animals. Saguaros grow better on bajadas, the gently sloping plains at the foot of desert mountains.

Growth is extremely slow and usually occurs during summer monsoons. By the end of its first year, a seedling may measure only one quarter of an inch. After fifteen years the saguaro may be a foot tall. It does not produce flowers or fruit until it is thirty years old. At the age of fifty, the saguaro may grow to seven feet. Its first branch or "arm" may sprout at seventy-five years.

By 100 years, the saguaro may have reached a height of twenty-five feet. If it survives to 150 years, the saguaro may grow to fifty feet and weigh eight tons. The bulk of the cactus is supported by a strong, flexible cylinder-shaped framework of wood ribs.

These slow growing "monarchs" symbolize the magnificence of our desert, and each one has its own personality for us to enjoy.

Part IV.

School Days: Fun, (almost) Flunking, a Master's Degree

While my father didn't teach me to play golf, he did share his love for football. In grade school, I cheered for the Wildcats in the top "coffin corner" of Arizona Stadium, paying 25 cents a game. Now, I'm a "50-yarder," I want the best seats whether it's football, basketball, softball, or any other sport or venue.

During the later '50s, when I attended Tucson High School, it was a predominantly Hispanic school. There were two other high schools in Tucson, Amphitheater and Salpointe, which later became Salpointe Catholic. Tucson High operated on two shifts, mine being 7 a.m. to noon.

I can't say that I spent a lot of time studying, but I sure had fun. I did get involved in leadership, being class vice president, but time was spent "boondocking" or drinking beer in the surrounding desert. On weekends, my friends and I went to Nogales, Mexico to drink underage on the main drag at the B-29 bar. Sometimes we went to bullfights, not so much to see the bulls (which I wouldn't watch today), but to drink beer. It is a miracle that we survived driving less than sober on Interstate 19, known as "Camino de la Muerte" or "highway of death."

I do remember, sort of, my best friend Gwynne and I going jigger to jigger along my parent's bar when they went to the airport to pick up friends. When they returned home, we ran to my bedroom as if we had been sleeping. Shortly, the room began to spin, and I was vomiting — all night long. How embarrassing when my parents went across the street to the neighbor doctor – the same one who offered the hot dog at the Himmel Park swim meet – to say, "Our daughter is drunk." He said if I didn't stop throwing up, I should go to the hospital and get hydrated. Fortunately, that wasn't necessary.

Another time, after a desert boondocker, my friends left me slumped on my front lawn. Fortunately, Gwynne's brother saw me and took me into the house. That put an end to my *over*drinking.

When it was time to apply to universities, I was rejected by Stanford and accepted to Northwestern in Chicago. New Orleanians Connie and Harry Kaufman were having dinner with my parents when I got this news. They highly recommended that I attend the late Sophie Newcomb College of Tulane University. I thought about the freezing cold Chicago weather and applied to Newcomb. Being the only applicant from Arizona, I was "geographically desirable" and accepted.

Believe me, college was the biggest wall I ever climbed. New Orleans was still segregated and the "white" and "colored" signs had a profound and negative impact on me. Then I learned, being a nice Jewish girl and proud of it, I could only join a Jewish sorority. I don't remember much about sorority rush, but I liked the Jewish gals at Sigma Delta Tau, and I was thrilled when they tapped me to join. Discrimination of any sort has never been an issue I experienced or accepted.

Even worse, I discovered that I had never learned how to study. I didn't get much of a high school education. I was miserable.

My mother had escorted me to New Orleans, taken me to the Roosevelt Hotel for a famous Ramos gin fizz, then cried when she saw my tiny shared un-air-conditioned room at Josephine Louise Hall. Then she left.

I wrote and called my parents daily. I wanted to come home. Harry Kaufman sat me down and said, "Mary, you can pack your bags and go home, or you can buckle down and consider this a challenge." By now, you can surmise that I did the latter.

Shortly thereafter, I met a football star and life became a lot more fun. Now I could sincerely root for the Green Wave, an obscure nickname based on a 1920 fight song. My maternal cousin, Charles Simon, attended Tulane, on the same campus, and he began dating my roommate Lynda, a relationship that led to a marriage of 50-plus years before he recently passed away.

We became experts in fine dining, especially at the famous French Quarter restaurants. We had our favorite waiter, Kitri, at Antoine's, and entered through their private door. When people ask me about my experience at Newcomb College, I tell them that I majored in "Bourbon Street."

In the early '60s, Bourbon Street was at its best: Elegant strippers expertly twirled tassels with their breasts, and all the great jazz players jammed. Today's souvenir and T-shirt shops can't compete.

Having poor grades, and close to flunking classes like English and Spanish, I still managed to graduate in 1958.

Like many college grads, I have no idea what I would do next. As the hot, boring summer in Tucson passed, I decided that I wanted to go to graduate school at the University of Arizona. At that time, there was no entrance exam for graduate school. I knew the Dean of Admissions, David Windsor, and we had a chat. He told me that he would give me a provisional admittance with the understanding that I would make straight A's. I accepted that challenge and enrolled in the College of Public Administration with a major in correctional administration. I wanted to be a probation officer. That didn't sit too well with my family.

My dad set up an appointment for me to meet with the warden of Florence prison. Little did I know that the time would be spent showing me every shiv, knife, and weapon used by prisoners.

Studying subjects of interest to me, I was able to maintain the required good grades. When I was assigned a presentence report of a juvenile delinquent for a judge, I could only see a "no-win" situation. The kid would become a hardened criminal in jail, and on probation he would be back in trouble soon. I switched to social work, doing an internship at Tucson's Jewish Family & Children's Services and its affiliate Handmaker Jewish Services for the Aging. There was no school of Social Work in the state at the time, but I wanted to be part of the solution for the social problems I had observed.

About eighteen months later, I had a master's in public administration.

Now what? The previous February I attended a college friend's wedding in Chicago. I really liked her new brother-in-law, and we had a date or two during the short time I was there, and then kept in touch. Days after my graduation, former Newcomb roommate Pat Cohn called offering to share her Chicago apartment. I said yes and quickly packed my bags (see page 35.)

Part V.

The "Windy City," Marriage, and Parenthood

Pat was getting a divorce, and moving from Florida back to her hometown of Chicago. She had an apartment, fully furnished, in a newly built Near North building, Carl Sandburg Village. I flew to Chicago and landed a job as an adoption caseworker at Illinois Children's Home and Aid Society. My caseload was primarily unmarried mothers and foster parents.

I had a good job, a place to live, and Pat was a high school friend of (future husband) David's, who lived in the next building. While I could walk three blocks to work, the agency sent me to work at their location in Waukegan, a 45-minute commute each way. They trained their new hires there. I remember being there when President John F. Kennedy was assassinated.

The first day it snowed, I spun out on the highway. I then recalled passing on admission to Northwestern University because of the cold weather. Driving in snow and ice still scares me. I avoid it at all costs. It's not an issue in Tucson, but can happen occasionally in Vancouver when we visit our condo at Christmas.

Life was grand in Chicago – unlike in Tucson, where there was little social life. I felt like I was slipping if I didn't squeeze in five dates during a weekend: brunch or lunch, and both an early and late date on Friday and Saturday. Introduced by Pat, David and I had several dates, but he was busy studying for the CPA exam, and sequestered himself for the next year.

A year or so later, I would run into David in our shared garage. He invited me out for New Year's Eve. That was fun, though I don't remember what we did. Shortly after that, Pat became engaged, married, and move out of the apartment with all of her furniture. Another male friend took me to a hotel auction where I bought a bed and few necessities.

One of my first dates with David was smelt fishing at Foster Avenue beach on Lake Michigan. Not unlike a snipe (is there really such a fish?) hunt, this is also an excuse for a party, but the sardine-like smelt were running, and we were catching them as fast as we could lift and lower our net.

Cleaning smelt is no big deal, but how would a nice Jewish boy know that? Just a squeeze to flush out eggs, no scraping out the guts. David was very impressed that I could "clean" fish.

My father came to visit me. When David, who I was now dating regularly, drove my 6-foot-4 father to O'Hare International Airport in his Volkswagen Beetle, my father was unduly impressed. Scrunched into the car, he felt the long commute to the airport in lots of traffic was beyond necessary. He told me, "Mary, this is a really nice young man – I think you should give him a second look."

It occurred to me that my dating life, which included a brief engagement to a Tulane physics student, plus dates with hundreds of other men, I never thought about kindness as a quality. I tended to like them better when they were less attentive. Little stuff, like not calling or being late, snagged my interest? If I complained to my dad, he would tell me, "Mary, in a year, you won't even remember his name."

At the time, I wasn't all that interested in David, but heeded my father's advice. I thought about the wear and tear of late hours of my social life. David and I started dating and we became engaged in February. I remember baking him chocolate chip cookies for Valentine's Day. I haven't baked anything for the past 55 years.

David's parents asked the typical questions: What does your father do, what does your grandfather do? Since I occasionally had a tear or tatter in my clothes, they assumed that based on my reply, "a dry goods store and a grocery store," that my dad was in retail and my grandfather sold groceries.

We were very shortly on the way with David's parents, Blossom and Sam, to Tucson to meet my parents. They must have been pleasantly surprised to find Levy's the most respected department store in Tucson, and later to discover that my grandparents were wholesale grocers in South Bend selling to Notre Dame, Sara Lee, and other big clients.

My dad offered us a paid honeymoon or a wedding, which in Tucson would include a huge guest list. Taking him up on his offer, we did extend a few invitations to Chicago friends, but let's be real. We were married on June 1, a very hot time in Tucson. A February wedding would have attracted everyone.

After our small wedding at Temple Emanu-El, where my Uncle Aaron was a founder, we had the first reception held at the new Tucson National golf course. Soon we were flying off to San Diego, while the reception was still going on. Entering our room, the phone was ringing. My father must have been worried about my virginity. I think he called me to see if all was well. Continuing on to San Francisco, we recognized the voice in the room next door. It was my father's friend, a lawyer who always told me that if I got arrested, I could call him any time, day or night. Were we being followed? Not really, it was a coincidence.

Our Chicago friends had generously given us a wedding wine shower, each couple bringing a bottle. A glass or more of wine nightly proved to be a fertility ritual. A year later, Suzanne was born, followed by Jeffrey three years later.

We moved to a small apartment on the south end of Glencoe after Suzie was born. When Jeffrey was on the way, we moved to Highland Park, the northern suburb where David was raised.

Back in those days, pregnant women were required to retire from work. Though who could better relate to an unmarried mother than a pregnant caseworker? I left and never went back. I was a stay-at-home mom until the children went to nursery school. I never used day care. By the time the children were in nursery school, I had figured out how to play nine holes of golf and an hour of tennis, and be home before school was over.

Shortly after that, David's parents moved to Florida. Without family, we thought more about the cold winters. When my father got wind of those thoughts, David was offered a job as chief financial officer of Farmers Investment Co., a large farming business in Sahuarita that grew acres and acres of pecans.

I didn't want to live in then-remote Sahuarita without having any medical care available for the children, so we lived in Tucson. After a year, David opened his own CPA firm in Tucson.

Suzie and Jeffrey loved growing up in Tucson and attending summer camp in Northern Minnesota where they developed a deep respect for nature as well as lifelong adventure skills: backpacking, canoeing, fishing, hiking, and horseback riding and wilderness camping.

Jeffrey Peachin and wife Kristin Byrd with boys Ben and Zachary

Developing independence and a love of wild places eventually led Suzie to a 30 -year career in public education guided by a philosophy around developing the whole child. Currently, she works with high school students in the Pacific Northwest, focused on helping them explore their own interests, skills and passion for learning into a career they love. When not working, she enjoys traveling with friends and family, volunteering in her community, and fly casting for trout in the beautiful waters of western North America.

Jeffrey was in the Tucson Boys Chorus and went to The Gregory High School before attending the University of Pennsylvania and Montana State University. Family adventures included biking, skiing, fly and deep-sea fishing, house boating, kayaking, camping, rafting and off-roading in an RV in Monument Valley. Jeff's wife, Kristin, and grandchildren, Zachary and Ben, join them for new family adventures.

Suzie Peachin

Part VI.

My Turbo Era

8. My Cessna Turbo 210—N9327S

Cessna T 210 , Photo: Tucson Airport Authority

Sometime in my middle thirties, perhaps inspired by my cycling and diving adventures, I had what many might consider a "mid-life crisis." It had nothing to do with my marriage, family, or home. It was a lust for speed. When I was in high school, I did some drag racing using a friend's Model A hydraulic clutch Ford. Races in the late 50s were held on the Air Force base at Davis Monthan. If you're wondering, my family never knew. Since I also swam on the YMCA men's team who trained there, going to Davis Monthan was never questioned.

A decisive woman, I walked into Stillwell's BMW car dealership, and drove out with a bright red bi-turbo Maserati. I was thrilled, but it was short lived. When I received my first insurance invoice, well, to me there was no car worth that kind of insurance money.

That didn't slow me down. Onward and upward. Having my single engine rated commercial-instrument pilot's rating, I bought into a third of a Cessna Turbo 210, the fastest, high speed and performance single engine aircraft.

Now I was the ultimate "free spirit." If the weather forecast looked good, I gathered my friends and we flew to Mexico to fish or dive or both.

My partners were great. I only knew their voices, one worked for IBM, the other Raytheon. They knew their vacation schedules a year in advance, I knew mine the previous day. Let me share that flying, like scuba diving, was a "big wall" to climb over.

Cessna taxiing at Ryan

Roger Cutter, my flight instructor had radioed Tucson's flight control for permission to take off. Then he jumped out of the single engine onto the edge of the runway leaving me alone to make my first solo flight in a two-seater Cessna 150.

When an aircraft controller gives permission for take-off, an immediate departure is required. Aircraft typically land every three minutes, and a plane sitting on a runway is a disaster waiting to happen.

Tears flowed down my cheeks as I pushed the throttle quickly reaching take off speed to fly the pattern to make my first solo landing. I did it!

Roger knew that I was capable of flying the airplane, but that I was terrified to do it myself. Once I overcame that hurdle, it was smooth flying through the flight requirements to earn my license plus a commercial/instrument rating.

Always a fair-weather pilot, there were times, when I made an easy decision not to fly. Sometimes it was as simple as high cross winds. I recall heading to Mexico for a weekend trip with friends when I heard an unusual noise coming from the turbo. I made a 180 turn back to the airport with the support and appreciation of my friends.

9. A Snakebite Kit and a Gun: An Emergency Landing in Yuma

During the '80s, my friend Jeanie was in the interior plant landscaping business. I owned an art and framing gallery. Both of us worked together on a number of commercial business installations.

Hired to install artwork and plants in a Yuma, Arizona bank, we decided that I would pilot us in a rented Grumman, along with my hand-clenching "fear of flying" frightened framer, Jack. We would send the plants and art in Jeanie's truck with her installer.

We met at Tucson International Airport, with Jeanie bringing pastries, a new-to-the-market Walkman with dual headsets, a snakebite kit and a gun. Her father had taught her during childhood to always be prepared for emergency landings in the desert.

Yuma is about a two-hour flight from Tucson. Above the city of Gila Bend, the radio stopped transmitting. Quickly realizing that the airplane had lost its alternator - in other words, all its electricity - I handed Jack, who was having a nervous conniption, a map and asked him to search for emergency landing sites.

It was about a forty-five-minute flight to Yuma. Despite having no air-to-ground radio communication, we decided to try to make it to Yuma's airport. Emergency procedures include flying over an airport's tower and wiggling the airplane's wings. Flight control then guides the aircraft having an emergency to landing by using light signal instructions.

After following these procedures without receiving any control tower signals, I decided to enter the landing pattern. Marine jets, practicing landings, probably distracted the tower from seeing my small aircraft.

No electricity meant that I had no flaps to slow the plane. I put the plane into slow flight knowing that I could only stop by using the brakes. Happy to land, I took the first exit off the runway and taxied into McDonnell Douglas aerospace company. I knew that I couldn't turn off the engine because it would not start again. I asked Jeanie to keep her feet on the brakes while I went into the company's office to call the tower.

The men jokingly asked if we were participating in a Powder Puff Derby. I wasn't feeling so humorous when I asked the tower if they had seen me make an emergency landing. They hadn't noticed, but said they would send a fire engine to escort me across the field to the nearest FBO (flight base operator). And to think that I had expected them to have a foam-covered runway awaiting my landing.

Turning off the engine, I opened the cowling. There was a misplaced ruler inside. How could they be so careless to put our lives at risk? I called the FBO in Tucson to tell them they could retrieve their airplane. Pat, Jack and I then went to the bank to install the artwork and plants.

At the time, there was a small intrastate airline named Cochise. We decided to fly commercially back to Tucson. It was about that time that I remembered that Jeanie had a gun with her. I warned her that if she got caught, I was going to act like I didn't know her.

With our installation complete, we made an uneventful return to Tucson. It was prior to the days of x-ray security. No one saw the gun, and Jack chose to return home in Jeanie's truck.

10. Getting Lost Flying in the Colorado Rockies

Once I obtained my instrument license, I never flew VFR (visual flight rules) again. David, (also a pilot) and I were planning to fly to Aspen with another couple. He had traveled there in a private plane a few weeks earlier. He told me, "Mary, I'll do the navigating for you, I know the way."

All was good until we flew into the state Colorado. When I saw CB (Crested Butte) etched into the mountain, I knew that we were in the wrong valley.

As the elevation rose, I was aware that N237S had supplemental oxygen for only the pilot and co-pilot, a FAA requirement at 12,500 feet. As we neared that altitude, I put on oxygen masks for the two of us. I called Aspen Tower, declared an emergency, and told them I would fly to the Red Mountain VOR navigation signal so they could vector me in to the Aspen airport. On the way to Red Mountain I saw the Aspen strip and made a safe landing.

Concerned about my passengers, they were sleeping from the experience of having less oxygen at a higher altitude, but later said they were OK and happy to be on the ground. It was only recently that Kathy said she thought she was going to die and Paul, now deceased, had taken a Dramamine and fallen asleep. As for David, I "fired" him from any further navigating.

11. Flying Adventures in Mexico: Commandant's Curiosity

Late one afternoon, I was flying my friends to San Carlos to go diving.

Mexico flight regulations do not permit general aviation pilots to fly at night. We were just squeaking the bewitching hour, when Hermosillo tower radioed to advise all pilots that they were closing the airport because the President of the State of Sonora was landing.

I explained that I was 30 minutes from landing, which I needed to do before dark. I don't know what happened to the President, but they allowed me to land.

Entering Mexico requires that you land and clear customs at the first international Port of Entry. Returning to the United States, the Tucson flight control provides a number for you to "squawk" on your radio prior to crossing the border.

Every commandante, until they got to know me, would ask me when I entered customs, "Where is your pilot." I would respond that "I am the pilot." It wasn't long before I was on a first name basis with those in Hermosillo, and Loreto.

Meeting my pals Mark and PK to dive in Loreto, the commandante told me that I shouldn't, as a woman, be flying alone. I never paid a bribe or "mordida", a practice that many pilots spoke of. On one occasion I brought a bottle of wine to the commandante in Hermosillo on that fateful Christmas brake fire trip. (see below.) It was a holiday gesture.

After Mexico City's National Museum of Anthropology was looted in 1985 of 140 priceless Mayan, Aztec, and other artifacts, all aircraft headed north towards the United States were searched. I always had more issues returning through customs in Tucson. The officers didn't seem to understand why I had nothing to declare. Routinely I showed them my diving and fishing gear.

Years later when I applied for a Nexus card, a Canadian equivalent to Global Entry, I was asked why I flew back and forth to Mexico without making any declarations. We had bought a small condo in Vancouver and the Nexus officers knew my entire history spanning the past twenty years.

12. Landing in Mazatlán with My Brakes Catching on Fire

Earlier I mentioned that I had two compatible partners with advanced planned vacations. I was not immediately aware that one of them sold his interest. One day while taking off, I saw an object fly off the dashboard. After checking, I didn't think much about it.

It wasn't a crisis until I flew to Mazatlán, Mexico for a family Christmas vacation. As I landed on the runway, the airplane brakes caught on fire. My new partner had obviously been working on the plane, and he left oil on the brakes.

N-9327S had a retractable landing gear. Returning to Tucson, feeling that it was safer, I left the wheels down. It was a longer, slower flight, but it was me that was fuming. When I returned to Tucson, I gave the new partner a choice of my selling my interest independently, or he could buy me out. He chose to buy me out.

I later heard that the two partners leased the plane to a flying club. While rented for a trip to Vegas, N327S unfortunately crashed with its passengers losing their lives.

After that experience, I rented airplanes until 9/11 when the FAA restricted General Aviation aircraft from major airports, and would not allow them to fly into Mexico. That ended my flying career.

Part VII.

Sport Fishing for Game Fish: Offshore and Fly Fishing

13. "The Gringa" of Barra Del Colorado, Costa Rica

Tarpon, Photo: Pochy Rosario

I didn't earn the nickname "Gringa" without merit. It almost cost me my life while tarpon fishing in the shark-infested waters of the brackish Barra Colorado.

Let's fast backward. How did I get to Costa Rica's rainforest? I flew in a small plane from San Jose to Barra del Colorado's dirt strip, roughly 40 kilometers north of Tortuguero in the northwest part of the country where it borders with Nicaragua.

A group of my Tucson fishing buddies had an annual trip to Barra Colorado to fish for tarpon in the Rio Colorado. When I asked if I could join them, I was told, "Mary, we'll put you on our waitlist." After several years I came to the conclusion that there was no waitlist, they were just putting me off. I told myself, what the hell, I don't need these men. I can make this trip by myself. I never expected that it would lead to one of my closer calls with death.

Arriving in San Jose late in the evening, I would spend the night before catching a small single engine aircraft into Barra Colorado's dirt strip. Soon after I checked into my airport hotel, there was a knock on my door. Assuming that it was the bellboy, I opened the door. It was a man who followed me down the hall to invite me to the bar. Slam! I learned another of my "traveling alone" lessons along with not going out of my hotel for dinner at night in strange places.

My trip became an annual fishing adventure for about a decade. I became passionate about tarpon fishing, and I was an admirer of the fishing expertise of my guide Juan. He must have felt a similar bond with me, when one year he carved a wooden tarpon for me to take home. We would leave at sunrise hoping the seas were calm enough to motor through the mouth of the river into the Carribbean Sea. It was much easier to catch and release tarpon when I could follow them in the boat instead of having them snag then break off on the river's bottom scattered rocks and sunken tree trunks. Sometimes, the smart, prehistoric fish just headed for the ocean when weather-wise we couldn't follow them.

On one trip, the weather was unstable, and feeling frustrated, the second day, I asked Juan if we could try to get outside on the ocean. I think Juan might have been a bit macho. He carefully timed the incoming waves as we headed out. Then a rogue wave slammed into the panga. The engine stalled, and trying as hard as he could, he couldn't get the engine started.

Wherever tarpon is fished, sharks gather, and it's a shark feeding frenzy with the angler usually pulling in only a head. Bill, the lodge owner, cautioned us time and again, not to get in the water for any reason. As chance would have it, a tarpon on an angler's rod did jump into my boat. With lighting speed, I jumped on the seat to prevent being injured by a thrashing tarpon.

I mention this because I knew being in the water was a last resort. Motionless in the incoming waves, the boat began to fill with water. We were at the mercy of the sea. I remembered the old saying "always stay with the boat."

With each wave, more gear flew out of the boat. We sank deeper and deeper. I had a firm grasp on each gunwale watching my gear being swept away. As I got closer to being up to my neck in the boat in the water, I saw a beach maybe less than a mile away. I could make that effort before we flipped out and I was swimming with the sharks anyway.

Out of nowhere, a boat appeared with two guides to rescue us. They had witnessed our swamping, dropped their anglers on the beach I had thought about swimming to, and sped out to save us.

Pulling up to the beach, the guys fishing were happy clams. They had no idea what was happening as they cast their lines. I apologized to them, then I asked Juan to send for another boat.

It was only a few hours before word spread that a "gringa" fishing alone had swamped in the mouth of the Barra Colorado river. Boats of anglers were coming close to take photographs of me. I missed my gear, but Juan had clenched my rod in his hand throughout the ordeal. Worse to me was the loss of my sun glasses. The equatorial sun hurts the eyes, and finding a pair to borrow was very challenging.

Each day we visited the beach to find wrapped items washed up on the beach. The most important item was a camera that my friend Mark had lent me. It was gone and couldn't be replaced.

I figured if vacationers on cruise ships filed insurance claims, so could I. What was the difference between an oceangoing liner or my small panga sinking? The insurance company finally agreed to reimburse Mark. Several years later, while renewing his policy, the agent made clear to him that coverage did not include "sinking ships." Mark replied, "Yes, I know. That was my camera."

The following years that I returned to Barra Colorado, I was called "Gringa." That to me translates in some ways negatively to "a touristy woman," but the locals actually appeared happy to see me back. And they had put in place a rule stating that no boats could go out to the ocean without being accompanied by a second boat. I'll take credit for that.

14. Nicaragua's Sensational Silver Kings, A Sandinista Legacy

Exploding out of the water, as night began to fall, a 200-pound tarpon jumped. Minutes after dropping our lines in the jungle's waters, Bob hooked into this monster. Extremely fit, Bob struggled to gain inches on the fish. By now it was dark on the Río San Juan and we had one small flashlight. We had visions of Hemingway's book, *The Old Man and the Sea*, when the Cuban fought the marlin throughout the night. Bob brought the fish to the boat time and again, only to have it make another long run.

Our guide Chili and I made a group effort to follow the zigzagging tarpon with David holding the gaff and I prepared to pass a set of long-nosed pliers to Chili if he could secure the fish to the boat for a release.

After struggling for two and a half hours, Bob released the tarpon into the darkness of the night. The "release" was either Bob tightening the drag (line tension) or the tarpon's brutal strength breaking the line. We weren't able to see the silver king's beauty, its length or girth. Relishing the experience, under a crystal-clear, star-studded night, we motored downriver to Sabalos Lodge stilted above the river.

La Esquina del Lago fishing lodge owner Philippe Tisseaux had told us, "This is extreme fishing. You'll be fighting tarpon deep in the heart of the Nicaraguan jungle. The fish would be larger than the more typical hundred-pound size. They would be jumping within sight of our twenty-three-foot panga. Skill and luck would be required to catch them.

In uprisings dating back to the 1960s, Sandinista (FSLN in Spanish) guerrillas in Nicaragua tried to overthrow the U.S.-supported Somoza dictatorship by means of an armed struggle. Fear of guerrillas kept anglers away allowing the fish, which can live up to 50 years, to grow without pressure from anglers.

Their fear was well-founded. During the 80s, I was fishing in Barra Colorado, across the river in Costa Rica, when the Sandinistas kidnapped three American anglers, which they released a week later. Costa Rica's Red Cross had set up a refugee camp along the river's edge. I went there for a tetanus shot after a fishing pal hooked me in the thigh with a rusty treble hook. Bill, the owner of Casa Mar Lodge, where I was staying, was happy to fly in a tetanus injection from San Jose, and even happier to stick the needle in my rear.

Philippe thinks Río San Juan tarpon fishing is the ultimate challenge, but one for experienced and patient anglers. Or, as one guest more pointedly argued, "it's a knock-down drag-out brawl with the tarpon controlling you."

In 2003, Philippe bought a corner of land edged by Lake Nicaragua, Río San Juan and Río Frio and built La Esquina del Lago lodge. After a night spent at his lodge, which resembles an oversized houseboat, he sends his anglers into the jungle.

The journey begins in San Carlos, a nondescript village that once served as a Spanish fortress. After anglers land on a 1,500-foot dirt-and-grass strip, a transfer from a taxi to a panga ride to Philippe's lodge takes only minutes.

A puff of volcanic ash expelled from Rincon de la Viera, rising over Lake Nicaragua's horizon, dissolves into a beautiful orange-colored sunset. Approximately thirty-one miles in the distance, Costa Rica's forested mountains loom on the horizon.

In Nicaragua's Río San Juan jungle, most fishing is done in Reserva de Biosfero Río San Juan, a lush rainforest of towering trees, winding vines, exotic shore birds, monkeys, sloths, deer, nutria and other jungle wildlife concealed by the canopy.

It is also a birder's paradise. White egrets, roseate spoonbills, tiger and blue heron, cormorants, anhinga and jacanas are just a few species that territorially stalk bait-size fish along the river's bank.

Nighttime in the jungle is a symphonic cacophony. The repetitive shrill of an unidentified jungle bird screeches a cry that sounds like, "Where are you?" Different species of frogs and toads croak and gargle. Rain beats on the hotel's corrugated metal roof. Howler monkeys grumble in the distance. Dogs bark.

At six the next morning, my husband David, friend Bob and I climbed back into a 23-foot uncovered panga for five days of fishing with guides Chili and Chico. Just a few minutes from the lodge, we begin trolling four lines with different colored Rapala fishing lures. After a few runs without any strikes, we reel in. Chili and Chico said they knew better "hot spots" along the river.

Río San Juan flows southerly from Lake Nicaragua in San Carlos, past the villages of Sabalos and El Castillo, where picturesque ruins of a Spanish fortress tower on a hillside above a wide stretch of rapids. This natural barrier stopped marauding pirates, and in the 1850s gold rushers bushwhacked around them on their way to California. The rapids stop us as well.

Men in small wooden canoes fished with hand lines for bass-like guapote. They sell their catch to locals or the few scattered restaurants along the river. Other men fish along banks with nets, sticks or hand lines for mojarra. Women wash clothes and dishes in the river. Stilted houses, without electricity, are scattered along the river's edge. The friendly "Nicas" wave as we pass.

Industrious subsistence farmers, they raise livestock and grow produce. Occasionally a larger cargo boat carrying logs of mahogany, or maybe a truck or appliances, passes by.

My adrenaline spikes when the first tarpon strikes my rod four hours later. It's a big one, a six-foot silver king weighing approximately 155 pounds. Hooked in the cheek, it's a two-hour battle until I release him. David hooks then releases a toothy gar. Bob catches a snook, which Sabalos Lodge grills, providing us a very delicious lunch. Nicaragua is not a foodie's destination, so we relish every bite.

Having been told to bring enough clothes for one or two nights, we fished our way back to Sabalos Lodge, a two-hour nonstop trip on the Río San Juan. The wooden-planked hotel has small rooms along an open corridor stilted above the river. Like La Esquina del Lago, Sabalos Lodge has no hot water for showering, but their small rooms include a fan. We were happy to rinse off the grime of a day's sweat and suntan lotion. And, we stayed for three nights.

Dusk brings clouds of sayulas, a non-biting fly-like bug attracted to light. We dined on the dim outdoor porch, seated as far as possible from several green and red florescent ceiling lights.

Once again night rain pounded the steel corrugated roof. Measuring as much as 200 annual inches of rain, this area is one of the wettest regions in the world. Whenever a torrential downpour soaks us, it's cooling, and actually preferable to the blazing heat of the equatorial sun.

Chili tells us that five in the morning is a better time for the bite. Rubbing his stomach, he tells us the tarpon "Comida mucho." Grabbing a quick sip of coffee, we eagerly climb into the panga. Most of the day it's "fundo, fundo, fundo," or just snagging the bottom. We jump a few tarpon and miss the same amount.

After fishing Sabalos, we return upstream to El Castillo. The rapids north of the city are known to produce big tarpon. But not today. We jump several more and lose one.

We listen to the growling of howler monkeys, watch a sloth clinging to a treetop and admire white egrets fishing almost every hundred yards. Colorful jacanas dart around water lilies.

It's late afternoon when David jumps a tarpon and Bob releases one. They are two happy anglers. I've spent a frustrating day without a single strike. Most of the day we fished below the rapids of El Castillo. During the midday sun, we take a break in town at El Topal restaurant, eating a typical lunch or dinner: chicken and pico de gallo (salsa) with a fried mixture of beans and rice.

Median and her 82-year-old husband Enrique have a compound, connected by a rickety boardwalk crossing a swamp like area. Multiple buildings house what they claim are their twenty-four children. It is obvious that the homestead, built by Enrique, expanded with each addition to his family.

Phillipe has an arrangement for his anglers to stop there for lunch. Seeing some passing fisherman in a canoe, we buy guapote from their iced container. Median cooks it up for us on her wood-burning stove rather than serving us chicken. The lunch, including beans, rice and plantains, costs $2.00 a person. We then returned to La Esquina del Lago lodge for our shuttle back to Managua.

My initial thought of going to Nicaragua was one of concern. Was it safe? I was pretty sure that David would back out, which is why I invited Bob, who is an avid angler. I got lucky and we ended up as a trio. We did not go into the city of Managua except for dinner the evening before our early flight out. We had the hotel cab wait for us. We were told that there is so much gang activity in the city that it is not a safe place for tourists. In spite of the fishing being mediocre, I'm happy I got to visit Nicaragua and fish while exploring this amazing rainforest.

15. Fly Fishing for Mako Sharks off San Diego

Fly fishing for mako shark, Photo: Michelle Woo

Exploding like a torpedo, the mako blasted from the Pacific Ocean's surface, its wide-shoulders making a triple acrobatic leap before stripping 250 yards of fly line as he sounded rapidly into the depths of the Pacific. Fighting a mako for forty minutes is not an unusual outcome — more like the rule.

It is hard to match the thrill of visually casting to a mako shark. In addition to the aerobatics associated with casting to other large saltwater species — sailfish, marlin, and tarpon — the angler must contend with the mako's brute strength, while admiring the beauty of its sleek, compact body.

Fly fishing for mako shark is at once terrifyingly active and deeply philosophical, one of the most challenging (and, some feel, frustrating) examples of conservation fly fishing. Even when hooked, the shark always wins: The sandpaper coarseness of its skin and tail either breaks the fly line (usually during a jumping episode), or the fish is reeled in and released at the side of the boat.

Once a mako is hooked, the boat follows the direction of the shark — otherwise the shark would strip the reel. If the angler is successful in bringing the mako to the boat, a custom-made gaff clipped to the line gently pulls the barbless mackerel-patterned fly from the shark's mouth.

A cousin to the great white, the shortfin mako, colored olive to cobalt, is considered a top-of-the-pyramid ocean predator. The species, members of which have been clocked at speeds up to 40 miles per hour, covers a wider range than the great white. And like their more famous cousins, mako hunt and feed primarily on live prey.

I was aboard guide Conway Bowman's boat, in the middle of the "Mako Triangle" — an area known to anglers as the "California Bight." Located in the Pacific Ocean between San Clemente, California, and Tijuana, Mexico, deep-water canyons have become prime habitat for mako spawning. After a gestation period of two to three years, the mako give live birth to as many as 15 pups. If the pups survive without being eaten by their mother or another mako, they are ready to prey.

Schools of sardine, herring, and mackerel feed the sharks until they weigh between 400 and 500 pounds. At maturity, the sharks leave for destinations unknown — amazingly, nearly nothing is known about their maturity or adult whereabouts.

The 50-minute boat trip off San Diego, aboard Bowman's 18-foot Parker outboard, is a bone-jarring roller coaster of a ride, not for the faint of stomach. Despite the jarring trip, on my first mako excursion, Bowman and I finally arrived at the fishing grounds. Bowman proclaimed, "This looks like a great mako day." The dark gray Pacific was shrouded by fog, and three-foot southerly swells collided with a cross chop. I swallowed hard and nodded in a way that I hoped appeared enthusiastic.

A third-generation San Diegan, the 34-year-old Bowman is a beachboy at heart. When he isn't fishing or working at his other day job, managing the Murray Reservoir in nearby La Mesa, he takes the surfboard off his car and heads for the waves. But fishing is his passion. He grew up fishing for bluegills, then graduated to calico bass. Always fascinated by mako, Bowman developed his technique over time, experimenting with a variety of flies and bait. Now he's a huge mako fan, with serious interest in conservation of the species. He has strong feelings about, anglers who catch and kill fish for food.

Bowman is a true angler, doing it for the joy of fishing. That doesn't mean he's not serious. He's recorded the exact location of each mako release from his boat. He begins each trip with information gathering. On our trip, he used his GPS (global positioning system) device to check the depth (less than 100 fathoms), water temperature (70 degrees), and current drift (southerly). This information is not just statistical — Bowman knows exactly where he wants to fish and, more importantly, the direction he wants the boat to drift.

Slowing the boat, Bowman lowered a chum bucket filled with mashed bonito tuna. Particles of fish began to drift out of the bucket, clouding the water with fish particles and oil. "Power chumming," we motored until the chum line stretched about half a mile. The location of the line was highlighted by a flock of terns and a few shearwater and Hermann's gulls, all looking for a feast along the chum line. While we waited for the mako to arrive, Bowman talked about his love for the shark, their strength and beauty, all the while tying steel leaders using his homemade flies.

The first mako approached the boat in less than an hour. Fishing for mako is visual fly-fishing. The angler uses the same baiting and casting routine for each shark. Bowman began with a spinning rod, baiting it with a mackerel head to entice the shark closer. Once the mako takes notice and begins to follow, he tossed chunks of mackerel, trying to lure the mako within casting distance. If a shark is about three feet long, Bowman recommends a 12-weight rod; larger sharks require a heavier 16-weight rod.

The mako came closer, eating the mackerel chunk. Bowman warned me to keep the fly off the water during this process: He doesn't want the mako tempted too soon, or too close to the boat. If the shark leapt into the boat, explained Bowman, "It would be disastrous. The mako would tear this boat apart." Yikes!

The mako receded a bit and at Bowman's signal I tossed the fly — but to no avail. Usually, if an angler succeeds, the battle begins. Mako don't usually give an angler a second chance, but this one was different. Contrary to the rule, the mako returned, majestic as ever. This time, after another taste of mackerel, it grabbed the fly — and I hooked it with all my might.

I'm an experienced fly fisherman, and an accomplished diver. In fact, I had dived with mako sharks, which, while intimidating, soon came to seem serenely beautiful in that quiet underwater world. But neither experience helped me here — maybe they even served up a false sense of security.

All security went out the window the moment I hooked the shark. It reared up, heading full-steam toward the boat, which offered negligible protection with skimpy two-foot gunwales. I was all reaction and adrenaline, wrestling for control for maybe ten seconds—and then the shark stripped the line, which spun from my reel with a high whine. It took me a few minutes to recover, and quite a bit longer to digest the fact that my opponent was a shark half my size, a three-footer.

Conway passes on hooking larger mako to protect both his boat and angler. Larger ones can be too dangerous when hooked.

During two half-day trips, a photographer, Bowman, and I had the opportunity to catch and release six mako, each of which reacted differently to our presence. Some did aerobatics; others circled the boat as if we were the prey, and a couple "bulldogged" (a term used by tuna fisherman for sounding or heading down). That's one of the reasons Bowman loves to fish for mako. Not only is it a visual sport that doesn't require trolling, each fish has its own personality, all are aggressive and unpredictable.

When the next mako approached, I gracefully yielded to Bowman, giving him an opportunity to prove his angling prowess. After that I released several other three-footers, each time feeling more confident, and each time reveling in the rush of the release.

Four hours later, the chum bucket was empty, and our day of mako fishing was over. I endured another rough ride back to the marina, this time with every muscle aching from the fight. Bowman was quiet, but I did catch his tune, "California Dreamin" –a tune in which the thrill and majesty almost overwhelm, and in which the shark always wins.

16. Zihuantanejo: Roosterfish and A Fish for All Seasons

Mary with Captain Adolfo and roosterfish, Photo: David F Peachin

Not too many captains will fish the rolling edge of tall breaking waves – those that surfers would consider the place to be. Instead, the isolated beach south of Zihuantanejo is beautiful and uninhabited. We are the only panga fishing there. Perhaps the lack of a road makes it totally remote. Captain Adolfo matter-of-factly tells us that missing the roll of a wave would mean a dangerous crash onto the beach. November is the season to be there so we have come to try for roosterfish.

He has a young, strong mate nicknamed "Gorilla," who can throw a bait farther and faster than almost anyone, including David and me. Roosterfish will chase a live bait as long as it's moving. "Gorilla" can bring them closer to us.

We can also troll for them, and this enabled me to catch and release what had to be a record-breaker. Adolfo estimated that the roosterfish, so called because of the quill-like feathers on its dorsal fin, weighed 90 pounds. (see photo.) They are rarely fished, seasonal (July-November), and most offshore anglers prefer the better odds of catching a billfish. In addition to my trophy roosterfish, I've had many other great fishing adventures with Adolfo.

Paseo del Pescador, the municipal fishing dock that serves Zihuantanejo and Ixtapa, is hopping at daybreak. The frenetic activity continues all year round.

Awaiting turns to board their chartered boats, anchored on buoys off the paseo, anglers' eyes snap open at the action-packed scene. Women sit on the dock selling Big Eye scad and another bait they refer to as corineros, a small, hearty green jack used for trolling bait. Feral cats rest patiently as if trained to wait for any leftovers. Captains, and a few gringos, pause at a stall to load up on coffee, burritos, and tortillas.

As the sun rises over the Pacific, the departing fleet of fishing boats turns either north or south for inshore fishing or westward, motoring about ten miles toward blue water to troll for billfish, dorado, and tuna.

It's a rare treat to be ocean fishing with my family. Both my husband David and daughter Suzanne occasionally are *más o menos* "faint of stomach," so we follow the shoreline.

Trolling less than a mile offshore on super panga *Dos Hermanos I*, Captain Aldofo Virrueta Barragan tells us that we are liable "to catch anything." He considers his panga *super* because of its size, speed, and comfort. I prefer to toss my vote to its open-air simple head (toilet), shielded from view by a half-wall. He also has two fishing chairs, which swivel and rock to provide flexibility to an angler. and two long cushioned benches, perfect for a nap during the hour or so ride back to the dock.

Captain Adolfo prefers the faster response time of the panga's tiller, the usually preferred side console. It's better for maneuvering between breaking waves, a skill definitely required for roosterfish. The fiberglass panga has cushioned gunwales to brace the angler. A shaded covering protects from the sun. Adolfo proudly maintains and annually overhauls the 50-year-old boat formerly used commercially by his father. His is not the typical panga found throughout Mexico. It is less expensive than the fancy yachts offered, but it is faster, more comfortable, and overall, more efficient.

The area's abundant schools of sardines and anchovies attract multiple species of fish. For several hours, we troll, rapalas reeling in a dozen or more Spanish mackerel, bonito, and skipjack.

With plenty of fish caught and released, we are distracted by the beauty of the area. Circling Potosi, a rocky island off Ixtapa, we admired saguaro-like cardon cactus. Frigates glide on wind currents, brown-footed boobies nest. Waves that pound remote beaches in Ixtapa could be a surfer's paradise.

While ocean conditions are usually calm in these waters, we awoke to our second day of fishing to gusting winds and a weather prediction for ten-foot swells with chop. My family quickly bailed on me.

Meeting Captain Aldolpho on the paseo, we motored more than an hour to reach blue water. That's where you find game fish like sails, marlin, dorado. The chop and big waves bounced us like kids on a trampoline. Gaviotas or gulls swooped around us as Adolfo rigged the outriggers with bigeyes dressed with a plastic pink lip, just an added attraction for the billfish. We trail two squid teasers.

As a school of dolphin circled the boat, Adolfo rubbed his nose indicating that they were bottle-nosed. It was hard to believe that his GPS read that we were 24 miles from shore. Near an international shipping lane, we watched cargo-loaded freighters heading to and from the Panama Canal. Coincidentally, weeks later I would see one of those boats motor into Vancouver's harbour. Zihuantanejo's larger but slower yachts appeared to be staying closer to shore.

Within minutes, the outrigger snapped. A Pacific sail, weighing about 100 pounds, performed multiple jumps before I brought it to the boat. Adolfo doesn't back the boat down on fish so I had a 25-minute workout. He asked me to hold the sail's bill as it revived. Before we released the fish, Adolfo asked me to feed some bait to the sail. "I want the sail to have good thoughts and happily return another day."

Ten minutes later, Adolfo looked at his watch then grabbed his GPS. *Dos Hermanos I* had drifted an additional five miles, and we were now 29 miles from the dock. We could see the coast of Baja across the Sea of Cortés. Before we could pull in the lines, both outrigger lines zinged, a "double" hookup. Adolfo placed one rod in the holder as I grabbed the other, reeled in a 105 pounder, then picked up the second rod to release an even larger sail. What a way to end a day of fishing.

During fall months, casting a pencil popper toward a comb-like fin weaving through breaking surf is likely to produce a fifty-pound roosterfish. Early winter into late spring, schools of black and blue marlin and large yellowfin tuna arrive. Resident Pacific sailfish sometimes take a migratory break during March and April. Snook anglers will sweat it out fighting the tasty fish during warm summer months into fall. Schools of dorado, while less frequent during spring (and which, for some unexplained reason, seem to disappear during October), are usually caught offshore. For anglers who just want to catch fish, annual species include grouper, barracuda, bonito, and shark.

When you are fishing the shoreline one day, then trolling miles off the coast in blue water for billfish, and have the opportunity to catch multiple species year-round, the question comes up: What attracts so many different fish to the twin fishing villages located in Mexico's southwestern state of Guerrero?

Rich nutrients attract bait to Zihuantanejo coastal waters, plus the area merging inshore and deep waters makes an ideal habitat for game fish to feed and congregate. Underwater, within 25 miles of shore, a curving 1,000-fathom drop creates a "highway" for migrating species. Shoreline rivers and lagoons provide a sheltered environment for juvenile growth. Most of the productive fishing range is between five and 15 miles offshore, which eliminates long runs to the fishing grounds.

What angler doesn't relish easy access to deeper water, calm seas and an abundance of species? And, comparatively speaking, Adolfo's quality of boat and tackle is at an affordable cost. That suits me to a T.

17. Heli-Fishing Among Grizzlies for Salmon

Grizzly fishing , Photo: Mary L Peachin

"Hey, grizzly!" Grabbing his bear spray, fly fishing guide Logan Wilkins shouted careful instructions: "Patricia, start walking slowly down the beach … now!" Resting against an immense log, she did not have a view of the grizzly standing above her. The bear peered from its sanctuary in the rainforest. Pat, who had been oblivious to any danger, instinctively responded by scooching slowly down the beach toward the river. The bear reacted to Logan's command by retreating into the forest.

I was wading in the Khutz River for pink salmon (known as humpies because of their rounded back) when I saw Logan with bear spray in hand. I immediately got the message. Yikes! Although my thighs continued to quiver after the incident, I remained in the river throwing my fly rod at salmon. The frightening encounter had lasted only minutes.

We were casting into the bears' fishing hole, one they use each fall to bulk up before winter hibernation by feasting on migrating salmon. Just minutes before, two grizzlies had ambled along the beach toward us. At Logan's alert, we watched as the bears, after spotting us, detoured from their salmon fishing grounds into the forest.

While sharing the same fishing grounds with grizzlies may have added some excitement, fly fishing the Khutz was more than just another great fishing experience. We enjoyed one of those rare days in the Great Bear Rainforest when the sun was shining, the cold water of the river crystal clear, and the temperature an unusual high of 70 degrees.

As I shed my long underwear, I wondered if the grizzlies might be hunkering down in the alders to avoid the heat of the day before emerging when the temperature began to drop. Throughout the day, we had, somewhat nervously, scanned the beach and hillsides without a further bear sighting. But we knew they were there. Enormous paw prints and scat littered the river's edge.

Khutz River heli fishing aerial, Photo: Mary L. Peachin

After helicopter pilot Chad Friesen lifted off the now-closed King Pacific's Lodge dock, the thirty-minute flight took us skimming over rugged peaks and glacial lakes, then swooshing through narrow valleys.

Pat Werner, her husband Bill and I talked through our headset intercom of our anticipation of a day of heli-fishing, and the probability of seeing grizzlies, a species not found on Princess Royal Island, the location of the lodge. While black bear and the rare white spirit Kermode subspecies are frequent sightings during lodge adventures, the grizzly is known to inhabit only the mainland of British Columbia.

The Bell 206 Jet Ranger set down on the beach next to the Khutz River – Tsimshian for "long inlet in a steep valley" – on the mainland. Without shutting off his engine, Friesen lifted off as we turned our backs to flying sand. We had arranged a pickup for mid-afternoon. The four of us were now totally alone in the wilderness of the Great Bear Rainforest.

That wonderful "mood of the mountain" offered fog-banked crevices with steam rising from wet sandy areas on the beach. Closer to the river, the cobblestoned beach was covered with rocks and boulders of various sizes. The river's crystal green-and-blue glacial water provided great visibility of numerous schools of spawning pink salmon migrating upriver.

While they are spawning, salmon, including pink, chum, and Coho, the latter who hang in the deeper, more protected eddies of the Khutz, stop feeding once when they enter a river system from the Pacific. Focused on surviving until they spawn, they become very territorial. A colorful pink showgirl streamer pisses them off, and they strike furiously whenever a fly is presented.

In the river, their bodies soften, scar and begin to deteriorate. The jaw of the male becomes hooked. When their spawn is complete, they die, leaving easy pickings for bear, wolf, eagles and gulls.

The gentle flow of the water and a sandy bottom made wading easy. The fish seemed oblivious to our presence or the quality of the fly presentation. While casting in those conditions might be easy, the catching was another story. The fish averaged about six to ten pounds, and with an eight-weight rod, they put up a decent fight. The challenge was not to snag a fish that might take a while running in circles around your legs. It was cast, hook up, fight, and release … one fish after another, all day long. That is the reason Pat took a break next to the log. We were all suffering from biceps burnout.

After three hours of fighting fish, Logan suggested that we stop to "pecker," or enjoy a picnic lunch. Retrieving our food, cached in a tree, we munched hungrily as we pondered the bear paw prints in the sand.

Long before we could see it, the echo of the helicopter's rotor bounced off cliff walls. The day had passed all too quickly. How rare are those days when everything is perfect including the weather, fishing, plus the added excitement of grizzly bear encounters?

Quall River

During another fall spawning season, pilot Paul Tosczak skimmed the bright red Bell 260 helicopter just above the treetops into British Columbia's Quall River inlet so we could search its crystal-clear water for pink salmon. Spotting a school making their way upstream, Paul hovered, then lowered the four-passenger helicopter gently into a green meadow filled with colorful late-summer flowers.

Hopping out with the rotor still spinning, guide Wayne Boles assembled two 8-weight fly rods with pink showgirls, a feathery fly that resembles a leech when moving in the current. Fellow angler and photographer Carl Duncan and I walked the short distance from the meadow to wade into the river.

"These fish aren't interested in feeding. They are on a mission!" Wayne said. "They'll go for that flash of pink on the fly whenever it is placed in front of them." Sure enough, on the first cast I hooked into a six pounder, sea lice still attached to its tail. "This fish just entered the river from its ocean journey – lice don't live long in fresh water."

The clear water of the Quall enabled me to watch the salmon and brightness of the fly zip through the water. As I waded waist deep on the river's sandy bottom, I could see the salmon swimming by my feet. I followed them with the tip of the rod.

A thunderous sound echoed off the canyon wall. I wondered if a storm could interrupt this glorious sunny day. "Oh, no," Wayne explained, "That's just another avalanche caused by melting snow on the higher peaks of the Coastal range."

As we continued to hook into fish, Wayne noticed clumps of grass floating in the current, indicating "a bear upstream." Having listened to his bear safety lecture (give them their space and back up), I queried as to whether he had brought a gun. "No, this time of year they're interest in bulking up by eating. As more salmon enter the river, this place will be loaded with bear."

Nearby, we could hear a hooting owl above the ripple of the current. When we had fished out the pool, Wayne suggested we move on. Thinking we would be wading upstream, Wayne pointed me toward the helicopter, and once again we lifted off. After passing over the bear grazing upstream from us, we again began aerial scouting.

The day went quickly and as the sun began to drop behind the snow-capped peaks. Our departure was expedited when Carl and Paul spotted a black bear headed our way. We gave him his fishing hole and headed back to the lodge.

The scenic 15 to 30-minute flight passed over breathtaking fiords and inlets. After a day of heli-fishing, it's hard to imagine wading side by side with bears or even other anglers trying to hook fish. Heli-fishing, which allows access to inaccessible locations is a special fly fishing experience.

18. Langara Fishing Lodge, Pioneer Fishing in Haida Gwaii

Eagles outnumber Heermann's sea gulls dive bombing bait balls of schooling frenzied herring feasting on plankton krill. Nearby humpback whales breach and fin as if waving to busy salmon anglers who barely have time to take notice of the cetaceans. Someone radios that three black bears are grubbing for food in Bruin Bay. For the serious angler, the rugged island of Langara is as close as it gets to the heavenly fishing kingdom in Haida Gwaii (formerly known as the Queen Charlotte Islands.)

"You should have been here yesterday (…when the fishing was really great)." Yeh, all anglers know that fishing story. But this one was different. Mark McAneeley was guiding anglers when 40-some killer whales (orcas) surfaced. Suddenly the pod divided and ten of these magnificent creatures, frolicking and blowing bubbles, circled Mark's boat. Their intention was to eat a fighting hooked salmon, but they took their time. After ten minutes, they suddenly grabbed the fish and sounded, leaving Mark, an amazed angler with a straightened hook.

Humpback at Langara Haida Gwaii , Photo: Mary L Peachin

Fortunately, these orcas were a migrating pod. When these voracious hunters pass through a fishery, they devour both salmon and bait. Fish that escape head for the unknown. It may have been an awesome sight for anglers who observed them, but it made for a slower day of fishing for 28 arriving guests at Langara's Island Lodge.

Located 200-feet on top of a hillside of old growth forest, the cedar lodge, a smaller, more luxurious version of Langara's fishing lodges, overlooks wind protected Henslung Cove. An eight-person ski hill-type tram carries guests between the dock and the lodge. River otters swim beneath the dock playfully welcoming newcomers.

Not a moment is wasted. Brunch is ready for arriving anglers and after satiated appetites, they head to the fishing grounds. Boats are 25-foot custom made aluminum boats with two 90-hp 4-stroke engines. It's a fifteen-minute motor to speed anglers to the popular fishing grounds of Cohoe Point. The stable boats have high transoms providing greater rod leverage for fishing. A compact, flushing head, so convenient for women, is located under the center console.

Several dozen boats mooch (trolling slowly with weighted lines using barbless hooks with cut-plugged herring bait) the protected cove because high northwest winds churning the surf don't permit venturing further west along the rocky coastline.

Minutes after lowering the lines 17 pulls or about 35 feet, a 20-ish pound Chinook (spring) salmon nibbles. Waiting patiently while feeling the bite, Mark watches the rod bend then says "hook it." Twenty pounders are medium-sized because during the week, five tyees (30 pounds) were caught including a 52-pound release and a 65-pound trophy fish.

Wearing a toque over his fishing cap for warmth and surgical latex gloves to protect against the salty brine of herring bait, Mark is an experienced guide requested by anglers from all over the world.

Unlike many other fishing destinations, the guides at Langara don't hook biting fish for the guests. Hooking any fish is the challenge and the fun part of an angling experience and, here, the novice has the opportunity to learn. Single action Islander reels (rather than the easier level-wind type) with lighter 20-pound test line adds more sport than down rigging at deeper depths method used by many fishing operations.

Mooching requires more skill for the angler to hook the fish, and the guide has to determine the depth where the fish are hanging out and feeding. If the angler doesn't anticipate the run of the fish during the fight, the handles of the reel, well, they're called "knuckle-busters" for a good reason.

There wasn't much time lapse between fish and another Chinook on the line followed by a jumper who was successful in unhooking himself. When the fishing slacked off, we had time to admire bald eagles as they fished. When herring splashed in the water like raindrops on a windshield, Mark caught them on bare hooks to use as tomorrow's bait. "They have to be stiff with rigor mortis to spin through the water correctly, so I catch them today to fish with tomorrow."

As Mark described it, we were fishing in the "last frontier." These salmon grounds are as far north as you can fish in British Columbia. On a clear day you can see the southeast panhandle of Alaska. In Mark's estimation, there isn't a better place for salmon and halibut fishing.

Before quitting time at 7:30p, we stopped on our return to the Lodge for a few minutes fishing in Bruin Cove. We were hoping to see a black or grizzly bear, but this is also the spot where sizable salmon hang out. A red-footed pigeon guillemot swam by the boat, a robin-like marbled murrelet dove quickly, while brown white-bellied rhinoceros auklet dived for herring.

Langara is not for "fair weather anglers or the faint of stomach." Gale force wind (+30mph) can whip the ocean swell as high as thirty feet. Leaving the protection of Cohoe Point or McPherson to fish favorites like Andrews Point or the island's west coast Lighthouse and No Name Point requires a calmer day.

In Solide Passage, the passage along Lucy Island and the route to the fishing grounds, a young humpback played in 24 feet of water. The barometer was rising and so were the salmon. Now able to navigate the waters to reach McPherson and Andrews Points, we had access to different salmon fishing grounds. Another day when the wind shifted, we headed southeast passing Cox Island stopping to search for bright-beaked puffin nesting on cliffs. The island is unusual with its interesting rock formations and a hole in the rock.

Changing winds also allowed us to fish southeast in the open ocean on the west coast near Lacy Island and the Lighthouse. We didn't have time to watch the Heerman gulls and bald eagles feeding or another humpback finning and breeching. Our time was spent with ten consecutive double hookups, fighting Chinook ranging from 20-30 pounds for three solid hours.

Aching biceps cried for ibuprofen and a soak in one of the lodge's two hot tubs. Stripping off the bright red survivor suits worn by all anglers, the warm water was perfect even in the rain. On the hillside, Sitka black tail deer nibbled the grass like lawnmowers.

The island of Langara is uninhabited except for four fishing lodges and a remote lighthouse on the northwest side of the island. This beacon, built in 1907, is lit by a 500-watt bulb. The lighthouse, manned by a couple, is the first land sighting seen by ships visiting North America. The rough waters along this portion of the rugged coast frequently make the trip by boat impossible. The red-topped lighthouse beacon is accessible by helicopter and our A-Star six passenger helicopter landed in the front yard.

Five of us were given a tour of the lighthouse including its tsunami reader then welcomed into the home where we were served spiced ice tea and blueberry cake. Before returning across the trail-less island, we landed briefly on the white sandy beach of Lepas Bay.

Thirty years ago, Vancouver school teacher Rick Bourne and his partners, the Noble brothers lived their dream. In 1984, they became aware of some great salmon fishing statistics from commercial operators around Langara. Rick sold his charter boat, and he and Richard, Robert, and John Noble started a small fishing lodge. They brought in a floating barge which they converted to a lodge.

Ten years later, they built the upscale (complete with Aveeda amenities in the bathrooms) twenty-eight guest Island Lodge. Little did Bourne know that his small twenty-four guest floating lodge would become one of the most popular salmon fishing lodges in North America.

He soon expanded the Fishing Lodge to hold fifty guests and added the 200-foot tram to carry guests up and down the hillside. Today, despite some rough weather and seas, four- or five-day trips allow as much fishing as the guest can handle. And while the fishermen play, the staff at the lodge rescue a newborn sea lion, its umbilical cord still attached. It's just another day in the Haida Gwaii, one of salmon fishing's "last frontiers."

19. Chilcotin Fly In-Fly Out Fly Fishing

Blue Ribbon Trout Dean River BC, Photo: Mary L Peachin

Beavers line the small pier that serves half a dozen rustic lakefront cabins. Not the wide-tailed furry type, but the 1950s-era Dehavilland aircraft. The six-passenger single engine float-plane is the workhorse of remote Canada, with the capability to lift off and land in a short distance while carrying a heavy load. It is the perfect vehicle for a wilderness fly fishing experience.

Stewart's Lodge, built in early '50s style by Robert and Virginia Stewart, had its beginnings as a rustic tented fishing camp. Today, the lodge, five hundred road miles north of Vancouver, in the Chilcotin region of British Columbia, offers anglers a selection of nicely appointed cabins from which they are able to enjoy fly in-fly out fishing. The area, which is surrounded by the snowcapped glacial peaks of the Coastal range, is isolated with the exception of the small village of Anahim Lake.

Pacific Coastal Airlines flies into its 3,500-foot airstrip, depending on the season, one or twice a week to bring anglers from Vancouver. The small logging and farming community of Anahim is home to 700 Chinook-speaking Ulkatcho Indians.

Each morning Duncan Stewart, who now owns the lodge, checks the weather to plan fly out destinations for the day. His experience is the only method of weather forecasting in this area.

After breakfast, the Beavers are loaded with passengers (carrying their fishing gear and a bag lunch). After a ten- to twenty-minute flight, the pilot lands on the water dropping anglers at a small pier, one of many nearby lakes (boats are cached at each) or a blue-ribbon trout river like the Upper Dean or Blackwater.

Chief pilot Doug Clarke, a resident of nearby Williams Lake, has been flying float planes for 20 years. Taking a break from fishing, we are treated to some aerial sightseeing. Majestic blue-ice glaciers with jagged peaks trickle snowmelt into jade-green glacial lakes. Another day, we circle Hunlen Falls, a waterfall that empties from its lake into a gorge before becoming a fishing stream. We flew along the Rainbow Mountains, a collage of red, yellow, and black covering a concentration of minerals including copper and iron.

Chilcotin loon, Photo: David Lovitt

Dry flying on the Upper Dean, one of BC's fine fisheries, can yield results of releasing forty to many as a 100 trout in a single day. Over the years we have seen these fish grow in size. Swift currents and slippery algae-covered boulders make the wading tricky. Jumping from the Beaver pontoons to the river bank, we took a motorized boat upriver to one of Stewart's five outpost cabins. Anchoring the boat, we hiked a trail to begin our wading. A Bald eagle with its ruffled chick stared at us from a tall lodgepole pine. A flock of goldeneye ducks, chicks in tow, swam by.

Another day we tackled the Blackwater, a more rugged trail – challenging wading, but a great fishery.

While the trout did not seem to discriminate between flies, red seemed to be their color of choice. On one day the "hot" fly was a flashy wooly bugger black/olive size 6. We found the muddler most consistent, but other anglers swore by leeches.

A young bull moose, his antlers still in velvet, swam in Lake Eliguk before settling down on the boggy shoreline to warm in the noonday sun.

As we trolled for brilliant speckled rainbows, glacier-covered mountains loomed behind a thick forest of black spruce and lodgepole pine. Circling the small pontoon boat near marshes, the trout seemed to be more active. Late in the afternoon pilot Doug Clark returned to our pick up scheduled for a certain time.

Mary fly fishing Dean River British Columbia, Photo: David F Peachin

Lake Hotnarko is about a 15-minute flight from the lodge. I took the smaller of two available boats cached in the woods. Having only a 3- horsepower engine, a strong wind, with only my weight, had me whirling in circles. After David and my daughter had a good laugh, I docked my boat and joined them in their small boat which was able to troll in a straight direction. We were upwind from the dock when we ran out of gas and had to paddle back to dock. A mother grouse scrabbled her chicks from our intrusion of their nest located where the gas tank was cached.

Outpost cabins are pristinely placed along shorelines and beaches at remote lakes and rivers. The lodge drops you in with basic supplies for several specified days. There is no communication with the outside world. Provisions include food, linen and chopped wood for the campfire. There is a wood burning stove.

Our favorite cabin was built on a sandy beach in a private cove. The lake, elevation 4,200 feet is surrounded by the snowcapped peaks of Mt. Davidson. Snowmelt creates springs to feed the lake. Once you come to terms with the bear-claw scratches on the window, it's easier to settle down – or is it? Two wooden beach chairs with a tree stump for a table offer wonderful views of the mountains. A small motorized boat is tied to the pier, a canoe rests against the cabin. Cooking can be done on the outdoor campfire, a wood burning stove or a propane stovetop. As a precaution, we carried water from the lake in buckets to boil. The cupboard is filled with canned provisions, and the lodge provides staples like eggs, milk, potatoes, salad, and T-bone steaks.

Before bedtime, we stoked the wood burning stove and made our routine "mosquito patrol." We wanted to eliminate any mosquitos still remaining in the cabin so we could sleep without being buzzed or bit. Snuggling up under our duvet-covered beds, we fell asleep listening to the distinctive call of the loon. In the middle of night 30-year-old Suzie cried out, "Dad, there is a mouse crawling on my stomach." Let's say, we were tight with nature.

Our final day we spent fishing Hunlen Creek. Noted for its cutthroat trout, we hiked a mile from our drop off at Turner Lake before casting our fly into the mouth of the stream flowing out of Cutthroat Lake. More than 30 trout were caught and released by each of us.

While fly fishing everywhere, with rare exceptions, requires a release policy, multiple summertime visits during Suzie and Jeffrey's college years, allowed us to observe the fish growing larger and more plentiful because of this conservation policy. Stewart's is unique in being isolated in a wilderness offering a unique ecosystem that provides views of bears, mountain goats, and other animals that can be seen while flying to the day's destination. Most fishing lodges have not been able to continue this option because of the high cost of insurance. Stewart's has the benefit of also flying for Tweedsmuir Park, both commercially and for those who come to camp or canoe.

20. Double, Double, Eagle! at Haida Gwaii's West Coast Fishing Club

Lori Mackstaller with guide and Chinook Langara, Photo: Mary L Peachin

Double, double, eagle! Say what? We aren't talking two under par golf here. Fellow Tucsonan Lori Mackstaller and I were fishing for salmon in a twenty-two-foot boat off Langara at West Coast Fishing Club's lodge in Haida Gwaii. It was one of those "anything can happen" days, and it did.

Trolling downriggers from a Boston Whaler we got a double hook up. Ensuing chaos erupted as we each followed our fish around the boat's center console to keep the lines untangled. A two-ton sea lion grabbed my fish, leaving its head, before grabbing Lori's fish. Before I could retrieve what was left — a twenty-plus-pound salmon head — a bald eagle swooped down, lifting it in his talons. This was a real close-up taste of the wilderness food chain.

We were so busy that when an announcement was broadcast over the radio, there wasn't time to reel in the fishing lines for a short motor to view a pod of twenty killer whales or orcas in the distance.

Lucky for us, we later got to see that pod of orcas after they swam through Parry Passage, where we were fishing. They appeared to be heading north, perhaps the fifty miles to Alaska. The bull, with his super-sized dorsal fin, and his mate swam some distance from the rest of the pod. During our four days of fishing, we also saw several lone humpbacks.

Monkey Puke and Betsy "dummy" flashers were tied to the boat, not the line. When I told guide Brent Maracle that I wanted to hook my own fish, he replied "At West Coast Fishing Club, all anglers are required to hook their own fish." How unique and refreshing not to have a guide hand over a rod with a hooked fish.

Fortune stayed with us. The sun was shining, seas were calm. We headed to the west side of Langara's Lacy Island. Not in the lee of the island, the water and wind here can be a real stomach churner. That is more typical of weather conditions in Langara.

During one of our fine cuisine dinners, Lori and I had the opportunity to dine with Fred Schuerenberg from Missouri. A widower, Fred was "bonding" with his new stepson, John Fuchs, over the weekend. He didn't bother to mention that he had just caught a potential season record-breaker 60-plus-pound Chinook.

When a sea lion chased his big salmon, Fred free-spooled the line while his guide hurriedly attached the line to another rod. Sea lions can't swim as fast as salmon.

An hour later, Fred measured and photographed the fish for the record book before releasing this granddaddy. When I asked Fred later why he didn't share this amazing story with the other anglers, he humbly told me, "I didn't want to sound boastful. This may be my first and last tyee." It wasn't, he caught another Chinook over that tyee thirty-pound requirement.

Maracle used cut plug herring for bait. West Coast uses the finest fishing gear: Islander single action "knuckle-busting" reels and Shimano rods. Knuckle busting? If you don't get your hands off the reel when the salmon runs, the spinning action of the reel on your fingers is going to cause a world of hurt.

For three days and two half-days, Lori and I released salmon while fishing Lacy and the calmer lee waters of Cohoe and Andrews Point. We enjoyed the wildlife, including pigeon guillemot and numerous bald eagles, and saw beautiful landscapes off Seath Point and Killer Bay. Uninhabited beaches and pinnacles included Langara's iconic Flower Pot and Pillar rocks. We were transfixed by bull kelp, white-sided dolphin, and numerous jellyfish.

Unfortunately, not all hook ups are good ones. A foul hooked (not in the mouth) or bleeding salmon is a dead one. West Coast offers flash freezing and packaging fish for their guests. Before we hit day three, we had limited out on salmon—the only choice left was halibut fishing.

Let's be honest. Halibut are some of the best tasting fish, but they aren't a lot of fun to catch. Then again, some folks may enjoy hauling what feels like a dead weight about two hundred feet to the surface. Not me. We were grateful when we caught "chickens," smaller and better tasting halibut.

Heading pass Egeria and Dibrell bays, we motored for about six miles. The combined smell of herring and salmon bellies from two other fishing boats acted like chum, helping to attract the halibut.

As we returned to Beal Cove, which the clubhouse overlooks, a humpback breeched out of the water. He then submerged, raising his tail fin. It was as if he was waving, "So long." It may have been the completion of our fishing journey, but not of those wonderful memories.

21. Patagonia River Ranch, A Fly Fishing Paradise

Becoming a member of Patagonia River Ranch's exclusive fly fisher's "Blue Label" Club is open only to those who release a twenty-five-inch rainbow or German brown trout. Argentina's premiere estancia, located in Northern Patagonia along the banks of the Chimehuin River floats anglers on six blue ribbon swift flowing rivers. Joining the Club is not unlike being a member of the "tyee" club, anglers who have caught a thirty-pound salmon, or a Caribbean salt water slam celebrated by releasing a permit, bonefish, and tarpon in a single day.

Fishing at the exclusive Patagonia River Ranch (PRR), while unparalleled in excellence, is not just a fly fishing hangout "for the boys." This is a luxurious "adult camp" estancia that offers as many activities as guests can pack into a twelve-hour day.

Located on a quiet dirt road, Patagonia River Ranch is forty-five minutes or thirty-six miles north of the village of San Martín de los Andes. Its gate, signed with the a discreet PRR brand, welcomes guests to an all-inclusive week of play: gourmet dining, a full bar and fine wines, everything including top of the line fishing gear. Emerged in a culture exclusively staffed by Argentines, it's all trophy fly fishing for trout, eating and, let's not forget, sleeping.

Argentina trout, Photo: Patagonia River Ranch

Owner Ken Gangwer is a Jackson Hole, Wyoming realtor and investor whose love for fly fishing took him to Patagonia more than thirty years ago. Returning year and year, in 1997, when told about the existing property in Patagonia, he bought the 650-acre estancia. He bought it for its location being surrounded by five blue-ribbon trout rivers that he could own, fish, and protect from poachers. That was just the beginning.

Temporarily side-stepping his love for fishing, he built a ranch and filled it with antiques that gave it the feel of an estancia of any well-heeled Argentine. To protect land erosion from destroying fishing habitat, he planted 24,000 cypress trees. He hired from the "get-go" only Argentines in order to support their economy. Anglers were attracted, not solely for the fishing, but enjoying its cuisine, wine and alcohol.

If Patagonia River Ranch is a well-kept secret, it's because Wyoming realtor Ken Gangwer doesn't advertise. His clientele is all word of mouth and repeat business. Local fishing guides cannot bring their clients to the Ranch to fish the six (Chimehuin, Caleufú, Aluminé, Malleo, Collón Curá and the Quilquihue area's rivers. Open between November and March, the ranch is totally exclusive for fourteen guests, there is no turnover during the week.

Those wishing to fish may head out with their guide at anywhere from five to eight in the morning. Hostesses Salome Audisio and Julia Volpe, who serve every guest's whim, divide their efforts taking one or both spouses shopping in the charming village of San Martín de los Andes, zip lining, kayaking, a Lago Lacar day long boat cruise, horseback riding, hiking, touring the Ranch's organic garden, or even taking a cooking class. A siesta can also be an option.

The fenced biodynamic organic garden covers a large area and includes several greenhouses as well as an orchard. When fresh produce, like tomatoes, are out of season, the best heirlooms are shipped from Buenos Aires.

Patagonia River Ranch, located in the Andes steppe of Neuquén Province, is landscaped by multicolored jarilla, neneo and coironales bushes along with Gangwer's introduced poplar and pine trees. River banks are lined with Creole or red willow roots stain. Knowing that a river can change its course by half a mile, over a decade, Ken planted 42,000 trees, all indigenous to Argentina, to protect the soil nutrients of his river front property.

The ranch house atmosphere is cozy with a living room and bar warmed by a large fireplace, a dining room with two large circular tables is adjacent to an extensive wine cellar and the kitchen. Gaucho antiques highlight the elegant accommodations and public space. There are several cabins for those wishing more privacy.

Ken's rose garden includes forty species grown in South America. The estancia's signature Papa Meilland® is a dark velvety and fragrant red hybrid tea rose. Buenos Aires growers did not expect it to grow in Patagonia because of the temperature variation, but it has flourished. Women guests are welcomed to the ranch with a rose.

Each day we were driven, raft in tow, to a river beginning with the Quilquihue, a river, known for its dry fly fishing, which merges into the Chimehuin River. Floating in a six-foot raft with two chairs and a standing bar and rowed by guide Mario Leyva, we used Orvis or Sage 9-foot rods with 5-6x tippet and Sage reels with dry flies: Adam parachutes, Fat Albert, caddis, grasshopper, mayfly imitations and beetle flies. We released rainbow and brown trout ranging between twelve and twenty-three inches.

Shore lunches, served on a plaid table cloth tables surrounded by armed chairs with a floral centerpiece of fresh roses and other spring flowers included a variety of food and wine or beer. One day, Chef Claudio Abraham, who has been at the ranch since it opened fifteen years ago, prepared a mini-asado of barbecued chicken wrapped in prosciutto, entrañas or skirt steak, and grilled pork, mixed green salad, grilled vegetables, peppers, eggplant, potatoes, and a mouthwatering crepe filled with dulce de leche topped with whipped cream and strawberries and a grilled peach. PRR was branded into the powdered sugar. Mendoza Zuccar vineyard's red Tempranillo was served. Satiated, as soon as the guides finished zipping yerba mate from their gourds, it was fishing time.

Dinner followed cocktail hour which lasted until everyone returned from their day's outing to the Ranch house. Typically served around nine, the entree might include a rib eye steak or marinated pork roast with grilled onions, mashed potatoes, freshly harvested lettuce, and a passion fruit tart. Sommelier Patricia Dalton introduced the nightly wine, always Argentine and frequently a Mendoza Malbec red.

David and Mary at Patagonia River Rancho asado

Another day we put in at the lower section of the Chimehuin. Its headwaters drain from Huechulafquen Lake in Lanin National Park before flow into Rio Collón Curá River. Snow melt from the Andes creates clear water which makes the twenty-five-mile Chimehuin River a habitat for large rainbows and browns. The hearty fish love its willow banks, big boulders, deep pools and frequent riffles.

A bonus was excellent bird watching highlighted by the northern carcara, black cormorant, lapwings, a variety of duck and geese, purple eagles, ibis, and more. Floating the Aluminé River along the stately cliffs of Piedra del Pilolil, a Mapuche translation for blue rock, we were unsuccessful in sighting condors. A two-hour drive south of Junín de los Andes village, the Aluminé becomes a tributary of the Collón Curá River.

El Manzano, in the upper part of Chimehuen, also offers large sized and quantities of trout. Three anglers drifted forty-two miles for twelve hours on the Caleufú River. Departing before daylight, they didn't return to the ranch until 11 pm. They released an average of sixty fish most of them ranging twenty or more inches. Another option was an overnight "luxury" camping trip on the lower Collón Curá River. Standup tents offered cots, mattresses and sleeping bags with a liner. Each tent had a toilet and hot shower. The large dining tent was formally set, a full bar stocked, an added bonus was the cooking expertise of Chef Claudio.

The week concluded with an asado in the patio. Chef Claudio spent the day grilling a side of beef and lamb over wood burning coals. The dinner also included chorizo sausage, empanadas, salad, grilled vegetables, and another scrumptious dulce de leche crème brulee dessert. The announcement of a presentation into Blue Label membership was a surprise to Tom Bosma. He knew he had released a large trout on the Collon Cura River while using a beetle fly, but he never considered it a contender.

All this speaks to the Ranch's solid booking year after year. Its word of mouth markets well. Whether two or five inches short of that magical twenty-five inch "Blue Label" qualification, another visit might provide the challenge for another opportunity, or, at the least, another exciting week at this luxurious "adult camp."

22. Kyoquot Sound: Fishing Beyond the End of the Road

Marilyn Murphy begins her orientation to salmon fishing on the stern of their liveaboard salmon fishing boat *Daleanne* at the same time a black bear lumbers onto the nearby beach. Kyoquot, she explains, ignoring the big animal, "translates to the land of many winds." Unfazed by her guests' distraction, she continues outlining British Columbia's salmon and halibut regulations to the dozen hard-core anglers. "Don't worry about him, that's just Boo," our four-year-old resident bear. "You'll see him scavenging for shells and seaweed during low tide."

It's just another everyday moment on Surprise Island, where the boat floats in the lee of a cove about five minutes by boat from the First Nations village of Kyoquot. For the next three nights, the 83-foot ship with ten staterooms, four shared baths, and two showers will be home to twelve guests, most of who are return visitors and *Daleanne* devotees. They welcome old friends with enthusiastic laughs and hugs.

The journey to Kyoquot has been an interesting one. After transferring from Seattle or Vancouver, anglers can fly or ferry to Campbell River, a village on the east coast of Vancouver Island. The adventure begins on the highway to Gold River, a two-lane road that winds through old-growth rainforest. There are beautiful views of emerald-green lakes, framed by Vancouver Island's snowcapped peaks. Black bear, cougar, and enormous Roosevelt elk inhabit the area. The road ends a few miles beyond Gold River. Since the town paper mill shut down three years ago, many have left; the main street looks deserted. At the end of the road, a two-hour drive from Campbell River, is Nootka Sound where Air Nootka's floatplane is docked. My next hour is spent flying 1,000 feet above the Tahsis Inlet, then winding north along the Pacific coast to Kyoquot.

With this crowd, the scenic journey is most likely taken for granted. These ten men and I have come to fish. Being the lone woman, Marilyn takes me under her wing, allowing me to stay in her house, and fish with her. The men are eager to meet their guides, jump into 17-foot boats, and head for some deep-water, downrigging and open-ocean salmon fishing.

Captain Marilyn Murphy has been fishing since she was a kid. She's been a guide for the family-operated Murphy Sportfishing almost half of her 26 years, and she can tie knots, set out lines, find fish, and out fish almost anyone. She was taught by "one of the best," her father Gordon who, at 76, was still guiding in Barkley Sound near Ucluelet.

Taking the sizable *Daleanne* through open seas in stormy conditions is not a trip for amateurs. Each spring for the past six years, Marilyn, who has a Master Limited captain's rating, has motored the ship from Kyoquot to the family's lodge on the Stamp River in Point Alberni.

We will be fishing in open ocean without coves to hid behind the elements. Twenty-five-knot winds are the norm, and Marilyn will fish 10-foot seas with northwester lies up to 40 knots. Offshore fishing can be rugged around Kyoquot.

Anglers with queasy stomachs can find calmer waters near the shore in the lee of the Barrier Islands, a group of lava rock formations that provides some protection from the elements.

Betty Johnson, who cooks for logging camps in the winter, spends her summers cooking for the Murphy's. Her small galley produces family-style meals with homemade breads and desserts. The meals are meticulously planned, as the provision boat comes only once a week. Anglers are always eager to taste some of her fresh salmon or halibut.

Marilyn's boat, the *Dolphin*, is a Campion Explorer equipped with a 150-horsepower Yamaha plus a 9.9-horsepower four-stroke trolling engine. She has a global positioning system, or GPS, radar, and a fish finder. Marilyn uses Shimano fishing gear, a single-action reel with 30-pound test line.

The captain scans the water, searching for fish as she guides the boat. She's looking for birds, especially murrelet, a species that dives to 120 feet. She's also looking for bait on the surface, or fish appearing on her fish finder. She knows the topography of the reefs and ridges, and where the salmon tend to feed. This area produces good fishing for salmon that have not yet headed to their spawning rivers, and anglers almost always catch their limits, sometimes in a single day.

Salmon fed on pilchards, needlefish, and squid, so Marilyn decides on a "hoochie" that resembles a squid, with a bright colored flasher to attract the fish. A twenty-pound chinook took the bait immediately, and while I was releasing fish, other anglers had some of their best fishing of the trip.

We start trolling in late afternoon and by the time we headed for home four hours later, Kyoquot was completely shrouded by fog. Yikes! Marilyn relied on the boat's radar to navigate shallow channels with treacherous rocks.

The second day, our target was hatchery-bred Coho, recognized because their back fin is clipped, and legal, if you choose, to keep. Marilyn gently releases them. This type of fishing produces a lot of better results, plus lighter tackle is a lot more fun to use.

We returned to shore hungry for dinner. In the village, hanging flowerpots mark Miss Charlie's, also a destination for recreational boaters heading up the west coast of British

Columbia to drop in for home cooking. Miss Charlie is a 37-year-old harbor seal rescued as an abandoned pup. Nursed in the bathtub of Esko and Lucy Kayra, she lolls on the rocks at low tide, visits everyone's dock, and chases pilchards in the bay when the tide is in. Charlie is the village mascot, according to the Kayras' daughter Sam, who operates the restaurant. There is no other business in town, not even a fuel dock.

Our final morning, we decide to fish behind the lee of Spring and Thornton Island. We begin by trolling for salmon with 9-weight fly rods, trailing flashers, and fly streamers called buck tails. I find the whir of salmon striking the fly even more exciting than the visual cue of the bent rod in deep-water fishing. I take a break and look around, enjoying the shore's black-lava rocks covered with gulls and cormorants, sea otters belly up with cupping sea urchins, spruce trees capping each small island, leaves of bull kelp gleaming in the sunshine.

Marilyn comes up at my side. "I love the smell of low tide," she says, inhaling the perfume of kelp, eelgrass, barnacles, and starfish. She takes another breath and smiles. "We'll be doing some gardening today," she laughs, referring to de-weeding our fly hooks.

Marilyn loves her life and loves fishing. Along with her brother, and four other guides, she'll work nonstop from June to August before heading the *Daleanne* back to Point Alberni. It's a long season, but she'll be ready for some fall river fishing, followed by winter steelhead fishing at their Stamp River Lodge. Sounds exhausting, right? Ah, but in November, she and her husband, take a month of vacation.

You guessed it. They go fishing in the tropics.

23. Vancouver's "Pin Popping Screamer" Fishing Derby

A "red alert" broadcast email warned anglers, "it's going to be *brutal,* dress warmly, don't wear runners (shoes)." Vancouver's weather forecast called for 100% chance of heavy rainfall and high winds. That would translate to 100 millimeters of drenching rain with 90-kilometer winds, a force so strong it produced horizontal precipitation.

Vancouver Chinook Classic Derby, an annual catch and release salmon tournament shouted out this foreboding forecast proclaiming a finality, "The show must go on."

Thirty-three boats from British Columbia carrying approximately 100 anglers moored their boats at Richmond's host Pacific Gateway Hotel and Marina on the Fraser River.

After gathering at five in the morning for a "fisherman's breakfast," anxious teams of three anglers boarded their respective boats to motor the Fraser River into Vancouver's Harbour. Heading the 26' Grady White into gale force winds, rock and rolling choppy seas, and full moon strong currents, I wondered what the hell I was doing there?

Vancouver Harbour, Photo: Todd Martin

My brand-new fishing buddies included two local businessmen, along with photographer Todd Martin, who would become an indispensable "first mate." The first "Pin popper screamer" occurred five minutes after lines were permitted in the water. Being gentlemen, I didn't hesitate when my buddies said, "Ladies first." I saw the line pop out of the downrigger, the spool going wild. I knew that this fish might be a contender. As someone yelled, "Reel, reel, reel" I knew not to "horse" the fish and risk breaking the line.

If the Chinook wasn't big enough to win, it was unusually strong for its size.

Bringing the Chinook to the boat, Captain Mike surmised that it looked like a high "teener." Probably not a winning size, it would be a waste of time to call then wait for the weigh boats to verify the catch. Derbies are usually won by Chinook weighing thirty (called a tyee) or more pounds. In stormy conditions, it could take the "weigh" boat a half hour or more to arrive. During that wait time, the fish had to be held in a net in the water and kept ALIVE.

Why did I agree not to call the weigh boat? As things would turn out, I probably released a winner. Mike was right except that he didn't predict the adverse weather conditions we would endure for the next eighteen hours, and its impact on the fishing.

Downriggers with cannon balls lowered sardine-baited barbless hooks to various depths. Only a sizable Chinook can snap a line out of a downrigger clip, a "pin popper" creating a whir-ring reel spooling fast and loud. In order to be in prize contention, the "weigh" boat volunteers measure the length and girth using a formula to determine fish weight.

Fishing was slow, currents tangled lines. Four trolling lines were reduced to two. There was a miscommunication about food and water being available on the boat. We were at the mercy of our stomachs for twelve hours. The food boat scheduled to bring out goodies to anglers couldn't handle the rough conditions.

We were fortunate to have a cover and a head, although it took us awhile to learn that the flusher was barely operative. One of our fishers, who did not have the required "cast iron" stomach, was saved by a Gravol seasick pill. With only two seats, one occupied by the Captain, the queasy angler wrapped his legs around me to hold me steady in the bow. His legs were shaking as they gripped around my waist. Was he uncomfortable about the weather-induced intimacy, scared, or just so cold he had the shivers? Knowing he was seasick, the thought of his barfing on my back dwelt in my mind. It was a very tough day of play with no entries to claim victory.

As conditions worsened, the radio announced more distant areas closed for fishing. When one of the guys asked about the location of life jackets, Mike assured us that they were in the hatch. Not totally comforting when cold water hypothermia can kill in minutes. We felt minimal relief seeing the Coast Guard hovering nearby. In fact, the only boats we saw in the entire harbour belonged to the Coast Guard. This was definitely a tournament that should have been canceled.

The only boats we saw fishing English Bay, Vancouver Harbour, Georgia Strait, T10, the yellow bell buoy, and the North arm of the Fraser were those participating in the Derby. Some boats were swept ashore, others lost equipment, or returned to the Marina.

Lines up! Returning to the Pacific Gateway Hotel late in the afternoon, all was dark. The worse summer storm in a decade, maybe the worse ever, had battered the Lower Mainland toppling drought-suffering trees into houses, cars, power lines. It would be several days before residents between metro-Vancouver and Seattle, Washington had power fully restored. The winning fish the first day was a mere 23 pounds. More regrets that we hadn't called the weigh boat. The $25,000 prize would not be mine.

Fraser River floated over their barriers creating "dead head" (milled trees) hazards for boaters. It was a slalom course to the harbour.

The second day was shorter, but rougher. Between strong currents and chop there were bone jarring, arm bruising troughs. Radio calls to the weigh boat were minimal. Then, a frantic call was heard ten minutes before the Derby ended at 1 PM. David Wei fishing on a Pacific Angler boat landed a 23-pound Chinook. With a "pin popping screamer," he snatched the title with minutes to spare.

My Own Fishing Captain

It goes without saying that the tournament was a nightmarish experience. I had seen fishing boats during my morning workout bicycling around Stanley Park, a bike lane that overlooks much of the harbour.

Decades ago, I worked with BC Tourism, Tourism Vancouver, and the Sport Fishing Institute visiting various lodges to write stories for U.S. newspapers and magazines. Sadly, money for freelancers ran out, and my popularity waned. Reading weekly reports from various camps indicated the ebb and flow of the salmon catch.

Vancouver Captain Lars Akerberg, Photo: Mary L. Peachin

I added my name to a few cancelation lists, and while there were a number of half-price opportunities, the offer was for two people. I would tell them that I could fish with anyone, but I didn't want to sleep with them.

After the Vancouver Chinook Classic Derby, I became aware that it might be possible to sleep in my own bed, fish during a shorter season for smaller salmon, but I would save money, and be out there.

Google comes into play here. After an intense search, I now have my own captain, Lars Akerberg, and I continue to release fish keeping the occasional one. I tested the skills of more guides, but settled on Lars in spite of having an historic day in Vancouver's Georgia Strait near the Fraser river with another guide. David joined me and the two of us had a non-stop day of double hook ups. I haven't nor did I expect to ever have that happen again, but for once, we were there on the perfect day.

Having Lars is the greatest. We plan a date when the tide looks favorable, I park in a friend's garage, and meet my Captain at his marina. We have had great fishing, and a better time. It's a luxury every angler should have.

24. Trophy Fishing in the Yukon Wilderness

Cirque of the Unclimbables, Northwest Territories, Photo: Mary L Peachin

Inconnu Lodge sits amid the vast wilderness straddling the Continental Divide in Yukon (formerly the Yukon Territory), Canada. The lodge is remote by anyone's standards. Its stunning wilderness landscape is punctuated by black and glacial-green rivers, isolated alpine lakes, jagged mountain peaks and flat-ridged mountains. During the summer, a rainbow of flowers peeks through the tundra-covered landscape.

The area is considered a "high eastern plateau," and except for the Mackenzie Mountains, many of the region's mountains, lakes and rivers are nameless. Offering both experienced and novice anglers a taste of Canada's best northernmost fishing, Inconnu Lodge, accessible only by plane, is 185 miles east of Whitehorse, Yukon's capital city.

Overlooking Lake McEvoy, the seven-mile headwater leads to a series of lakes interconnected by streams offering superb fishing for lake trout and Arctic grayling. Each day, there is adventurous fly-in fly-out fishing to remote places where it is possible to wade or drift rivers, and either fly fish or spin cast in alpine lakes for more species, including northern pike, Dolly Varden, or the rare inconnu, or sheefish, for which the lodge is named.

Next to its trophy-size fish, Inconnu's isolation and nameless destinations are its primary attractions. A five- to forty-five-minute flight drops the angler at one of about twenty lakes where eighteen-foot boats are cached, or at one of a dozen rivers fished by canoe, jet boats, or inflatable rafts.

Inconnu practices conservation by resting its fisheries for several days, weeks, sometimes even a season. They want to keep the fish wild and hungry. Having such great fishing resources to themselves, with no population within a hundred miles, they prefer to maintain the anonymity of their favorite destinations.

On a recent flight in the area, I saw four moose busily grazing on river weeds in shallow river rapids. Warren LaFave, who with his wife, Anita, owns Inconnu Lodge, crabbed his Hughes 500 helicopter into a hover before landing on a riverside bog. He dropped us near a cached canoe, and we paddled downstream for a close-up moose encounter. Unfortunately, the moose had wandered into the willows.

Casting five-weight rods tied with wooly bugger and leech patterns, we waded in fifty-two-degree water, releasing dozens of Arctic grayling and lake trout. After a shoreline picnic, guide Ken Richardson suggested we paddle to an area better known for its trophy-sized lake trout. Climbing into the canoe, I spotted a bull moose, one with sizable antlers. Ken and my husband, David, quietly paddled us toward the bull until we got within a hundred yards. The moose stopped feeding and we stopped paddling. After a brief stare down, he splashed out of the water and into the brush.

While fishing another lake for specimen (forty-inch) northern pike, Ken told us he was taking us to the "river of our dreams." Narrow and lined by a boggy bank, the sandy-bottomed river produced grayling and lake trout on almost every cast. Several times Ken used a tape to measure a twenty-inch release. This was definitely a day that ended too soon.

David holding lake trout with Guide Ken Richardson at Inconnu, Yukon, Photo: Mary L. Peachin

Another day we fished from inflatable drift rafts, with Ken manning the oars, down another river. Two captain's chairs with standing casting bars allowed us to cast three-weight rods for grayling. Exploring miles of relatively virgin water, whenever we reached a prime fishing pool, Ken would drop anchor to enable us to throw a fly into a nearby pocket or riffle structure.

At the end of our drift, Warren — piloting the helicopter — sighted us waiting along the riverbank. After using a sling to haul the raft back to the put-in, he picked us up for the short flight back to the lodge. It had been a unique and adventurous, fun-filled Yukon day, and a cold dip in the lake, a nearby hot tub and steamy sauna awaited our tired muscles.

Inconnu's 6,500-square-foot main cedar lodge includes a large dining room, a vaulted-ceiling lounge with game tables, a gift shop, and even a conference room with, believe it or not, satellite television and wireless Internet service.

Inconnu's Dehaviland Beaver floatplane is used along with the helicopter for daily fly-outs for fishing, heli-hiking, river drift trips, or seeing the natural wonders of Northwest Territories' Cirque of the Unclimbables and Virginia Falls.

Cirque of the Unclimbables, in Northwest Territories' Nahanni National Park Reserve, is a cluster of peaks and walls in the Mackenzie Mountains Natural Region.

A challenge for world-class mountaineers, the cirque is in the Ragged Range, near Glacier Lake. Its most famous peak, Lotus Flower Tower, is a must for every serious climber.

Virginia Falls is also in Nahanni National Park Reserve, on the South Nahanni River. It has a total drop of 315 feet, making it about twice the height of Niagara Falls. It consists of a single drop with an average width of 850 feet.

Waders, boots, and a small daypack (for rain gear) are the only essentials required for guests. The lodge supplies all fishing tackle, including spinning, level wind, or fly rods along with lures or flies for each guided day.

The LaFaves built Inconnu Lodge log by log by log. It took five years of hard work, grit and determination. Logging more than 1,500 freight flights, Warren flew in every piece of building material, in his Dehaviland Beaver.

Gracious hosts, Warren and Anita are "Jack and Jill of all trades." Each day, Warren flies anglers to and from their fishing destination. Anita, the "Martha Stewart" of the Yukon, warmly meets and greets clients. She plans gourmet four-course dinners, has the weekly provisions list down to a science, packs scrumptious picnic lunches, oversees the chef's and kitchen staff 's food preparation and service, and tends to other administrative duties.

Inconnu's nine cedar cabins, cozy with wood-burning stoves, overlook the lakefront. The Beaver floatplane and fishing boats are tied to a wooden dock lined with Adirondack chairs.

An exception to Inconnu's strict catch-and-release policy is a day of enjoying a shore lunch of freshly caught grayling. Ken, batters the fillets with corn meal, then grills them in a cast-iron skillet over a propane burner with butter and a splash of wine. Ribs, fingerling potatoes, Greek salad with arugula, and garlic toast are also served, on plates garnished with fresh strawberries.

Yukon is a great place to view wildlife. Moose outnumber the territory's entire human population by 20,000. Mountain goat and sheep climb steep, rocky mountain slopes. Grizzlies and black bears munch on wild berries, and more than 200,000 caribou migrate seasonally through the territory. Other wildlife includes wolves, wolverines, coyotes, foxes, beavers and marmots. It is also a birder's paradise with the region boasting more than 200 species of migratory and birds of prey.

It's difficult to imagine having easier access to twelve remote rivers and streams and seventeen lakes with the choice of fishing seven species of trophy-size fish. Fly fishing, spin casting or trolling can land beginner or professional anglers nonstop activity in the five- to thirty-pound class. When you are releasing different species of fish on light tackle on almost every cast, does it get any better than that?

Part VIII.

Scuba Diving Adventures

If you have paged through my fishing adventures, hang tight. Scuba diving is my first passion. When asked my favorite place, I find it a difficult question to answer. There are interesting and remote places, but I like muck (the ultimate critter) diving more than diving in a cage with great white sharks. I enjoy seeing thousands of elusive hammerheads as well as the tiny epaulet shark. Where have I've been? It's much easier to tell you what I have missed. If you exclude cold water diving, below 75 degrees, I regret that I have missed the mantas of Yap, the World War II wrecks of Truk, and while there are many places that I would enjoy, if I had to pick one, it would be Eastern Indonesia, give me two choices, add the Solomon Islands east of Papua New Guinea.

In recent years, I've been spending more time in the water with whale sharks. I love their polka dots and they are an easier to reach destination. The travel to get to Indonesia is a trip of four days with two overnights, one in Bali, and the other on an island in South Sulawesi. Getting to Bali is an 18-hour flight.

Bali used to be great, but now the traffic is streets crammed with motor scooters. Nothing is more melodic than the Muslim "Call to Prayer," but I can pass on the call at 4am. Not only are flights long, but unveiled, Anglo women alone (like me) stand out, an attraction for numerous I-phone photos. Another issue is one of 3am connections. Unable to explain a 1am wake-up call at a hotel in Makassar, I was afraid to go to sleep. Good thing, the hotel never called me. Expecting to be alone in the airport, I realized from locals cramming the airport it was Indonesia's typical flight schedule. I did try my ATM card to see if I could actually get cash without a fee. It worked, thanks BBVA.

Four exhausting days later, submerged in pristine waters with diverse geography, and fabulous fish and coral, you soon forget that awful experience of getting there.

25. Deadly Encounters: a Box Jellyfish and Blue-ringed Octopus

Experiencing a few irritating jellyfish stings over the years, I started wearing Lycra or a wetsuit, depending on the chill, and a hood. Jellies typically swim near the ocean's surface so as I ascended, I always circled making a swirl to swoosh them away.

Peter Hughes, an early scuba icon, invited me to join him when he launched his liveaboard dive boat in Palau, Micronesia. That's when, as his guest, I missed diving with mantas in Yap, a stop on the plane route.

Palau is known for its strong currents and fabulous diving. It is also the site of World War II battles, most famously the Battle of Peleliu. Palau's Blue Corner reef has been called one of the world's top dive site.

Blue ring octopus, Photo: Dave Jaskey M.D

Like Australia, known for its small but deadly box jellies, which can kill in four minutes, Micronesia has its share of these critters. After diving for three days, without sight of a jellyfish, and I always look, the water was warm so I wore a t-shirt over my bathing suit.

Divers at Blue Corner require a reef hook to stay in one place. There are up and down currents that can contribute to the bends while getting back and forth to the boat, neither great for unwanted nitrogen consumption. Tuna swam over the reef only to be gobbled by sharks, hundreds of them.

While swimming toward Blue Corner's reef, I felt a sting brush my biceps. Yikes! I didn't see it, but guessed it was a jelly. I continued the dive.

Exiting the water 40 minutes later, I told the boat crew that I thought that I had been stung by a jellyfish on my upper arm. Their first question was, "Mary, are you having trouble breathing?" That's when I realized there might be a problem.

It was the beginning of a 10-day trip, and I wasn't about to spoil it so I gratefully accepted help from the crew and guests. Literally everyone on the boat had some kind of medication to offer me for pain, itching or swelling.

The first symptom was the unexplainable swelling of the left side of one breast, then generalized body pain that lasted six weeks. When I returned to Tucson, I called the University of Arizona's Poison Control center.

That's when I learned about box jellies, and I haven't been unclothed in the water again. You might say it was a tiny brush with death. There are very few annual deaths because swimmers and divers make it a point to avoid contact.

When I was writing *The Complete Idiot's Guide to Sharks,* I learned about the blue-ringed octopus. Polka-dotted like the whale shark, the creature is just a few inches long. It has the reputation of being one of the most venomous critters in the ocean, another four-minute killer. It reportedly carries enough venom to kill 26 adult humans within minutes. Now I was intrigue by a search to see one.

At the time I wrote that book, 2002, there had only been one known death. Current fatality estimates vary, from three on the low end to seventeen at the most.

These octopus spend much of their time in tidal pools or shallow reefs, a young girl had stuck her hand in her scientist dad's bucket and she was bitten.

I knew that they tended to be nocturnal, and that they were found in Indonesia. One night near a dock on Kri Island, I spotted one. Diving with a group of divers, I began yelling through my regulator, "Shoot your camera." I flashed my light on the octopus, as its yellow spots started pulsating. They must have thought I was crazy. Another night, I saw a second one. This time my crewmates were thrilled and knowledgeable.

A few years later, my Chicken Diver buddies saw one during the day on the bottom of a shallow area. That was a real treat.

26. Solomon Islands: Saltwater Crocodile

Saltwater Crocodile, Mirror Pond, Solomons, Photo: Matty Smith

A dangerous saltwater crocodile had been previously seen in Mirror Pond, an underwater cave on Mane, one of many mangrove atolls in the Solomon Islands' Russell chain. "We do not know the behavior of this man-eating crocodile," stressed Scott Waring, then divemaster on the Spirit of the Solomons liveaboard dive boat.

"When he has been sighted, he is usually lying on the cave's ledge," Waring said. He told us that while the crocodile had previously attacked a snorkeler, it had never bothered a scuba diver. He urged, "When you follow me through the 250-foot underwater passageway, please leave me plenty of room to escape!"

Waring's wife, Diane, chimed in, "It's only a small croc and it isn't always there." Confidence bolstered, I decided that I was up to this scuba diving encounter. Perhaps foolishly, five of us felt that there was safety in numbers. Those aluminum tanks on our backs, if they scared whales, they also helped us feel invincible.

Our intrepid group included divemaster Waring, James Forte, a professional underwater photographer; Zim Gervais, a videographer; Karen Haugen, a nurse; and myself. Haugen and I brought up the rear. We figured in the event of a hasty retreat, it was "last in, first out."

Divers headed into Mirror Pond

Following in single file, we threaded through the twisting passage at a depth of sixty feet, carefully avoiding stinging fire coral growing on the cave's wall. Approaching the entrance to an underwater cave, the tunnel narrowed, leaving an open slot extending to the surface of the atoll. Coral-covered mangrove roots gripped the edges of the pond. Tree limbs cluttered the surface water's edge, providing lots of hiding places for a crocodile.

Waring quickly sighted the crocodile resting on a ledge and signaled for our attention. I looked up to see the six-foot man-eating crocodile lunge into the pond, swim across its surface, then climb onto another ledge. Yikes!

When I surfaced for a better view, the crocodile lunged back into the pond. Adrenaline pumping, hearts pounding, the five of us spontaneously back-finned out of the cave, retracing our path through the passage.

I had imagined the definition of Diane's description of "small" as a twelve-inch aquarium-size croc. What had I been thinking? Haugen later shared, "My heart was pounding when I made that 180 degree flip out of the cave."

Feeling secure after leaving the passageway, we continued our dive. Descending to deeper depths, we admired two Australian giant cuttlefish camouflaging their bodies to blend with the variety of colorful coral reefs of the Solomon Sea.

* * *

Ten years later, in 2010, I returned to the Solomons to dive on the Spirit's sister ship, the well-known and respected *MV Bilikiki*. Our first dive was at Mirror Pond, and it was déjà vu. Just the thought of a second encounter raised my adrenaline. But this time, there was no croc. It was a stunning checkout dive rather than the usual humdrum shallow dive to check our weights and buoyancy. I guess if you travel that distance, they assume you're an experienced diver.

In 1989, *MV Bilikiki* was the first full-service luxury liveaboard dive vessel in the Solomon Islands. She offered private showers and toilets in ten deluxe cabins. The 125-foot boat departed from the city of Honiara, Guadalcanal Island, cruising primarily the Russell Islands.

Its untouched soft and hard corals are home to hundreds of tropical fish and "critters." Each anemone seemed to have a symbiotic relationship with a different species of clownfish. Lionfish hung under rocks, while in the current, schools of neon fusiliers, batfish, bannerfish, damsel, parrotfish, and other fish swam. Blennies, mantis shrimp, octopus, cuttlefish, crabs, conchs and other shells guarded entrances to their sandy holes or crevices. Reef sharks, turtles, and occasionally eagle rays cruised reef walls.

In the midst of this spectacular beauty, which includes many caves, swim-throughs, and interesting underwater terrain, lie the sunken remains of the casualties of the Battle of Guadalcanal, one of the largest World War II battlegrounds in the South Pacific.

On one dive, I saw a World War II B-24 Liberator. It had shreds of a parachute hanging out its doors. When I posted a photo of it on peachin.com, my 25-year-old website, I heard from families around the world asking if I knew the N-number or plane's identification which are numbered according to the country of ownership. They had lost a beloved pilot during the battle, and they wondered if that was his plane. Time had erased the numbers, so unfortunately, I couldn't bring any closure to their grief.

The tremendous variety of nocturnal "critters" and gentle drift diving made for some fascinating night dives. Colorful crinoids were feeding as their arms waved in the current. Mantis and other shrimps, lobsters, and crabs crawled out of their crevices onto the sandy bottom. The water temperature was a comfortable 82 degrees.

The *Bilikiki* makes it a point to make an island visit during each voyage. With permission granted, we received a hearty welcome by the Karumolun Village chief. We were also given the opportunity to buy crafts displayed along orchid-lined paths.

There was a variety of carvings and bowls made from ebony and rosewood. Negotiations were standard fare and included a first and second price. Typically, a purchase included a request for additional "trade" items. AA batteries were a hot item, as were shaving razors, combs, and even a pair of socks.

Men, followed by the women, danced for us. This pre-arranged sing-sing followed a welcome with the chief asking us to stand in a line so the islanders could place flower leis around our necks. We were then escorted to nearby benches for the show. The conclusion of the dancing included the singing of Christian hymns in English.

During our ten-day diving trip, the warm water allowed us to spend as many as fifty hours underwater. Reflecting on the sites and critters as we returned to Honiara, we experienced what has become the *Bilikiki* tradition of "Popcorn Passage." Years ago, a bag of popcorn was thrown to some children. The approach of the dive boat now brings out many families. Paddling furiously in their dugouts, it is joyous to see their excitement when they catch a bag of popcorn.

Boarding our Air Solomon flight to Nadi, Fiji, all of us shared a very special feeling for the Solomon Islands. The scuba diving was world class, the *MV Bilikiki* and its crew and operation were superb, the people of the Islands were warm and friendly, the mangrove islands and its underworld was beautiful.

27. Cocos Islands: Hammerhead Diving in Costa Rica

"You'll want to be my dive buddy this week. Trust me on this." The young man looked at me quizzically, wondering why a smiley silver-haired woman would make such a definitive comment. Benji, young enough to be my son, didn't know that during the Okeanos Aggressor's routine check-out dive, while the diving crew assessed our underwater capabilities, I was evaluating the divers.

The crew of our mothership, a 120-foot converted fish trawler, divided the twelve us into two Zodiacs. Benji must have trusted me because he switched his gear into my assigned Zodiac.

When diving with sharks, "babysitting" an anxious buddy reduces the time spent at depth and the opportunity for an up-close experience. I wanted a buddy who could descend immediately after a back roll from the Zodiac without surfacing then get to depth fast. Benji was my man on this quest for scalloped hammerheads — he just didn't know why. He would appreciate my rate of descent and low air consumption after one dive.

Cocos Hammerhead, Photo: Bill Kimball

Sharks tend to not hang around, and frequently only the first divers get to see them. On our trip, they were also deep-swimming about 100 feet beneath the surface. No time to waste.

Twelve of us had endured an excruciating 42-hour boat ride to the Cocos Islands, 300 miles south of Costa Rica's Osa Peninsula in the Pacific Ocean, to dive with the "big stuff" — schooling hammerhead, whitetip and oceanic reef sharks, pilot whales, whale sharks, sailfish, marlin, manta and eagle rays, wahoo, and tuna. The steering on the boat was broken, unable to motor in a straight line, we zigzagged that long distance. The air conditioning was also broken; we all slept together on the roof of the top deck. The Aggressor Fleet refunded us partial payment for these inconveniences.

Contrary to their reputation, hammerheads — Cocos's primary attraction — are shy, elusive sharks that swim off at the sight or sound of a diver's bubbles. The normal water temperature of 70-72 degrees had been warmed by an El Niño current to about 82 degrees.

We entered the water and descended. This was serious open-water diving, no reefs or shark cages for protection. We had to navigate through strong, shifting currents; always aware of riptide-like surges that could smash us against boulders covered with long-spine sea urchins.

We could spend only minutes at depth looking for sharks before ascending in stages for decompression limits while exploring boulder crevices for lobsters, stingray, octopus and other sea "critters."

Benji's decision to partner with me was rewarded on the first dive of the weeklong trip. We were the only divers to see hammerheads. We also saw some interesting "critters," the most unusual being a camouflaged orange frogfish. When it was time to ascend, we drifted away from the boulders, once again searching the deep blue water for any glimpse of the "big stuff."

The islands teemed with a variety of other life. Scientists have identified 97 species of birds, two endemic species of reptiles, 57 crustaceans, 500 mollusks, 800 species of insects, turtles including black, olive and Indo-Pacific hawksbill, and five species of freshwater fish. While eager to see the island's 300 species of saltwater fish, we were focused on diving with hammerheads.

There are fewer than half a dozen dive sites surrounding the Cocos: underwater seamounts with names like Dirty Rock, Submerged Rock, or Sharkfin, which rises above the water in an iconic shape. The dive boat usually anchored in the calmer waters of Manuelita Bay.

Our divemaster, Jay, shared a number of diving precautions. When diving in surging water, he suggested, carefully observe the fish. "When they swim, you swim. They're used to the currents of the surge." Underwater currents in the Cocos can be horizontal or vertical, sometimes sweeping divers ten to 20 feet in any direction. Jay also cautioned about bracing against seamount boulders to avoid hitting them. "The boulders are covered with urchins and barnacles," he said. "Their spines do not feel good penetrating your body."

"Currents changed continually, and with visibility limited to 50 or 75 feet, Zodiac drivers can't follow your air bubbles," he added. "Be very careful when you surface, to avoid being run over by an inflatable boat." The warnings helped illustrate why the Cocos is a destination for only experienced divers.

Midway through the week, in addition to the hammerheads, we saw dozens of whitetip sharks, the larger, more aggressive oceanic whitetip shark (similar to the one that charged me in the beginning chapter of this book); yellowfin tuna, jack crevalle, marble and eagle rays, and turtles.

Schooling sharks in Cocos, Photo: Bill Kimball

A particular thrill was diving in the midst of a pod of pilot whales. We sighted them from the boat, and underwater could hear the dolphin-sized whales "sing." Several divers saw a school of yellowfin tuna precede the whales. Two other divers were ecstatic to glimpse a sailfish, its fin majestically unfurled.

A hike took us to a 200-foot waterfall near Wafer Bay. After riding in the Zodiac from the *Okeanos* to just beyond the breaking waves, we jumped into the ocean and bodysurfed onto the crab-covered rocky beach. During a rugged half-mile climb through the rainforest, we were cautioned about using potentially poisonous roots or vines for handholds, or stepping on logs, which might be rotted. Hot and sweaty upon reaching our destination, we jumped into the re-freshingly cool pool at the base of the waterfall with some of its inhabitants, freshwater shrimp.

At a second island location, beach entry was easier because the tide was low and the beach sandy. Large boulders strewn around the beach have names carved into them, including that of legend-ary diver Jacques Cousteau. The oldest "graffiti" we saw was dated 1880. We hiked up a creek and climbed over rocks splitting the stream. But time was limited and we were at Cocos to dive.

At the end of one diving day, several of us took the Zodiac out to fish for our dinner." We circled the island, using monofilament as a handline to catch 35-pound wahoo and a smaller jack crevalle. The evening ended with a pod of pilot whales circling us in the setting sun.

Like so many dive trips, buddies bond during the week and vow to stay in touch. Generally speaking, after returning home, and having to catch up on work, family, and life, that rarely happens, and when it does it is for a year or two. I feel comfort knowing that Benji was grateful that I asked him to buddy-up. It made the trip better for both of us.

28. Komodo Dragons, a Hike from the *Arenui* Indonesia Dive Liveaboard

It bites to kill. The Komodo dragon is the world's largest monitor lizard. Once it gets a taste of blood it is impossible to separate it from its prey. Its toxic bacteria saliva creates an infection that slowly kills the animal. Komodo's devour everything including the animal's hide. The famous indigenous species are found in the 17,000-island archipelago of Indonesia.

Four days into our *Arenui* Indonesia Liveaboard 12-day dive journey, we arrived at Komodo National Park where an estimated 2,500 dragons can be found on five of the islands. Swimming between islands, propelled by a long tail, they warm in the sunlight to reach an optimal temperature which increases their energy to hunt. They can smell prey at great distances. Close to ten feet in length, they weigh as much as 150 pounds. They have no predators. Females lay up to eighteen eggs which incubate for ten months.

Komodo Dragon , Photo: Mary L Peachin

The dragons congregate only when they are feeding. They fight with one another and frequently cannibalize their young, weak and old. Hatchlings, to avoid being eaten, live in trees for two years. Researchers have discovered that, like snakes, Komodo's also have a venom that interacts with their deadly saliva bacteria.

The island is arid and hilly. Two rangers took us for an hour and a half hike carrying forked sticks. Most dragons are seen near the ranger station. This is probably because they are attracted to the ranger's garbage. We saw several Komodos along the trail, one drinking from a stream. As we climbed the hill overlooking the bay and the *Arenui*, we saw their prey: water buffalo and Timor deer.

While hiking among Komodo dragons was a great thrill, diving off the *Arenui* ranks as one of the best boats and destinations.

The discovery of new destinations, knowledge of fish migrations, and identification research has taken divers to many new places. Liveaboards have improved from cockroach infested, unseaworthy scows to cattle boats, and are now, pricey small occupancy boutique liveaboards.

Our 12-day trip offered muck diving (see Chapter 29), strong currents requiring reef hooks, and bottomless reef walls. There was a lot of variety, including hard and soft corals, and even mangroves that included new sightings daily.

Departing, Bali, we rocked and rolled overnight in moderately rough seas and windy conditions through the Lombok Straits towards the west side of Lombok Island.

Our first two dives were on the east side of Lombok near the island of Gili (Indonesian for island) Lawang. We saw numerous species of shrimp and a robust pipe fish. Usually observed with his head protruding out of the sand, a hunting snake eel slithered along looking for prey. There was a school of striped catfish, ghost and Halameda pipe fish, crinoid shrimp, and a cockatoo waspfish spiny devilfish, harlequin shrimp, and a hairy angler, more commonly known as a frog fish. A carrier crab carried a piece of wood.

In Bima, a city on the eastern coast of Sumbawa in central Indonesia's province of West Nusa Tenggara, the island of Tanyung Sai had fine black sand with clear visibility unless kicked by a fin. Like silt in a cave, the area and critters were quickly obscured. We saw a coconut octopus eating a crab, one orange frogfish had lost an eye.

Other critters included a juvenile grey frogfish, tiny cuttle fish that squirted away like the flash of a strobe, reddish crinoid cuttlefish, a rare Melibe nudibranch appearing thin and limp like a piece of floating tissue paper, a shy mantis shrimp, eggs of a cuttle fish, and a pipe fish carrying her eggs. Little did I know that this was just "an appetizer" for what we would see later.

Pair of Halemeda pipe fish, Photo: Dave Jaskey

Gerry, my divemaster, studied different fish and critter behaviors. One the more fascinating behaviors we observed were two speck-like microscopic-size isopods who suck the blood and lives of clown fish. In an attempt to rid themselves of these life sucking killers, clown fish continually open and close their mouths trying to spit them out.

During our twelve-day trip, the water temperature ranged between 71-82 degrees. The waters around Komodo are consistently cold. I always wore a five-mil suit and added a skin or two plus a hooded lined vest.

Maximum dive time was 70 minutes, which we used almost every dive. While there was a flexible buddy system, partners usually stayed together. If divers wanted to see critters, they followed their divemaster. We ate when we weren't diving or sleeping. Morning and afternoon snacks included pizza, fish sticks, always fresh and delicious tropical fruit, an open cookie jar, and a fresh cake or pastry.

Hot rocks, a dive site at Sangeang Volcano, which is alive, but not active, has underwater sulphuric bubbles trickling from the sand. They definitely warm the water. A pair of cowries, covered with black mantles rested in a sponge, there were multiple species of nudibranch, a large black lionfish carried eggs on her spine, and a green turtle was eating an unidentified sponge, one that allegedly appears to give them a "buzz." Glassy eye fish rose in columns. There was a rainbow of thousands of crinoids and orange anthias. A yellow and black ribbon eel, burrowed in the sand under one of many table corals. A raging current swept the black sand making it appear like a Saharan sand storm. We drifted to a beautiful reef covered with every imaginable soft and hard coral. Seventy minutes later, we made our way up to shallow sand which offered a spiny devilfish. There was a variety of nudibranchs, and several blue painted lobsters.

At Crystal Rock, we made a direct descent in two to three knot current. Making good use of our reef hooks, we admired three-foot Napoleon wrasse, big eye trevally, surgeon fish, schools of fusiliers, several white tip sharks, one of which was pregnant. A couple of bottled nose dolphin were seen by several surfacing divers.

Castle Rock, also known as Takat Toko, is two submerged pinnacles located near Gili Lawalaut. We watched surgeon fish chased by trevally with sharks following close behind. We found ourselves surrounded by schools of fish.

Our next stop was Rinca Island's Hannibal Rock. It is known as one of the world's top ten dive sites. Discovered by the late Larry Smith, an Indonesia dive icon, if you like biodiversity, you'll love this pinnacle. The water temperature dropped to a chilly 72 degrees.

We found a giant pink frogfish, but couldn't find the paddle flap and weedy rhinopius, members of the scorpionfish family, that are frequently seen. We saw red sea apples, a species of sea cucumber. Some were closed while others were open and feeding. A yellow pygmy seahorse clung to a seafan.

Torpedo Alley was the site of our Rinca Island night dive. The fourth daily dive was after sundown. While we all participated in one or more, there were only two regular night divers. Camouflaged in a soft coral was a hairy frogfish. We did not see previously sighted electric torpedo rays. There were skeleton shrimps, a coconut octopus. A Bobbitt worm, named after the infamous wife who offed her husband's penis. We also saw decorator crabs, shrimp, nudibranch, and a painted frogfish. The bone chilly 71 degrees limited that dive to 40 minutes.

During a day dive at Torpedo Alley, we saw the same hairy frog fish. This sighting was topped by two mimic octopus, three painted frog fish, a ghost pipe fish, a small cuttle fish, and a friendly hawksbill turtle. A frog fish cuddled next to a leaf fish, while a zebra crab took refuge in a fire sea urchin

In Manta Alley, located on the south side of Komodo Island, we admired approximately ten large reef mantas on each of two dives. These mantas appear to have little curiosity and swam quickly away.

We were not able to find the wonderpus frequently sighted at Pink Beach. The site, however, did not disappoint. Colorful mandarin fish, doing their mating ritual, swirled in thick fields of staghorn coral. Burrowed in a hole was a white mantis shrimp, a yellow headed jawfish, mating nudibranchs, and a black ribbon eel.

Leaving the Park, we motored to Loh Liang Bay. There are strict rules about not touching or chasing mantas. In Takat Makassar channel between Flores and Komodo, mantas feed and clean in the 2-3 knot current. It was a roller coaster ride.

About halfway through the dive, mantas began appearing. Flying in the current, a few coming my way made for some close encounters. We saw about a dozen of them before surfacing. Tatawa Besar is a sloping reef that can have split currents. This is a place where divers have been swept away. Each of us was required to carry a safety sausage. Two large boomies or small pinnacles had schools of batfish and harlequin sweetlips. Turtles hung out near shallower water. It was a beautiful dive.

Discovery Bay, along the long island of Flores is a 19-hour motor from our dives around the island of Sabalon. Indonesian fisherman continue to blast fish. In populated areas, many reefs have been destroyed. The sound of a blast made miles away sounds like dynamite has been dropped above you.

We were returning to our final destination in Maumere so our best option was spending the day in black sand doing muck diving. Weird critters make their appearance at different times.

Discovery Bay was a real test of neutral buoyancy. One touch from a fin created a sand storm cloud mixed with dead leaves and twigs. True to its name Discovery, we saw new critters. Still unplaced in the genus octopus, the mosaic is cream colored with spotted arms. It has a unique darkish mosaic pattern and an extended mantle. There was also, a white "V" octopus, two more critters none of us had ever seen.

Our trip ended on the eastern part of Flores Island in the port of Maumere. In 1992, the area was hard hit by a reef destroying tsunami. It has a few reefs, about three hours away, which still shine with soft coral including a member of the Nephtheida family that grows downward. It is found in the top of deep shady caves dangly in the current.

After our final dinner, the crew performed a sing-sing. Dancing and singing, some wearing Papua headdress, they embraced us goodbye. New friends, great diving, beautiful weather, lots of new sightings, Komodo dragons, excellent food, great service and luxury. What else could a diver ask for?

29. Muck Diving in Lembeh Strait, Sulawesi

Hairy frogfish, Photo: Bill Kimball

Why descend 20 to 30 feet into water filled with stinging hydroids, and God knows what else, to scan a bottom covered with junk and scattered trash, a dozen varieties of empty beer bottles, old fishing nets and bamboo traps, discarded rice bags, and, perhaps, a coral bommie here and there?

At first glance scuba diving in murky water just doesn't make sense. Sounds like an oxymoron, doesn't it? Surely, this wouldn't appeal to any wall cruisin' big-animal-loving divers (like me.)

With good reason, experts flock to Lembeh Strait, renowned for its silt black lava sand low visibility diving. Well, muck diving is like exploring a landfill serving as a hiding place for the world's most incredible critters. Critters are buried or camouflaged in the sand, tuck into jars or cans, hidden in a small amount of vegetation. Lembeh Strait may be the frogfish and nudibranch capital of the underwater world. It took just one dive to realize that this is as fascinating as diving can be.

Kungkungan Bay Resort is located near Bitung City in Indonesia's North Sulawesi. Isolated and literally at the end of the road, 17 bungalows, bordered by tropical rainforest and surrounding coconut plantations, overlook the mile-wide strait. Other than a few mosquitoes, it's utopic.

The most jaded diver, one who has "been there and seen that" underwater, will agree that Lembeh Strait will just plain "knock your dive booties off."

At Nudi Retreat, flamboyant pygmy cuttlefish camouflaged themselves in gorgonians. A newborn, recognizable only by its shape and color changes, clung to a soft coral. Talk about underwater sensory overload! And, there was much, much more. On a single dive, we saw a longfin waspfish, spiny devilfish, leaf scorpionfish, an ugly sand-buried reticulated stargazer, plus a variety of living shells.

About a third of our group of 18, the infamous, fearless hyper-diving "Chickens," was international in scope. Inclusively growing from several Arizona "desert rats" led by Commander Pollo, the group included divers from the UK, Germany, Sweden, and a German ex-pat from Shanghai with a friend from Jakarta. Yup, for this trip, the "Chickens" spared one of their many squawking rubber mascots from its usual inclusion in a shark bait ball to go on "the ultimate critter hunt."

Several nights, the Chickens took advantage of nighttime explorations to see fully exposed flat-headed stargazers, the frizzy "bad hair day" bright orange hirsute hairy frogfish, and other nocturnal critters. Another night it was a crabfest: an orange and purple decorator crab carrying a live urchin. Even a red octopus showed itself. We saw critters wherever we aimed our underwater flashlight.

Yellow-headed, big snouted, creamy brown-finned, and a small pink eel were not like your ordinary moray eel. Mouthing their jaws in unison, they frequently shared crevices. Other uncommon species included the minor, barbed fin, white-eyed, snowflake, and a blacksaddle snake eel who poked his head out of the sand.

The "minefield" of creatures around the sites at Teluk Kambaku included many species of nudibranchs: leopard, heron Island, black-margined, obscure hypselodoris, turberculate mexichromis, eye-spot, and elegant nudibranchs. Larger than a tennis ball, a yellow-and-black notodoras minor looked like a ripened banana.

We learned a whole new underwater sign language, unique to those we typically used diving. We had new critters to point out to one another. A curled index finger signaled a seahorse, or a curled pinky indicated a pygmy seahorse. Two-handed index finger wiggles meant a fingered dragonet.

Many hues of clownfish darted in and out of multi-colored anemones, sometimes surrounded by schools of white-spotted, black-barred Banggai cardinalfish. The clownfish were very protective - a "Nemo" bit one diver three times during the week. Those cute little fish had a taste for knuckles.

Frogfish have different color phases during their life. We saw yellow, white, green, orange, pink combined with brown, and black. Some of them were as small as a lime, others as big as a football. A pregnant female, her belly bulging, hung near her mate on an abandoned anchor line. Like a piece of a sculpture, a chartreuse frogfish clandestinely fished from the stem of an elephant ear-shaped leather coral. In a split second, a black frogfish, tucked in a bommie, consumed unwitting cardinal fish.

Juvenile batfish glided in and out of bommies. A brown cockatoo waspfish could easily have been mistaken for a leaf. Different sizes and colors of zebra, dwarf, spotfin, deepwater, weedy, and demon lionfish tucked under corals, rested on the sand, or drifted slowly in the gentle current.

Scorpionfish were plentiful and included the long mustached ambon with horny growths above its eyes. Marked by white algae and sponge-like calcification, the humpback scorpionfish was equally weird. A brilliant yellow-fringed weedy scorpionfish drifted like an autumn leaf. To everyone's delight, the sand and rubble brought several sightings of the purple weedy Rhinopeous.

Jawfish with eggs in mouth, Photo: Bill Kimball

Fire urchins used two white front legs to march along the bottom like an army battalion. This was certainly not a good place to lose control of your buoyancy. Spiny devilfish, sea moths, and fingered dragonets so ugly that you wondered who would prey on them.

An octopus took refuge in an empty bottle. Striped zebra crabs fed on dead urchins. Two Pegasus seamoths crawled along the black sand. Banded coral shrimp scurried about openly. Golden bristle fireworms crawled through the sand, file soft-shelled clams used banded tentacles for swimming. The long spines of the Venus Comb murex were stunning.

Nudi Falls was a three-minute ride from the resort. A whip coral goby skipped up and down the thin coral. Nearby we saw a white-ringed black-spotted tail comet fish, orange and red warty pygmy seahorses in sea fans, a yellow soft coral crab hiding in gorgonians, and winged and ring pipefish.

At a mucky spot named Hairball, the smallest of the sharks: a six-inch black and white striped epaulet slept on the bottom. Overturning a rock at nearby Batu Merah, we found a second one: this time a three-inch juvenile.

Several malibi nudibranchs floated like plastic bags. A paradise mantis shrimp wasn't shy, while a pair of sailfish gobies ducked into holes. An orange juvenile puffer hung with a white frogfish. Whiskered eel catfish stirred up the muck as they fed in a school in the sand, rigid shrimpfish swam in vertically formation.

An option to a night dive was a dusk mandarin dive. Beautifully ornate with patterned dark-edged green and blue bands and yellow line markings on the lower part of their head, they are extremely shy. As the sun set, we patiently waited in the coral rubble at Batu Angus for them to swim out of the bommie to do their elaborate dancing mating ritual. We saw about a dozen fish, but no mating.

KBR's intimacy oozes charm, service, romance and atmosphere. Lembeh is a place worth traveling through countless time zones to endure the agony of horrendous jet lag.

Until 1990, KBR was a coconut plantation. When America's Supercuts heiress Kathryn Ecenbarger cruised through the strait, she found the place so beautiful, she mentioned to ship Captain Billy Matindas that the bay should be developed as a resort. He offered to help arrange for her to buy the land.

In 1991, Ecenbarger sent her son, Mark, a contractor, to build a resort. Mark was a diver, but after one look at the muck and poor visibility, he was not motivated to get wet. As time passed, he felt frustrated waiting for building materials to arrive. He descended into the Strait and began discovering critters he couldn't identify in any book. The realization hit him that the diving in Lembeh was unique. Three years later, a simple resort became a world class dive operation, a destination attracting worldwide experts.

We saw more new, unique critters in five days, that in several decades of diving. What didn't we see? To mention a few, there was Saron shrimp-red polka-dotted with yellow carapace and green halimeda ghost pipefish in fronds of halimeda seagrass. Lucky for them, some of the group saw a mimic octopus and orange hairy frogfish. Never thought I'd say this about muck diving, but Kungkungan was a highlight of my many underwater adventures.

30. Snorkeling with Humpbacks in the Silver Bank

I've seen many humpbacks, especially while fishing in the Pacific Northwest. It's always a thrill to see them breach, fin, spy hop, fluke up, and especially "bubble up" to catch and eat herring. But there is nothing like being close to a female nursing her calf. I love everything whale. Being in the water with them nursing calves and during mating season in the Silver Bank off the Dominican Republic is an extraordinary experience.

Humpback tailing, Silver Bank, Photo: Brett Sussman

It's a three-month sexual orgy. Humpback whales have migrated to the Silver Bank for millions of years, scientists say. Between January and April, the whales arrive near the Dominican Republic strictly to calve or mate. These shallow Atlantic waters are 85 miles north of the Dominican Republic and a similar distance southeast of Grand Turk. Here, you can observe the many behaviors of the humpback, the males breaching and finning as they solicit sex from females in estrus. Some bulls sing to attract females who might be nursing calves, and those without calves depart the Bank pregnant.

The Bank was named for Spain's *Nuestra Señora de la Pura y Limpia Concepción*, a galleon carrying 40 million dollars in silver bars. She sank in 1641 after colliding with one of the many towering coral heads submerged inches beneath the surface.

During the whale rendezvous, each bull is focused on the same goal: finding and copulating with an agreeable female. Their mission is so singular they stop feeding. Vocal cetaceans, they emanate birdlike songs mingled with groans and moans, chirps and warbles as they perform intricate exhibitions of courtship behavior. While many have witnessed this "foreplay," no one is known to have ever seen either the mating or birthing ritual.

The 120-foot *Wind Dancer* provides voyeuristic snorkelers the opportunity to snorkel with these whales from two fiberglass tenders. Little time is spent "whale waiting." There is surface activity to watch, and when hydrophones are dropped into the water, the songs of the humpbacks can be heard.

Silver Bank humpback breaching, Photo: Brett Sussman

The 10-hour crossing over open water from the Dominican Republic can vary from calm seas to 6- to 8-foot chop. Fortunately, we have the former, and we are being guided by expert Tom Conlin. Snorkel-only whale viewing is determined by weather.

A "fly-by" is a fast-swimming whale on a mission. "Blow and go" means the whale surfaces and moves on.

While interested in learning about the whales and their behavior, we're even more eager to get in the water with them. Tom does not want to put us into an aggressive rowdy group with bulls or fins slappers. They can travel at 20 to 30 miles per hour and stay down for as long as 40 minutes at a time. Tom might take an hour to get us a good encounter.

That's a challenge with the bulls positioning and soliciting, their testerone off the scale, females in estrus, with many nursing calves born every two to three years. Females are ready to breed again soon after giving birth, which occurs every two to three years.

Tom compares it to "Friday night happy hour at the rowdiest bar in town. By 2 o'clock in the morning there are only a few males left."

Two dozen males might compete for one female. They slash at each other with barnacle-covered dorsal fins. Breachers crash in midair.

Humpbacks are acoustic: The more noise snorkelers make, the greater the chance of frightening them away. We will make passive "soft-in-water" entries. We are taught to lie on the gunwale, making a seal entry by sliding headfirst into the water, gripping our cameras. Still in the water, we let the whales come to us. We swim slowly and quietly, turning by swiveling our hips, barely moving our fins. "Keep the noise down while looking down. This is the whale's domain, we need to respect that, and we are visitors here."

Whales sleep on the surface while their calves surface to breathe every four to five minutes. If a whale turns away twice, we leave them alone, giving them their space.

Sometimes the tender sends out a scout, who signals to the rest of us that they have sighted a whale. The most frequent sighting is of females with nursing calves. We observe all types of whale behavior. Then, in an instant, the whales take off. Some of our encounters last minutes. The longest is fifteen minutes. On our first day, the visibility is about 30 feet, with a cloud cover. The bright white of the whale's dorsal fins gleams through the limited visibility.

The next morning one tender has a dozen encounters, while the nine of us in the other boat enjoy some close-up "whale waiting." Even though we don't have the same adrenaline rush, the trip beats any commercial whale-watching outing on the east or west coast of North America. Those operations don't permit in water encounters, and loaded boats usually have to remain more than 100 yards away to not disturb the whale.

One day, there is a brief encounter with a school of half a dozen Atlantic spotted dolphins, many with newborns less than two feet long. Another time, four immature male humpbacks swim under and around our boat, giving us a close-up view of bloody dorsal fins from fighting with one another.

We follow a group of seven rowdies, their pectoral fins bloody from slashing and tailing one another underwater. Looking for a mom with a calf, we find one being followed by an escort, a young male hoping to court her. Sealing into the water, we watch the female, calf and escort below us. As they ascend to the surface, they circle us, one of our best encounters. Two more fly-bys and it is time to break for lunch. We have no idea what is in store for us that afternoon.

After we follow a mother and a calf for a while, she turns away twice, so we steer away. We find and spend close to three hours with one mother and calf. Our first of numerous encounters was probably the most exciting, as the calf played with and nuzzled with its mother at a depth of about 30 feet. After 15 minutes, or as guide Brett notes, the third time the baby surfaced for air, we wore out our welcome. The calf breached, missing us by a few feet. Then mom tail-breaches or tail-slaps the water, telling us, "Enough!"

When the whales "settle" we again enter the water. This time, the baby nurses and the pair snuggle quietly. The next time, we see her the baby is upright in the water as she surfaces every four to five minutes.

After several encounters, we call the other tender to share "our" whales (only 10 snorkelers are permitted in the water with one whale or mom-infant pair. We take turns viewing the whales the rest of the afternoon.

You don't need to be a certified diver for this trip, but sealing into the water, especially when there is a dozen or so encounters, is exhausting. It's belly in, swim 100 yards or so, then climb up a ladder back into the tender. The rewards are well worth the workout.

31. Tahiti's Fakarava Wall of Sharks

Multiple species of sharks were everywhere in sight. They weren't schooling like the hundreds of hammerheads in the Cocos Island or Galapagos, those timid appearing ones that disappeared at the sound of a regulator bubble.

Diving the slack tide of a channel in Fakarava South, Tahiti, a wall of more than 300 sharks is possible to see, but only when the currents aren't rushing. Crystal clear water filled with black, white and silver tip, lemon, gray, hammerhead, and reef sharks swim in every direction, a wall of them above or below one another. The Tahitian definition of slack is a strong up and down flowing current, one that I can drift, without any chance of swimming against it.

Gracefully, a giant manta added to this sensory shark overload along with schools of reef fish hanging in the current: jack, soldier and surgeon fish, big node unicorns, orange line and pompano triggers, blue-fin trevally, and more.

This visual overkill offered about 100-foot visibility. The fish and shark were so thick that I could have missed seeing some species. The rich diversity in this ecosystem of undersea hard coral mounts, myriad of reef fish, and countless sharks make Fakarava's Garuae Pass well qualified as an UNESCO Biosphere Reserve.

Rangiroa is an equally exciting drift dive, one that is better known in the dive world, but considered less challenging than Fakarava. Its Tiputa Pass is known for sightings of dolphins, marlin, grey, hammerhead, and other sharks, plus manta rays. I had been told that I wouldn't need a reef hook to hang on in the current, but I would have loved to have had mine holding me in place.

Grey reef sharks, Photo: Bill Kimball

How did I luck into this thriller? Having dived solo for decades, my husband suggested that we travel through French Polynesia on the *Paul Gauguin*. I jumped at the chance to "have my cake and eat it, too." While I would not have the option of 4-5 dives a day, I would have a cruise ship vacation, one that offered diving. Not familiar with cruising, the diving opportunity sounded good to me until I read the fine print saying "Diving on a space available basis." Yikes!

Nope, I wasn't willing to journey that far a distance after learning that less than satisfactory (too few, too shallow, too beginner, boring) dive options were not committed. HELLO, GOOGLE! I found a Tahiti land-based operator, *Topdive,* who were located at five of *Paul Gauguin* ports of call: Papeete, Bora Bora, Moorea (Society Islands) and the Tuamoto atolls of Rangiroa and Farkarava. I could begin diving in gateway Papeete prior to the ship's departure. I didn't have to stay at a depth of the ship's determination or dive when they felt like opening the dive deck. I booked *Topdive* with the understanding that they would meet me at each port of call.

Meeting on the dock, their truck drove me either to their dive shop or a place to meet their dive boat to head directly to the site. When we finished our diving, they return me to the port to catch the tender back to the *Paul Gauguin.*

It was a schlep to haul my gear. I disembarked, already dressed in a skin and wearing booties, on the first 8:30 am tender, but it would prove well worth it. Summing up accolades for

Topdive is easy. They had boats, of varying sizes, specifically built for diving, excellent English-speaking dive masters, excellent dive sites, and offered complimentary equipment: an Aqua Lung regulator and BCD, a three-inch shorty for the 82 degree water, Nitrox to breathe, plus a Suunto dive computer (I accidentally left mine at home.) After each dive, they served tea and water, fresh fruit or donuts. They were prompt and courteous.

I found it incredible when *Topdive* advised me that the magnifying glass (used to inspect critters) that I left in my vest in Papeete, was delivered to my next stop in Moorea, before I realized that it was missing.

The expertise of their crew was evident and necessary when it came to the speed and direction of currents in both Fakarava and Rangiroa. Tides and currents are charted for a period of three plus weeks. The narrow width of these two passes, both of which have reached cult status in the shark diving community, create strong currents flowing in every direction. Off the beaten Polynesian path, less traffic attracts serious, experienced divers providing those who make the effort an awesome experience.

Drift diving these currents is more than just a great float. Exact timing of the incoming tide is crucial and divers have to deal with upwellings, and side currents in order to not get swept away. In Rangiroa, while diving with a Japanese couple, the divemaster had to hold on to the woman to keep her at depth. I am not sure if it was an issue of not wearing enough weight on her belt or a lack of buoyancy control.

This was a new dive experience for me. I was using equipment displaying bars and meters rather than psi (amount of air) and depth, and diving daily with non-English speaking nationalities. Over a ten-day period, I briefly dived with one American. The other divers were German, French, Japanese and each was friendly in spite of our limited or almost non-existent ability to communicate. Fortunately, my low air consumption meant I didn't use more than half a tank of air. I never had to worry about reading gauges or having to signal a half tank turnaround. Many divers not sharing my years of experience would find these gauges difficult to understand.

Everything appeared seamless in spite of the ship's 8:30 chronic tardiness. Topdive was aware of the *Paul Gauguin* schedule, they watched the tender make its typical ten-minute shuttle to the dock.

Without giving me an explanation, Topdive canceled my diving in Moorea. Luckily, I had gone to the effort to fill out *Paul Gauguin's* extensive paper work, so I signed up to dive with them during our two days in Moorea. It reinforced my decision to have made my own arrangements, but I didn't want to be "dive-less" in Moorea.

32. Night Diving in Wayag, Sulawesi

Mary jumping off dive boat

With a diver's giant stride, we plunged into the depths of the Halmahera Sea. As we dropped down to the reef wall on the western end of Wayag, West Papua, we enjoyed the feeling of weightlessness. It was as if we were skydiving without speed, wind velocity or feeling the abrupt g-force when the chute opens or bungee jumping without a rope tied around our ankles.

Departing Biak, West Papua, in Indonesia, it was a twenty-four-hour ride on the liveaboard dive boat to reach Wayag. The atoll was so small it was not even a dot on the map, the closest marking was the island of Waigeo.

The site of this incredible dive was nameless. Its bottomless reef started in about ten feet of water. A virgin wall appeared untouched, as if other divers had never seen it. Covered with soft corals, there were sections with avalanche-like sand shoots flowing to overhangs above immense canyons. The wall topography was spectacular.

Mary diving in Sulawesi, Indonesia

My buddy and I dived off the top of the reef quickly equalizing our ears on the sand chute before plummeting through iridescent schools of silversides until reaching a maximum depth of 100 feet. We loved the feeling of being neutrally buoyant as we headed into the depth rather than drifting with the current at a level depth.

After several "freefalls" we leveled at sixty feet to closely explore the reef. A variety of anemones hosting schools of clown fish and black spotted damsels swayed in the light current. We saw many species of colorful nudibranchs. Lionfish clung to the undersides of cliff overhangs in underwater canyons. Schools of jacks, tuna, and triggerfish cruised the wall while an occasional reef shark swam by. Lobsters and eels hung together in rocky crevices.

The reef wall at Wayag was not a typical location for a night dive. It had no bottom, or underwater landmarks that a diver could recognize from an earlier day dive. After spending several hours on four previous dives, my buddy, Peter Matthews, and I decided that we couldn't miss the opportunity to dive the wall at night. We had spent too much time diving off the sand chutes instead of fully exploring its length. Our vision would be limited in the dark, but we knew that the night "critters" would be fascinating.

We agreed on a short twenty-minute night dive. We thought Wayag had been a great dive during the day, but we never expected the ultimate night "critter hunt." Lionfish were out in force, their poisonous fins swaying in the current. The reef was covered with peacock rays, filefish, large pencil urchins, and banded shrimp, just to name a few. The ugly tasseled Woebegone shark and a green crocodile fish rested camouflaged in a sandy location. Every inch of the wall was covered with a different "critter" or soft coral. An unidentifiable yellow ball, looking like a Christmas tree ornament, appeared unattached to the reef. Perhaps it was a type of algae, fungus or egg sack.

Suddenly, our twenty-minute night dive plan had exceeded an hour. We were neither tired nor chilled; we were totally distracted by the beauty of the wall. After spending more than a total of three hours on this nameless wall off the western point of Wayag, we concluded that this remote reef wall was the most beautiful and diverse site we had ever dived.

West Papua (formerly known as Irian Jaya) is known for the beauty of its islands and rain-forest. Its people, the Dani and Asmat, were known as headhunting cultures. Indonesia has a great deal of diversity, culture, and religious customs. As fascinating as the country might be, my buddy and I will forever treasure our night dive on the gorgeous reef at Wayag.

33. Cenote Diving in the Yucatán

Cenote Diver at Chac Mool

"More than two hundred divers have died here." Our flashlights scanned the sign of a skull and cross bone emblazoned with the word "peligro" or danger. The chill of the 78° water and the message gave me the shivers. I knew that our lives were in the hands of Pedro, an experienced certified cave diver. We would not stray from his lead.

That was easier said than done. Where the crystal freshwater of Chac-Mool, one of Yucatán Peninsula's 3,000 underwater caves blended with saltwater seeping into its interior, my first thought was that my vision had blurred. The halocline mixture of fresh and salt water reduced visibility to only a few feet. I kicked faster to keep up with Pedro. I could barely see his light.

Campeche, Yucatán and Quintana Roo comprise the Peninsula. A low, flat landscape located between the Gulf of Mexico and the Caribbean Sea, the Mexican state lacks rivers or streams. Its scarcity of surface water dates back 3,000 years when Mayans explored the cenotes as a primary water source.

Mary cave diving in Yucatan cenote

The cenotes were used for more than just drinking water: they provided "virgin" water for religious rites, and burial and sacrificial sites. Mayan pottery shards, charcoal, torches, and petroglyphs can be found in most of the explored caves. The cenotes were sometimes used as a place of refuge as well as a source for clay and minerals.

A dzonot, the Mayan word for "cavity of water," is formed when rainwater seeps through cavities in the Yucatán's porous limestone. It is estimated that only 1,400 cenotes have been explored. Turquoise or green water flow through these irregularly shaped caves. Some open into surface pools, others remain hidden in underground caverns or deep fissures in the jungle. In

Dos Ojos, curtains of surface light beamed into the cavern illuminating thousands of unique stalactites and stalagmite formations. It is spectacularly beautiful and scary.

Three of us had signed on for a day of diving in the cenotes with Scuba Cancun. Picking us up at our hotel, they drove us about 45 minutes south into the remote jungle. Our bumpy ride along a narrow road was soon interrupted by ATV dust of tourists on a tour. They, too, had come to look at the entrance of Dos Ojos, one of the cenotes that surfaced into a pool. Dos Ojos got its name because there are two adjacent cenotes.

After donning our wet suits in the steamy jungle, we wandered down a dirt path that led to uneven stone steps down to the pool. Pedro gave us a serious briefing including cave hand signals, that would be used with flashlights in the darkness. If we were to get separated, there were arrows pointing to the exit of the cave. Throughout the day, I never saw one of those arrows. Each of our two chilly dives would last an hour, and while not deep—perhaps a maximum of 40 to 68 feet— the clammy warmth of the humid jungle made us eager to shed our wetsuits

As we followed Pedro, we occasionally sighted black mollies, catfish, and three-inch freshwater shrimp. A total of forty species have been identified in the cenotes including 38 crustaceans and two species of fish.

Dos Ojos has a platform with a ladder for jumping in and climbing out. By the time we reached the van, we quickly ungeared and ate some sandwiches. We continued another thirty minutes to cenote Chac-Mool or "little brother."

Plunging back into the cold water we followed Pedro past the danger signs. Chac-Mool has a large dome where you can surface to observe roots hanging from the earth's surface. Bats cling to the ceiling. After a brief look around, we submerged to encounter another low viz halocline. My fins flapped into high gear as I followed the weak beam of Pedro's light.

And then it was over. To be underwater water in such a surreal environment was an incredible experience, one that will last a lifetime. I felt no inspiration to learn technical cave diving.

34. Archipelago Los Roques, Venezuela and Angel Falls

After logging more than 100 dives, I was looking for a dive site that would provide good diving, but wouldn't necessitate days of travel. This was before I wrote the book, *Scuba Caribbean* (University Press Florida), and I had never heard of Los Roques. In March, I received a last-minute opportunity to review a boat for *Undercurrent*, the *Antares III* in Archipelago Los Roques, Venezuela. I did not know the problems this great offer would bring until the end of the trip. It was Semana Santa or Easter weekend in Caracas. I would become stranded in a politically unstable city.

Los Roques is a refreshingly different Caribbean dive destination. There are chalk-white sandy reef walls, numerous varieties of fish and sea creatures, and lots of soft coral that enhance Los Roques' beauty. There were very few divers or tourists there, and I could reach it by taking a three-hour flight from Miami.

Archipelago Los Roques is a 40-minute flight north of Caracas, Venezuela. I had booked the trip with liveaboard dive operation *Antares III*. Environmentally protected by Venezuela's government, the Archipelago boasts a variety of undersea settings including walls, pinnacles, caves, and coral gardens. All of these can be accessed by beginning and intermediate divers, who are treated to gentle, easy drift diving.

The main island in the archipelago, El Gran Roque, is colorful and charming. When the Venezuelan government banned commercial fishing in the archipelago, local fishermen colorfully painted their casitas and converted them to guest posadas to serve tourists who visited primarily for fishing and diving. Several catamarans offer daily tours with lunch and snorkeling. Línea Turística Aereotuy airline's central kitchen provides food to serve posadas, day dive boats, and sailing catamarans.

For divers spoiled by large schooling fish and the pelagics of the South Pacific, Cocos, Papua New Guinea, or Indonesia, scuba diving in Los Roques requires an attitude adjustment. This is not "big stuff" diving. During the week I saw two nurse sharks and caught a brief glimpse of five spotted eagle rays.

The pleasures of Los Roques are small and numerous. There are many varieties of grouper, snapper, angelfish, butterfly fish. We saw schools of horse-eye jacks, African pompano, Spanish mackerel, grunts and damselfish. There were green, spotted, and tiger eels. Large midnight blue and rainbow parrotfish swam by, as did a wide variety of trunkfish and filefish. We saw blenny, goby, porcupine fish, hogfish, hind, and even several barracuda. About the only undersea fauna we missed were turtles.

Underwater, we signaled the presence of spotted drums using "beating drum" hand signals. At one site, three juveniles hovered in front of a huge moray eel, while an arrow crab looked on. I even saw bonefish in shallow water. The Venezuelan government issues catch-and-release licenses on the outer islands of the archipelago to bonefish and tarpon anglers. They have done a good job of keeping the paradise of Los Roques a fisherman's secret.

The stationary life we saw matched the variety of fish. Sponges included orange, yellow, olive, branching tube, stovepipe, azure vases, barrel, black and orange balls attached to encrusting and calcareous coral. Giant anemones housed Pederson cleaner shrimp instead of the more usual inhabitant, clownfish. We saw many colored worms including feather dusters, Christmas tree, and spaghetti. Coral types included fire, sea fan, feather plumes, black, whips, staghorn, elkhorn, yellow pencil, star, brain, lettuce, and saucer coral.

Crustaceans were numerous, and seemed unafraid of divers. We saw large Caribbean spiny lobsters, averaging four to eight pounds each, and several species of octopus. They were joined by a variety of crabs, including the small yellowline arrow and the tasty Florida stone crab. Shells included queen conch, flamingo tongues, and murex. We were amazed to observe a murex eating an oyster. There were fiery orange fileclams, winged oysters, black, white, and combined white-black long spiny urchins, plus crinoids, tunicates, and sea cucumbers.

The incredible variety of sightings was enhanced by the professionalism and warmth we experienced from the crew of the *Antares III*. In eight days, we made more than 25 dives, three of them being night dives. Our route, taking us from El Gran Roque to Punta Salina, Dos Mosquises, Casqui, Carenero, and Boca de Cote, was smooth, with almost no current and only occasional wave action – most of it experienced on the 10-minute boat ride to each dive site.

Antares III divers make a minimum of three daily dives. Divemaster Ron Hoogesteyn and his crew change divers' gear after each dive and wash all of their equipment, including wetsuits, a nightly service that can quickly spoil a diver.

Ron led the dives, carrying a line with a floating buoy so the peñero (panga) could follow his drift. Backrolling into the water, we did our exploring. After each dive, we handed up our gear, then climbed a ladder back into the peñero.

The 76-foot yacht *Antares III* is a converted trawler. It has six cabins, each with two beds and a private bath. The decor of the main salon includes beautiful lacquered wood floors, cactus arrangements, artwork, a library, and a shell collection, all evidence of the care taken by this family-owned operation.

While Los Roques is restful and charming, there is little else to do on the island. But, for the serious diver who wants a unique experience, beautiful scenery, and the hospitality offered by the *Antares III*, a trip to Los Roques is well worth it.

Jungle Visits and Angel Falls

When we asked about visiting the villages of Arekuna and Canaima, Línea Turística Aereotuy, told us, "It's a two-hour flight, and there's no bathroom on the plane." Another dive writer and I booked the flights, landing in a Cessna twin on a dirt strip near the Pemón Indian village of Arekuna, in the Gran Sabana of southern Venezuela's Guiana Highlands.

The flight was not for the faint-hearted. When the pilot made his landing approach over the Caroní River, he turned downwind instead of making a standard upwind landing. The scenic flight had taken us from the Caribbean to Venzuela's inland flying over Guri Dam into mountainous jungle terrain. We arrived intact, and were soon on our way to our first stop, Camp Arekuna.

The camp consisted of a hill called a tepuy surrounded by 10 churuatas or palm-thatched circular huts surrounding a dining room. Its elevation provides a glorious view of the jungle and Caroní River. During dinner one night, we saw a reflection of the planet Venus shining in the river's currents.

Each of the churuatas, many with river views, is divided into two units, separated by a half-wall. While this allows minimal sound privacy, the half-wall allows air to pass through the huts. Each unit has an entry/dressing area with a bathroom that includes a cold-water shower. A bedroom, with three comfortable mattresses, are set on concrete blocks. Colorful woven bedspreads with matching pillows are covered with alpaca blankets. An oversize hammock is strung decoratively across the room. While there is no air conditioning or fan to move the air, the cool breeze is sufficient. Electricity is provided only between 6 to 11 p.m.

A petroglyph relief is etched on the room wall, a reference to the those left by pre-Columbian Caribe tribes living along the Caroní River. The interior design is charming, an unexpected contrast to the churuatas' plain exterior.

"Shake your clothes and check your shoes for centipedes, fire ants, and scorpions," a sign in the room advises. Arekuna is a camp for the adventurous traveler.

Each day we took excursions into surrounding areas. Colorful, flat-topped sandstone mesas dot the landscape with many tepuys rising majestically out of the rainforest in the indigenous Guiana Highlands.

One hike takes visitors a quarter mile up a tepuy to a view of Angel Falls in the distance. The falls, on the 270-square-mile Auyantepuy, is the highest waterfall in the world. It's 3,212 feet high with a 2,648-foot uninterrupted drop into the Churun River.

The falls were named after U.S. pilot Jimmy Angel, who, while searching for gold in 1937, landed his plane on the boggy tepuy. The indigenous Pemón Indians call Auyantepuy the "Mountain of the God of Evil."

Another excursion allows guests to float the Caroní River in a bongo (a Pemón dugout canoe,) then paddle downriver to Las Babas rapids, named for small crocodiles that used to inhabit the river. We took this option, following it with a hike along the path that follows the river and leads down to a view of several pre-Columbian Caribe Indian petroglyphs. After our hike, we swam in a small bay along the river.

The next day we walked through the jungle to the Antabaras River. We were met at river's edge by a guide in a bongo. He took us upriver to view more rapids before returning to the fork of the Caroní River. During this excursion we saw Guacamayo macaws, red-bodied with blue and green feathers. The canopy of the rainforest bloomed with purple, gold, and yellow trees called apamate, bucare, and araguaney. We then visited a small conuco – a Pemón farm site cleared in the jungle. The family grew manioc, bananas, chilies, and sugar cane.

Next on our itinerary was a flight to Canaima, located ten minutes from Arekuna, which serves as a base camp for trips to Angel Falls. In Canaima, we stayed at Jungle Rudy's Camp Ucaima on the Carrao River. Our excursions were led by a young Pemón Indian named Priscilla, who took us first to Sapo Falls, where the hiking trail runs under Sapo falls, drenching hikers and everything not protected in the guide's plastic bag.

We then took a bongo excursion up the Carrao to Orchid Island. We were visiting during the dry season (which runs from October to May,) and the river was too low to travel beyond the island. To get to Angel Falls, we hiked another four hours upriver in the river before a two-hour hike on a trail leading to the falls. This excursion, called Pozo de la Felicidad, stops at a pool with a small waterfall. We swam while our guides cooked barbecued chicken for our lunch.

Camp Ucaima, where we stayed that night, featured cabins facing the Carrao River. Although the decor was more basic than that of Arekuna, the food served on Ucaima's outdoor patio was tastier. We were most grateful that we had brought insect repellent. The Canaima-jejen (no-see-um) bites and itches like crazy.

The journey had been unique in the sense of enjoying some good diving, but Venezuela's jungle is not geographically accessible, and the country's political climate is unstable.

When I arrived back in Caracas, I faced multiple dilemmas. Landing at the international airport, 75 miles from downtown, following my initial arrival, we had flown directly to Los Roques. I was unable to get a return flight to the United States, so I took a shuttle downtown to the Hilton Hotel. It was then that I learned that it was Semana Santa (Holy Week/Easter) and most people living in the city spent the holiday in Miami or beyond. It was during the reign of Hugo Chávez, and businesspeople visiting Caracas, and those who stayed at the hotel, had bodyguards to protect them. I was told that I had to stay in the hotel until I could get a flight out.

There I was, trapped in a hotel in a violent city with nowhere to go and nothing to do. Additionally, almost the entire staff had left the property to celebrate the weekend. Finally, I decided to enter the executive offices and use their computer to write this story. The following Monday, I was on the first flight back to the United States.

35. Banded Sea Kraits, Hunter's Seamount, Philippines

Black and silver-striped sea kraits possess a highly toxic venom. Though alleged to be shy and reclusive, hundreds, maybe thousands of these kraits occupied an 80-foot unmarked seamount near Philippines' Apo Reef National Park.

During a spring dive trip to the South China Sea, Hunter's Rock, about 12 miles off the west coast of Mindoro Island, was an overnight destination. It seemed strange, but exciting, to be motoring to a dive site solely to observe snakes. It certainly gave me pause for thought. Kraits have to surface to breathe. What if I jumped on one as it was surfacing for air?

Assuring myself that wearing a wet suit, booties, hood, and gloves would protect me against the snakes' small mouths, I took the plunge.

Banded Sea Krait, Photo: Bill Kimball

Descending in strong current, for which the seamount is known, I leveled at a depth of eighty feet. I watched snakes, sometimes accompanied by goatfish and trevally, patrolling for a meal while wiggling their way to the ocean's surface for air. They were oblivious to me. After a while, I began to wonder how long can one just watch snakes moving up and down. Perhaps, during their July mating season, it might be more interesting. The experience itself wasn't as odd as knowing I was surrounded by extremely venomous snakes.

Little is known about these snakes that frequent coral reef areas. Bites are rare. Their heads are short without a discernible neck. They have wide, paddle-shaped tails. Their eggs are laid on land. Known to be nocturnal, fewer are seen during the day. They breathe air at least once every six hours.

Kraits are not fast enough to catch fish, so they usually hunt prey by hiding in coral. The sea krait also forms hunting alliances with yellow goatfish and bluefin trevally, who flush prey from narrow crannies into the reef. The highly venomous bite then paralyzes its prey.

I wasn't so keen on jumping in the ocean with snakes during the day, so I certainly wasn't eager about a night dive when they are more active. During dinner, my buddy Dena had a few too many drinks, which boosted her confidence. That's a real no-no as your first drink means you've enjoyed your last dive. As for me, I chickened out.

Part IX.

Bicycling Tours, Emerging into the Culture of a Destination

36. Two-Wheel Global Adventures

Throughout my childhood, I rode my bicycle to school daily. I didn't have handbrakes, gears, nor did I wear a helmet. Cycling was a great substitute to walking five blocks. My junior high and high school was too far away to bike so I took the public bus. Those were the days before parents escorted their children to school for security reasons.

After my introduction to bicycle touring which was a 45-mile ride from Taos, New Mexico, the high or lowlight of it being that our catered lunch along a highway rest stop was stolen, and following my two years of riding across Arizona, David and I started traveling on bicycle through various countries including a self-contained trip to Japan.

This book could have been focused entirely on fishing, bicycling, diving, and other genres of adventures in the pages ahead. In order to move along to bears and aerial adventures, I'd first like to share some bicycle highlights.

There is an expression in Montana that says, "If you sleep late on the 4th of July, you are liable to miss summer." We understand that. During a July bicycle trip through Yellowstone National Park, it snowed! We covered our cycles, and rented some horses for a day ride.

We have cycled through much of the western United States including many of national parks, the vineyards of California, Oregon, the San Juan and Gulf Islands (the latter just across the Canada border,) Alberta, and British Columbia. We have made the effort to find a bike tour in almost all of Canada's provinces.

In Europe, in addition to the chapters on the Czech Republic and Puglia, we traveled to several destinations in France, Italy and Sardinia. We date back to when Tom Hale, owner of *Backroads,* led his trips.

The best trip was one of our first, Hokkaido, Japan. Never knowing where we were was an adventure by itself. The worse, was a tent camp ride between Banff and Lake Louise in Alberta, Canada. The scenery was fabulous, but the weather made it impossible to enjoy. Rain and sleet keep both our tents and us wet and frozen for the week. I might add, I should have remembered, how I felt about sleeping on the ground (even when it was dry), during one of my Grand Canyon to Nogales rides.

The national parks of Glacier and Yellowstone have some very long, steep rides. *Going to the Sun* is a 50-mile two lane highway that climbs steeply, an estimated 5-10 % grade, to the village of St. Mary. Waterfalls cascade off its rocky side while the edge steeply overlooks lakes, glaciers, forests and more mountains. Any cyclist who has made this ride should consider it a badge of honor.

Beartooth Pass rises out of Yellowstone leading to Red Lodge, Montana. Coming out of Mammoth Hot Springs, I had biked about 30 miles when I saw a bison in the center of the road lumbering towards me. There was a car jam behind him, and in spite of not wanting to turn around and ride downhill, what choice did I have? Bison are the number one tourist killers in the Park.

I rode to the nearest turnout and hid behind a boulder. The bison was getting closer and closer. Please, I said to myself, let him keep going. He did, and somehow, with lasting trepidation, I stuck out my thumb and hitched a ride to the top.

A trip in Provence, France was going to be canceled because there were only four riders signed up. As it turned out, the other couple was a dentist and his wife. He was adamant that he had booked a year in advance to accommodate his clients. The trip went, and fortunately, we had a great guide and they were enjoyable to be with.

Multiple times we have unintentionally strayed from the map, but somehow, someway, we found our destination or the guide found us.

Several trips have included century (100 mile) days in addition to the one shared in the chapter on Newfoundland. Two that I best recall was a ride from Cedar City, Utah through the national parks of Bryce, Arches, and the Grand Canyon. The road was a downhill ride in the summer heat of Arizona. David had a tire blow twice, the second was replaced by the guide's tire. I did my personal best of 90 miles, arriving to see my naked husband taking a shower in the public park water faucet in Jacob's Lake, Arizona.

There have been good times and great times, not to mention road rash, sore butts, and chowing down—all a part of bicycling.

37. Cycling Arizona from the Grand Canyon to Nogales, Mexico

500 miles! Yup, this is a chapter that will leave you wondering about the boundaries of my sanity, if that hasn't already happened. David bought me a new bicycle with 18 speeds. When I signed up for the Grand Canyon to Mexico bike ride, I didn't know how to shift a gear, or the importance of going uphill in the lowest gear to make it easier or using a high gear downhill to gain distance. I didn't even have a callus on my tush. Yikes!

At the time, The Greater Arizona Bicycling Association (GABA) offered this annual ride each October. I remember the year, 1983, because David was horseback riding with Los Charros, a cowboy-type men's club, on an annual horseback ride on a southeastern Arizona ranch. The southern part of the state was floating in a deluge of rainy weather.

Cheerfully meeting up with about 75 cyclists, my friend Mark and I set off from the Grand Canyon headed for the highway towards Flagstaff. I really appreciate the friendship when I think of Mark looking at my BUTT for an entire week. That's a real friend.

It was easy going downhill into the Flagstaff area, but I would later remember that what goes down must come up and vice versa. It was not like it sounded — all downhill.

In our midst were renowned writer, the late Chuck Bowden and photographer Jack Dykinga. This was a "piece of cake" ride for them while they enjoyed an occasional toke. Not for me. I was at the back of the pack for the entire week. I still cannot believe that not one cyclist gave me a lesson on gear shifting. I was on the road for as long as 12 hours "in one day."

Our accommodations were not great. We had a sport vehicle (for carrying our sleeping bags and personal items) and we had set places along the route to lay down our heads or to sleep or camp. These were locations, not all familiar to most: Mormon Lake, Strawberry, Roosevelt Lake, Mammoth, Green Valley, and Nogales.

One killer day, we rode from Lake Roosevelt up a 10 percent grade to Globe, ending at the schoolyard in Mammoth. Our tents were squished together, it was a sleepless night spent listening to snoring and farting.

My thoughts focused on giving my bike to an orphanage in Nogales. I couldn't wait for the ride to be over. By the time we arrived in Oracle, not far from Tucson (where I could bail,) I remember that I thought it was flat between Green Valley and Nogales.

Not so. It's all uphill from Green Valley to Nogales. By the time I arrived, the big celebration was all but over. There wasn't time to find an orphanage before the bus left returning us to Tucson.

A few months later, doctors told me I had to have a hysterectomy. I heard snippets of conversations like "Mary is all through." Not so! I was back on a horse in six weeks (more on that later), and signing up for the next year's ride, along with my friend Mark, in six months. I did some training before and following the surgery, and I learned how to shift my gears.

The route between the Grand Canyon and Mexico was similar, with some different stops. The best part was an option to stay in on-the-route hotels, not fancy, but a real bed.

Still, riding at the back of the pack had some advantages. I never saw the dog that bit a rider, nor the sadness of a seeing a rider killed by logs hanging off a truck that hit him on a mountain road. Never arriving in time to mingle or make friends, I didn't ask circumstances of the fatal accident or the rider's name or who was bitten by the dog.

The memory dream of leaving my bike at a Nogales orphanage returned, but once again, catching the bus back to Tucson took priority.

38. Hokkaido Island, Cycling Along the Sea of Japan

Sea of Japan

The message, written in Japanese on a laminated index card said, "Hi! Our names are Mary and David. We are bicycling from Hakodate to Sapporo? Will you help us? The first time we used the card, we realized that the cards (written for us by a student at the University of Arizona) would be our sole means of communication during a self-contained bicycle tour along the coastline of the island of Hokkaido in Japan.

Following the reader's stare of amazement, we would use sign language to indicate if we were tired and in need of a hotel, or hungry and looking for a restaurant. The hospitable Japanese people, after carefully trying to interpret the card, always honored our request.

Before leaving the United States in early June, we went to our local bicycle shop to bone up on basic bicycle maintenance. We revisited fixing flat tires, adjusting brakes and derailleurs, and rehearsed packing the bicycles for airline cargo and re-assembling the bikes on arrival. We gathered quite an audience in the Hakodate airport as we unboxed and readied the bicycles for our tour. Asking directions to the nearest hotel, we were pointed toward the trolley. We followed the tracks to the nearest hotel.

Our bicycle tour began early the next morning. Not adjusted to local time yet, we pedaled away from our last western-style hotel at daybreak. Planning to have breakfast along the road, we followed Highway 228, the route to the village of Kikonai.

Japanese restaurants do not serve breakfast. By mid-morning, our growling stomachs in-spired us to stop at a fire station. We were a real curiosity to the fireman. They were not used to seeing Americans much-less traveling on bicycles. They offered us a tour of the station. When they showed us their lunchroom, we pulled out our laminated index card that said, "where is the nearest restaurant?" Knowing that we wouldn't find a place serving breakfast, they opened their lockers to share their lunch with us.

Tummies filled, we hit the road again, this time stopping at a bicycle shop to adjust a brake. The mechanic was so excited to work on a Japanese bike (most are exported to America) that he practically gave the bikes a complete overhaul.

We made a fortuitous discovery in a small grocery store. The owners usually lived in the back of the store. If we engaged them in sign language, we were invariably invited into their home for a cup of tea or coffee.

This insight was important because most Japanese restaurants do not open until after noon. Since we were unable to read any signage, we would have to continue riding until we actually observed people eating, our way of identifying a restaurant.

Ordering a meal was challenging. In the countryside of Japan, there are no plastic meal samples nor is there any English translation. We were served a variety of dishes whenever we ordered "ramen" (noodles), the one word we could say in Japanese. It didn't take us long to learn to check out what other diners were eating, walk over to their table, then point it out to the waiter.

A good example of our "hotel" message card came in Kikonai. Stopping at a car dealership, a salesperson led us slowly by car to the nearest minchiku (business hotel). We slept in futons on the floor, shared a unisex bathroom with a non-westernized toilet. We enjoyed our first introduction to the ofuro (hot bath), a daily ritual in Japan. My efforts to book a room were fruitless. David had to do it, not proper etiquette for a woman evidently.

Our journey following the Sea of Japan began in Fukushima. The two-lane road was either flat or gently rolling with wonderful views of the ocean on one side and an occasional waterfall on the right. Every ten miles or so we would pass through a small fishing village. The countryside was litter- free, garbage left for pick-up along the side of the road was neatly packaged. Garbage trucks had loud speakers that played classical music

The absence of restaurants was due, in part, to the tradition of hotels serving both dinner and breakfast. Japanese delicacies include raw eggs, whelks (snails), cuttlefish, seaweed and other unidentified creatures of the sea. These delicacies require a cultivated taste. I managed to surreptitiously discard a number of raw eggs and shovel some of those raw delicacies under my rice. Bicycling in Japan was not going to be a gourmet journey, it would be a "rice trip."

In the town of Matsumae we stayed at our first ryokan. The Japanese-style hotel room included two futons and a private bath. The large shared ofuro was unisex and located in the public space. Breakfast and dinner were served in our room. Today, staying in a ryokan is one of Japan's most luxurious experiences.

Road construction was always a problem. It was impossible for us to understand the posted signs. We didn't know if the road was impassable or the number of miles under construction.

We found it a challenge to match words on our English map to the Japanese symbols for road signs, we could barely identify a town.

When we encountered road construction, fatigue, or miserable weather conditions, we would stick out our fingers to hitchhike. We soon learned that a more successful technique was to stand by the side of the road, then cross and raise both arms to indicate to the driver to stop. Japanese drivers didn't understand the thumbs up signal for hitch hiking. Another challenge was finding a vehicle large enough to carry both the bicycles and us.

During the trip, we found ourselves occasionally hopping a ride with delivery vehicles carrying packages, fishing nets, and sugar cane. Confronted with what appeared to be serious road construction, I flagged down an empty sand and gravel truck. After stopping a double-decker truck, the driver climbed up to loaded our bicycles, as I climbed into the cab. It is a Japanese custom to remove shoes prior to entering a home. The cab was decorated with knickknacks, fringe, and fancy carpeting, it looked like the interior of a home. Pointing to my dusty shoes, the driver indicated for me to leave them on. The driver was wearing slippers, so I wanted to be respectful.

Yikes! Distracted, I wasn't aware of David's absence until the truck was driving down the road. This was going to be a harrowing experience. I didn't know our destination, was not carrying a map, and didn't have a cent of our $500.00 cash. Our reunification was in the hands of the driver.

Soon I heard giggles as the driver chatted on his CB. I realized that a second truck was following in tandem. Hopefully, David was riding in that vehicle. At a fork in the road, the truck stopped, and the two of us were happily reunited.

Between the towns of Matsumae and Kitahiyama, less than 300 miles, we would have to cycle through approximately fifteen poorly lit, rutted tunnels. Prior to entering the tunnels, we affixed flashing beacons on our backs. If we could see the light at end of the tunnel, we tried to time our ride when there were no oncoming vehicles. Not only were the fumes noxious, we were concerned about our safety.

We stopped to sightsee whenever our curiosity was aroused. Along the road we toured the Seikan Tunnel Museum, the Setana Aquarium, and the Chizaki Rose garden. The garden featured a wonderful collection of bonsai trees. On one occasion we were given a tour of a "factory" harvesting cuttlefish, another one of those acquired taste delicacies.

Sometime prior to our fourth night on the road, we lost our handy Japan Airlines paperback dictionary. It included both English words and Japanese symbols. Arriving in Esahi, a somewhat larger town, we spotted a sign for Japan Airlines. While it turned out to only be a billboard, our hostess for that night called an English-speaking Zen Buddhist monk to interpret our questions.

The monk arrived at our ryokan with a Japanese map. He showed us a symbol for "spas" located along the coastline. This information would make our daily hotel queries much easier.

After a city tour of Esahi, the monk took us to his monastery. He was so pleased to have American guests he asked David to speak English to a classroom of children.

During our first week of riding, we had enjoyed perfect weather and ideal riding conditions. The only downside was riding through the tunnels. As we rounded the bend into Sutsu Bay, we encountered the only rainy day of our ride. Our last night on the coastline was spent at Moiwa Hot Spring, a coastal spa. Our route then turned inland toward the city of Otaru.

Along the road there were deep ravines with gushing waterfalls. We stopped to visit an aquaculture trout farm. Once again, the pavement ended abruptly. This time there was little traffic; we were in an isolated area. Finally, after walking our bicycles several miles, we were successful in hitching a ride with a farmer. We had to remove the front wheels of our bicycles to make them fit into his small truck.

As we headed toward the city of Sapporo, there were signs of civilization. Road traffic increased and tunnels became longer. We decided that it would be safer to hitch the final twenty-five miles into the city of Sapporo. This time we stopped a driver hauling fishing nets. He dropped us at the Grand Hotel in Sapporo.

The bright neon lights of Sapporo snapped us back to reality. There was an Olympic site visit, beer gardens, and many of the same department stores found in Tokyo. Streets were designed either numerically or alphabetically which make excursions easy. There were cosmopolitan restaurants and western hotel beds.

We left Japan with wonderful memories of friendly, helpful, and hospitable people. We had felt safe and secure riding with cash and leaving our bicycles unlocked. Bicycling through tunnels and eating a diet of raw food grew wearisome. It was a few years before I enjoyed eating sushi again. We both agreed that this incredible 400-mile bicycle tour around the island of Hokkaido was an adventure of a lifetime.

39. Chile to Argentina, Pedaling through the Andes

A 285-mile bicycle tour through the Andes from Puerto Montt, Chile to Bariloche, Patagonia, Argentina, sounds crazy, doesn't it? Not so: On this journey, the bikes "rode" *over* the towering mountains on the roof rack of a Backroads touring van, while cyclists took a bus and ferry through the lake district between the two countries.

Chile, a long country follows the spine of the Andes, is often overlooked as a tourist destination. All I knew about travel in the region was that serious mountain climbers go there to climb Mount Aconcagua (22,841 feet), the highest summit in the Western Hemisphere. Frankly, the Andes seemed an unlikely area to tour on a bicycle.

Looking further, the brochure rated the bicycle trip good for "energetic beginners, who might require an occasional van shuttle," as well as for intermediate and advanced riders. The terrain was defined as "mostly rolling with both level and long grades." It was the "sapphire-blue lakes curving around snow-crowned volcanoes and the rugged Andes" that caught my attention.

That sold me. I gave them my credit card. I didn't know that the bicycling would prove just as interesting as the post fishing trip that attracted me to South America in the first place.

A sunrise view of the snow-capped Andes from the airplane told me I was in Chile as we prepared for landing in Santiago. The city's charm surprised me, and I wondered if I should have scheduled more than a day there.

A military band playing in the plaza interrupted my jet-lag morning nap. I lunched at the fashionably late hour of 2 p.m. at a local parrillada restaurant, El Novillero. Customers, mostly men dressed in coats and ties, cooked steak or chicken on small grills (parrilladas) next to their tables.

After lunch I wandered the cobblestone streets of the financial district. Businesspeople scurried from one marble-faced office tower to another, talking intently on mobile phones. When I strayed from the business district to walk through a local market, a pair of policemen approached me, expressing concern that someone might want to take my camera. They escorted me back in the direction of my hotel.

A 6 a.m. wake-up knock the next morning gave me an hour to catch a shuttle to Arturo Merino Benitez national airport. An hour later, a Ladeco airline jet delivered me to Puerto Montt, where I settled into the 25-room Hotel Viento Sur. The following day, I would meet eighteen riders joining the Backroads tour. I spent the additional day visiting Chiloe, a small southern port city overlooking the Gulf of Reloncavi in the Pacific Ocean.

In my hotel, I had noticed men in the dining room wearing earpieces. Hmm? Was this a drug deal going down? Later, when I walked to the local craft market, I looked up to see former President Gerald Ford coming towards me. I introduced myself, as if he should remember me - he had given me the Alex de Tocqueville award (for charitable efforts) at the Kennedy Center. Suddenly, I was surrounded by Secret Service, the same men staying in my hotel while the president was offshore staying on some dignitary's yacht.

The route began on a dirt road along the north shore of Lago Llanquihue, the third-largest lake in South America. The autumn sun illuminated captivating views of the snow-clad Osorno and Calbuco volcanoes, so often obscured by clouds.

We were soon guiding our wide-tread mountain bikes along rolling (and sometimes steep) gravel roads. Mountain bikes require more effort than smooth-tread touring, or road bikes. In many places, lava-rock gravel (used to provide fill for potholes) made the roads slippery and challenging.

Our first two nights were spent in the villages of Frutillar and Ensenada, both settled in the mid-1800s by German immigrants. The architecture in the villages is preserved, while the people have been fully assimilated into Chile's culture.

The scenic lakefront Hotel Salzburg in Frutillar was a welcome sight after 30 miles of bumping over ungraded, washboard-textured roads. The Hotel Ensenada, 53 miles farther in Parque Nacional Vicente Perez Rosales at the base of the Osorno volcano, is a hiking destination for many Chileans.

The next day's journey was a short 10 miles to Petrohue. By this time, our group had bonded enough to make the decision to share the cost of a half-day river-rafting trip down the Petrohue River. "Adelante! Vamos! Alto!" Row, hurry, stop! Our rowing lesson came in Spanish. It was a fun and relaxing afternoon, a nice break from the bike saddle.

After rafting, the day came to cross the Andes. At our morning briefing, we learned that guide Suzie would take our bicycles on top of the van for a 10-hour ride over the Andes at 12,000 feet. The rest of us would take the Cruce Internacional Lagos Andinos, a daylong journey by ferry and bus through the Lagos Todos los Santos.

Ferry across Lago Todos de los Santos, Photo: Mary L Peachin

What a relief! Our scenic ride through lakes and forest named in honor of "all of the saints" was a welcome alternative to an uphill grunt over the Andes. Several hours later, we crossed from the Chilean national park of Perez Rosales into the Argentine Parque Nacional Nahuel Huapi. We were amazed how well the two countries coordinated the ferry and bus journey, without delays or losing our baggage. It was the first rainy day of our trip, yet through numerous transfers, our luggage remained dry.

A layover day at Llao Llao resort, where we were reunited with our bikes, gave us time to ride the popular "Circuito Chico" route, a 33-mile ride through rainforest that passes several lakes. The highest scenic lookout, Punta Panoramico, features a view of Mount Tronodor (11,520 feet), the highest Andean peak in the region.

From Parque Nacional Los Arrayanes, it was a 12-mile pedal along the Arrayanes trail to Villa La Angostura. Arrayanes is a native tree with peeling cinnamon-like bark and myrtle-like leaves. The trail required some technical expertise and, as a result, there was a lot of walking bikes around roots and under low branches. Where the trail washed into Lake Nahuel Huapi, we had to edge along the side of the lake, walking our bikes. The van shuttle couldn't follow along on this two- to three-hour ride.

By this time, our group was beginning to show some "road rash." At one time or another just about everyone hit the ground. We were looking forward to another layover day after a 37-mile ride to Villa Traful.

We found it overlooking Lake Espejo at the Hosteria la Posada in Villa La Angostura. The hotel is frequented in the winter (our summer) by South Americans who come to ski the Cerra Bayo ski basin. Our visit provided a picturesque view of the hotel's terraced gardens, which included lavender, poppies, roses, and many other flowers.

The small village of Traful was fronted by a newly built lakefront pier, chocolate factory, police station, forest fire commissioner, two small stores, and the fishing lodge where we stayed: El Rincon del Pescador. On our layover day, most riders headed for the chocolate factory, while others took an energetic hike around Lago Traful.

It was hard to believe that our final day, a 62-mile ride into the town of San Carlos de Bariloche, could offer more scenic enticements than had the previous 10 days, but it did. Rocky spires combine with sandstone and flagstone to create scenery similar to the colorful Bryce and Zion national parks.

Parque Nacional Los Arrayanes tree, Photo: Mary L Peachin

After the last 25 miles, a dirt road along the Rio Traful, we arrived at the paved highway leading to San Carlos de Bariloche. About this time, the strong Pampas headwinds began to blow as the skies darkened - as though Mother Nature knew our tour was coming to an end. Just as I approached that little yellow road sign, the one with a drawing of a car going uphill, the Backroads van pulled along beside me. With a sigh of relief, I climbed into the van with the other riders as a torrential rain began. It was perfect timing, a fine end to a challenging and rewarding trip.

The trip would end in Bariloche, a destination of anglers' dreams. Virgin streams offer blue ribbon fly fishing for rainbow and brown trout. Searching my wish list for future adventures, I had found an October '96 Forbes article about an Argentinean estancia, Arroyo Verde, titled "The World's Best Fly Fishing Lodge. Period!" Here I was, right in the neighborhood. I had arranged a trip to Arroyo Verde, 800 miles southwest of Buenos Aires, a place where I could fly fish and ride horses to my heart's content.

The Southern Cross and Orion, constellations prominent in the Southern Hemisphere, sparkled as rainbow and brown trout jump to take the fly. According to my Argentine fishing buddy, Buby Calvo, "The Rio Traful is the most productive after sunset. Larger ten-pound brown trout are more inclined to take a fly in the evening hours when they can't see the angler's reflection in the river."

Calvo is the nephew of Meme Larivière, owner of the luxurious Arroyo Verde estancia south of Bariloche. The gentle Rio Traful meanders through the ranch. Calvo has fished the Traful most of his life and knows every fishing hole in the river.

Unique to the river is the spawning of Encerrado (landlocked salmon), stocked in 1903 by the U.S. Fish and Wildlife Service, which at the time provided food fish to various states and some foreign countries. The salmon thrive along with rainbow and brown trout. With the fish feeding on shrimp and pancora, a small crab, their meat is pink and tasty. The trout, both rainbow and brown, have been weighed in at a high of 10 pounds.

Fish populations have thrived because of the estancia's catch and release policy. The trout served for meals come from the river's hatchery. Unlike most rivers, there are no insect hatches on the Rio Traful. The result is that the trout feed and will take a fly almost any time of the day.

Sections of the Rio Traful have swift current and large mossy boulders, but many good fishing pools have gentle currents. The riverbank is void of "fly-catching" trees. The Rio Traful varies in color from pewter gray to malachite green. The cordillera of the Andes provides breathtaking views around every bend of the river. An occasional eagle will soar, a flock of geese will honk overhead, or a kingfisher may swoop down to catch a fish.

Arroyo Verde is in Patagonia's spectacular lake district. The snowcapped peaks of the Andes surround seven lakes. Rivers flow through primeval forests. Black volcanic rock blends into the red-orange hues of incredible sandstone formations. The 15,000-acre estancia is in Nahuel Huapi National Park, one of the last strongholds of the Araucanian Indians.

The estancia derives its name from a small arroyo (dry stream) running through the property. The original bridge spanning the Rio Traful, built 75 years ago, is visible from the dirt-road entrance. The trip from the paved highway into the estancia is a journey into the tranquility of years past, one without telephones or television, of beautiful scenery and starry nights. There is no light pollution. The main ranch house, renovated in 1976, is furnished with antiques. The estancia was so desirable that former Argentine dictator Juan Perón confiscated it in the 1950s. Later it was returned to the Larivière family.

In a break from fishing, we rode Criollo horses from pampas to mountains in search of condors, led by Pachanga, an Argentine gaucho. Criollo horses are descendants of Spanish stock, a mixture of Arabian, Barb, and Andalusian stock. Gaited, they provide a smooth ride. They are strong and able to carry weight with great endurance.

Andean condors are the world's largest birds able to fly. Weighing up to 33 pounds with a 10-foot wingspan, this Argentine flag symbol needs help from the wind to keep them aloft. For that reason, these birds prefer to live in mountainous Andes windy areas where they can glide on air currents with little effort. Sadly, there was not enough wind to provide them lift during our ride.

Maita, Buby's fiancée, reached into her saddlebag, and after pouring some vino tinto (red wine), she served up some homemade sausage and cheese, and tortillas. Argentine tortillas, made with potatoes, tasted more like a quiche. That was followed by chicken Milanese.

Pachanga gathered wood to build a fire to boil water for his yerba mate. The highly stimulating herbal tea is passed in a gourd holding a silver straw with a strainer, which separates the loose herbs from the tea.

Red stag were in rutting (mating) season. The call of the red stag is distinctive from the "bugling" sound of an elk. At night I fell asleep hearing the mating calls from my estancia bedroom window. It was special to enjoy this estancia experience after riding a bicycle 285 miles through the Andes.

40. Cycling Newfoundland's Great Northern Peninsula's Viking Trail

Our six-day Freewheeling Adventures' Newfoundland bicycling journey, a journey known to locals as riding "The Rock," began in the village of Deer Lake, one of Newfoundland's few airport gateways.

Guides Dan and Riley picked us up at the Lake View Bed and Breakfast to shuttle us to our bicycle tour meeting point in Gros Morne National Park. After a stop at the *Newfoundland Insectarium*, where we viewed a collection of butterflies, tarantulas, beetles, and bees, the guides stopped at Bonne Bay. They whipped together one of the weeks many picnics. Restaurants in Newfoundland are few and far between.

After a night's rest, we peddle an hour or so to *M.V. Emm-Cat* catamaran to take a tour through a sapphire blue fiord that merges into the Gulf of St. Lawrence. White-sided dolphin and a moose eating saplings were a few sightings. A highlight was the view of Gros Morne mountain. Some of the 10 cyclists on our trip hiked the mountain making an eight-hour climb that took them through the forest then hand over hand rock scree. They said it was a rugged climb, but they were rewarded by a wonderful view of Rocky Harbour.

Bonne Bay Marine Station's (aquarium) guide David Forsey emphasized how precise Captain James Cook charted the adjacent glaciated fiords carved 15,000 years ago. Located as the Southern boundary for Arctic creatures, the aquarium displays include eel pouts, snow crab, stripped and Atlantic wolfish and a blue lobster.

The next day we took a small ferry from the Bonne Bay landing to Woody Point. Cycling to Discovery Centre, Kim Thompson provided an introduction to Gros Morne, a UNESCO World Heritage Site since 1987. Woody Point is a small village featuring a single street dotted with a few coffee shops, bar and an art gallery.

Heading from the Discovery Centre to Trout Lake, we rode along the barren Tablelands. Located between Gros Morne National Park's Trout River and Woody Point, ultramafic rock or peridotite illustrates a unique landscape, one thought to have originated during a glacial plate collision in the earth's mantle about several hundred million years ago.

Overlooking Trout Pond, Dan and Riley put together another picnic lunch. This time they served Trout Lake bakery's homemade pea soup with warm bread.

A two plus mile walk to Western Brook Pond along a dirt trail had boarded walkways covering bogs and marshes. Approximately 9,000 years ago, Western Brook Pond became landlocked. Because of this enclosure, it is not considered a fiord.

Newfoundlanders originally call it a pond because they weren't familiar with the word "lake." Its waters are home to land-locked salmon, brook trout, and arctic char. The surrounding peaks with tumbling waterfalls are the northern end of the Appalachian Mountains.

We shared the two-lane Trans-Canada Highway 430, *The Viking Trail*, as it is Newfoundland's only route for vehicles. Small patches of fenced land, some with scarecrows served locals as vegetable gardens. Highway lanes are wide, with no shoulders, and drivers and truckers politely gave us wide berth. It was unbelievable to spend much of our riding time with the added benefit of a strong tailwind. The road was edged by fields of wild flowers dominated by brightly colored fireweed.

This ride is considered 2 black diamonds, a challenging ride for experts with two one hundred-mile (century) days, was way beyond my comfortable level. Electric bikes were just being introduced, and I didn't hesitate to claim one. I could coast downhill and motor up. Lucky me.

After departing Entente Cordiale, a small inn along the highway, our lunch was served next to lobster traps, stored for the summer, in a field of lupine. Our meal included seafood chowder, Montreal beef (corned beef), pickled herring, and fine cheeses. The lunch was expedited because the day's distance was 112 miles. Ontarian Claire Coire rode the entire route from Portland Creek to Tuckamore Lodge.

L'Anse aux Meadows, a National Historic Site and UNESCO World Heritage Site, dates back 1,000 years ago when Leif Ericson or Eriksson's Norse expedition from Greenland landed in Newfoundland, a region they called Vinland. The group, estimated to number between 60 and 90 landed in Strait Belle Isle not far from Labrador. Here, they built sturdy underground camps covered with turf for protection against the frigid winters. They explored as far away as New Brunswick.

Newfoundland Viking Trail David Peachin cycling, Photo: Mary L Peachin

During their North Atlantic voyages, they encountered Innu, Beothuk, Mi'kmaq aboriginals as well as small colonies in Greenland and Iceland. In 1960, a local fisherman led Norwegian explorer Helge Ingstad to an "an old Indian camp". The site turned out to be the 11th century ruins of Eriksson's Norse building complete with ancient Viking relics.

Our final night would be in one of the few remaining Canada lighthouses. The Inn, located on Quirpon offers the unique island experience of staying in a 1922 lightkeeper's home on the northernmost tip of Newfoundland.

Getting to our accommodations at Quirpon Lighthouse Inn Island was its own adventure. The innkeeper's twelve passenger zodiac was out of commission so he was operating a six-passenger outboard to shuttle guests the forty or so minute ride through Iceberg Alley. Stopping at a primitive rubber dock, we then hiked fifteen minutes up a wet, gravel road. In addition to the lighthouse the innkeeper's home has six guest rooms, plus a dining room for twelve. A second house offers an additional five guest rooms, plus a sitting room. There is no television or Wi-Fi.

Late afternoon was spent in a glass fronted building built to view whales. While bountiful most of the time only a single minke was sighted. The island has a population of twelve red foxes. The alpha female we saw was scrawny possibly from nursing a spring litter of seven.

One last meal of tasty Atlantic cod was enjoyed on our last evening. While we were staying in Iceberg Alley, where whales and icebergs congregated, and at the tip of North America, we evidently arrived too late in the season to see either.

Howling wind, pouring rain and choppy waves hampered our departure. Owner Ed English's large Zodiac had not been repaired. He was forced to shuttle guests to and from the island on the small fishing outboard boat. This meant a longer trip with fewer guests. On the day of our departure, twenty-two guests were returning to their home destinations.

Traveling with Freewheeling is all about adventure and while only one person was successful riding the 112-mile day, we all got to bicycle our limits, hike, and take scenic boat rides. The trip was long, but fascinating and a great introduction to a more isolated region of Canada.

41. Secrets of Nova Scotia's South Shore Bicycle Tour

Ten cyclists from the United States and Canada met in the seafaring town of Chester to learn *Freewheeling's* "secrets" of the rugged North Atlantic coastline. The quaint fishing village, founded in 1759, is located about 45-minutes south of Halifax.

Arriving late on a Sunday afternoon, locals sat in their vehicles, car doors opened while others reclined on lawn chairs as they listened to a late afternoon pop concert. A band struck up some oldies under the whitewashed gazebo next to the yacht club. Our base for the next two nights was The Captain's House, a four-room inn. Visitors and locals mingle with houseguests to enjoy their fresh gourmet seafood served nightly.

David Cycling Nova Scotia, Photo: Mary L Peachin

The first day of cycling secrets began to unravel as we rode a 40-mile-ish loop around the Aspotogan Peninsula. Goldenrod, Queen Anne lace, wild iris, roses and orchids, black-eyed Susan, fireweed, and rosehips, the size of cherry tomatoes, lined the hilly two-lane road. Our bicycle route weaved through forests of spruce that seemed to separate beach-fronted fishing villages.

By the time we had cycled 25-miles to Mahone Bay we discovered that "keeping up with the Jones" in this part of Nova Scotia is a homeowner's pride of their garden. Lawns were covered with white hydrangeas, homes sparkled with recently painted red, green, purple or yellow shingles. Beaches at Blandford (a former whaling station) and Bayswater may have been a chilly 60-degrees, but locals swimming in the surf took advantage of a sunny day. Nearby, many stopped at a flower-filled memorial to pay tribute to the victims of Swiss Air 111 flight.

Stopping for a picnic lunch in Bayswater Park, we noticed that Freewheeling's secret was shared in part with other cyclists. With more than 4,625 miles of coastline in Nova Scotia, Backroads, a US bicycling touring company and Canadian Bicycling were sharing the same picnic site.

Fresh flowers adorned our picnic table complimented by colorful china plates and linen napkins. The buffet lunch included a whole smoked salmon, homemade olive tapenade, hummus, chutney, and salmon pate. Freewheeling's owner Philip Guest believes the coffee he serves his guests should be freshly roasted and hand ground. In fact, the coffee grinder was attached to the picnic table and served in espresso cups.

Freewheeling, based in nearby Hubbards, knows the Maritimes and Atlantic Canada well. Their guides are local and knowledgeable, daily schedules are less structured. Guests can vary their route and there seem to be more flexibility than itineraries offered by larger cycling companies. There is no morning "route rap," and while daily instructions and maps can sometimes be confusing, that's part of a Freewheeling adventure.

It was a stroke of coincidence that we ran into Bucky, and his mates, Wayne and Ozzie, as we rode past a dock in Mill Cove. They were boarding their trawler, *Capt. Pooch M & T*, to check their tuna trap. Asking if we could join them, we watched as the three, beers in hand, joyously celebrated the morning's catch of a 250-pound tuna. If they were lucky, the fish would fetch $20 a pound and shortly be on a charter flight to Japan to be sold for sushi. The summer had yielded few monster-size fish. In the past they would have fattened up the tuna before shipping it off so the additional weight fetched more money, but times were lean. If a tuna gets caught in the maze-like trap which descends to the bay's bottom at 95 feet and is anchored to the shore about 1/4 mile away, they shoot the fish and tow it to a nearby air strip across the bay. Bucky has caught fish weighing more than 1,000 pounds during the two-month tuna season (he traps lobsters during winter open season months).

Colorful village of Lunenburg, Photo: Mary L. Peachin

This experience gave me pause for thought. We would never have had that opportunity if we weren't traveling on bicycles.

Jumping back on our bicycles, we finished our ride in Hubbards before vanning back on the highway to Chester. Continuing south on our 27-speed Trek hybrids we continued to follow the Lighthouse Trail (which doesn't directly pass by many lighthouses) around Mahone Bay to Lunenburg.

Along the road we stopped to watch Bill Lutwick restore wooden boats in his traditional shop. At a "whale carvings sign, we met Peter Redden. His father passed down the craft to his son who now carves sharks and penguins rather than the whales that brought local fame to his father. At the Innlet Cafe in Mahone Bay, their burger was made with fresh Digby scallops. The restaurant buys their seafood directly off fishermen's boat.

Settled in 1753, Lunenburg was designated a UNESCO World Heritage Site in 1995. The port city, built on a hillside was once a fishing and shipbuilding center. The Bluenose schooner (preserved on the back on the Canadian dime) was built here in 1921. The town received notoriety for its rum-running trade during the 1930s.

Our quads screamed on a "monster" hill on the outskirts of Lunenburg. We followed a peninsula winding around a golf course. A glimpse behind was a landscape of the colorful wharf front of Lunenburg.

Along the way, we stopped at Ovens Natural Park. A path high above the slate covered beach was the location of Nova Scotia's brief 1861 gold rush. A cable ferry motored us from the peninsula to LeHave, where we stop for lunch in the village's well-known bakery.

Another highlight of our Lunenburg visit was a boat tour with *The Lobsterman*. While lobster fishing was not in season, Captain Barry Levy hydraulically hoisted six traps out of the bay as mate Jason Greek told us just about everything there was to learn about the tasty delicacy. In order to run these tours, the Lobsterman has an agreement Canada's Department of Fisheries to tag the shellfish in order to trace their migration. Today, most lobstermen used metal traps that better withstand winter cold water conditions. Levy referred to the older wooden variety, frequently displayed on house lawns for sale as "tourist" traps. Each trap Barry lifted had as many as half a dozen lobster weighing up to three pounds.

After a van transfer to Crescent Beach, we continued south along Lighthouse Route passing over one-lane iron bridges then winding back to Broad Cove, Little Harbour, and Mill Village. In the early afternoon we stopped to enjoy another gourmet picnic at Geese Haven.

Our final night was spent at the rustic (built in 1928) White Point Beach Resort. We fell asleep, our windows opened, so we could listen to the crashing waves of the North Atlantic. The next morning was spent hiking the beach in Kejimkujik National Park. Deer and black bear dig insects from seaweed left on the beach at low tide. The endangered piping plover nests on this beach, harbor seals colonize along shoreline rocks.

Brief as it may have been, we all came away with the feeling of friendly people, beautiful landscapes and a curiosity to explore more of Nova Scotia.

42. Puglia, Cruising Among the Trulli in Italy's Boot

Trulli of Puglia, Photo: Mary L. Peachin

Narrow roads weaving through century-old groves of twisted olive trees serve as paths for bicycle riders pedaling in Puglia (Apulia). Scattered through many vineyards and vegetable fields, unique white-slate beehive-shaped trulli are homes. Along the blue waters of the Adriatic, small boats unload copious amounts of fresh, tender octopus and squid.

During a nine-day Ciclismo Classico cycling trip along southern Italy's "spur" and "heel," boot bordered by the Adriatic Sea to the east and the Ionian or Gulf of Taranto on the south, we saw no tourists other than several other riders. It was early fall, and we found the absence of tourists appealing.

Bari, the capital of Puglia, had its day of glory as a Byzantine stronghold. Today, the port city serves as the gateway for catching the ferry to Greece. Here, we met twenty-five Americans and Canadians for our 19-mile shuttle ride to the small village of Polignano a Mare, the start of our bicycle tour.

The city's 16,000 inhabitants live on a plateau with sheer cliffs overlooking the turquoise waters of the Adriatic. The open window of our Hotel Grotto Palazzese room was a straight shot to the water. From a nearby room, an avid angler dropped a fishing line a hundred feet or so into the ocean. Offshore, evening fisherman in small boats used lights to attract fish and calamari (squid) to their nets.

After fitting our bikes and listening to a safety briefing – "Point your hand in the direction you're turning, hold your bike line straight, and angle your arm down if you're slowing" – we took a warm-up ride through narrow cobblestone streets. Your arms could almost reach between the homes lining the streets. Stopping along a scenic shoreline spit, our guide Sheri pulled out a map to give us a preview of trip highlights.

As if doomed to a dungeon we descended a narrow stone circular staircase. Ten stories below, a walkway above the sea led to a stunning grotto, the hotel's dining area. Under the concrete floor, birds flew to nest overnight as waves crashed against rocks.

Bicycling between Polignano a Mare and Alberobello, a distance of 30-some miles, we rode through a variety of vegetable fields. Each plot appeared to be anchored by century-old olive trees, plus almond, fig, plum, apricot, pear and orange trees. The few vegetables we could identify included arugula, broccoli, fennel, cabbage, parsley, onions, garlic, and corn.

The area surrounding the city of Alberobello, a UNESCO World Heritage site, has the greatest concentration of trulli in Southern Italy. The steep grade of the single-lane road had a distant view of the Adriatic. The beehive-shaped trulli dotted the fertile landscape. The whitewashed conical, pinnacle-roofed houses, built without mortar, are concentrically tiled in gray slate. Pinnacles and sides are frequently painted with astrological or religious symbols.

When we stopped for a delicious homemade lunch at Azienda Agrituristica Biologica Serragambetta, where owners Domenico and Perna family-owned eighteenth-century villa. They serve prearranged lunches and has seven small rooms for overnight guests. Today, the ancient restored farmstead is known as "I Monti." Its two-bedroom suites and foyer are built trulli-style. After a challenging day of riding, it felt great to relax in this unique accommodation.

Mary and David bicycling Puglia

Locorotondo, a circular village perched on a hill, was our destination for a day loop ride. Cycling again through fields of grapes, olives and fruit trees with rows of vegetables, we stopped for lunch in Martina Franca, a village founded in the 10th century by refugees fleeing the Arab invasion of Taranto.

Buildings of Baroque architecture surrounded its cobblestone plaza. We wandered into a cafe for homemade pasta mixed with delicacies from the sea –mussels, squid, and octopus. Families drifted in after Sunday Mass, while others headed home, leaving the streets empty. The city of Alberobello is divided by two hills that were once separated by an ancient riverbed. Its trulli village is on a steep hillside surrounded by almond and olive groves.

The residents of Alberobello have lived on this porous land since the late 11th century. Their trulli, built with sheets of slate known as chiancole and no mortar, were free from property tax because they were allegedly moveable. Ferdinando IV of Bourbon absolved the payment of this tax.

The Cubana Café, tucked by the roadside, featured a deli case brimming with fresh anchovies, octopus, mozzarella, prosciutto, eggplant, olives, rolls, salami, and Parma ham. Buying a variety of goodies in many small plastic containers, it suddenly occurred to me that I might have "bought the store." When the storekeeper added up the tab, the grand total amount to six Euro.

Riding through the small fishing port of Savelletri, we passed the city of Fasano to reach San Domenico. Picnicking on a rocky outcropping overlooking the crystal-clear blue Adriatic, we enjoyed our deli antipasto.

Masseria San Domenico is one of Puglia's destination resorts attracting golfers, spa-goers and – would you believe? – bicycle riders. In the middle of an olive grove, the whitewashed accommodation was the first place we encountered tourists, three bicycle groups: Backroads Active Adventures, Toronto-based adventure company Butterfield and Robinson, and a private custom group.

One night we dined elegantly at San Domenico; another night we enjoyed a hearty four-course dinner along the shore of the Adriatic. Dinner was followed with a program by young costumed folkloric dancers from Alberobello.

The whitewashed city of Ostuni has the appearance of a North African city. A 15th century Gothic cathedral towers over the central plaza. The village is a tangle of narrow cobblestone streets and arched stairways.

After we had ridden six days in glorious weather – 70-degree days (50 at night), the sky poured torrential rain. Lucky for us, it was a day of shuttle travel. Some of our group on the "mini-tour" headed home, while the rest of us loaded into several vans for a five-hour shuttle to Gargano – the "spur" of Italy's boot.

The hilly promontory coastline beckoned us with crashing waves on beautiful beaches. The riding graduated from rolling hills to steeper mountains. Instead of winding through ancient cities and olive groves, we followed a two-lane highway from Vieste to Peschici, a hillside town surrounding a picturesque bay. The white buildings of the city looked Greek or Mediterranean in appearance.

A white limestone rock monolith, Promontorio del Gargano, or Pizzomunno, looms as the gateway to the city of Vieste. The mammoth rock appears as if it had calved from the steep cliffs of Vieste.

Frederick II built a castle at the town's highest point. Now used by the military, it is closed to the public. Most visitors come to Vieste to enjoy its beaches rather than learn its history. Much of the area is in Gargano National Park, a pine forest mixed with maple, beech and lime trees. The plan for our second day in Vieste was a boat ride to view scenic grottoes dominating the coastline. Unfortunately, the storm of the previous day churned the seas, canceling our trip.

Once again, we mounted up and cycled the coast viewing scenic cliffs and a World War II military tower. All too soon our eight days in the bike saddle were over. We celebrated our final evening at Enoteca Vesta feasting on tender octopus and squid marinated in Puglia's extra virgin olive oil.

After an early morning shuttle to Foggia, we said our goodbyes and exchanged emails before going our separate ways, some to explore more of Italy or head back to the States.

While each bicycling touring company provides a daily rap session to give riders route direction, Ciclismo Classico provided a very detailed itinerary:

Route Rap: Ciclismo's Best of Southern Italy

- **Day 1:** 6.6-mile Polignano Loop ride to Grotto Palazzese
- **Day 2:** 29.8 miles from Polignano to Balsente with lunch at Agriturismo Grotte to Masseria Fortificata I Monti, 2 nights spent in trulli-like accommodations.
- **Day 3:** 32.8 Locorotondo Loop Ride from I Monte, lunch on own in cellar in Martina Franca
- **Day 4:** 30 miles to Savelletri, Fasano to San Domenico with picnic lunch on Adriatic. Masseria San Domenico resort in Savelletri di Fasano for two nights.
- **Day 5:** 38 miles to Ostuni with picnic lunch and walking tour. End of mini-tour.
- **Day 6:** 5-hour shuttle to Vieste, "the spur of the boot," with a visit to the 900-year-old cathedral of Trani, the only Italian cathedral built by the sea.
- **Day 7-9:** Hotel Degli Aranci in Vieste in Gargano region. Three nights at hotel then transfer to Foggia to train to Naples then to the Amalfi Coast.

43. Czech Republic, Family Cycling and Walking through Prague

The directions read, "Veer right at the green post pointing to Krybniku, turn left at the Y-intersection away from the parking sign, right at the Y in front of the trash can, left at the Y intersection near the nice block of granite on your left, left at the next Y, veer left then pass through the low concrete pillars." Miraculously, it was only at this final juncture that 24 bicycle riders got lost riding through a city park to the plaza of Ceske Budejovice.

My family was on a six-day Backroads bicycle tour through the Czech Republic. In a country where you don't speak the language, getting lost adds to the adventure. Czechoslovakian road signs are few and far between and communication was difficult. Finding anyone who could speak English, showing them the map, then trying to understand their instructions, was always a challenge. Eventually, our group found a woman on a bicycle who indicated that we were riding in the wrong direction and triumphantly led us into the plaza.

The gateway for this trip was Prague, where we took a bus south to the medieval town of Kasperske Hory, the starting point for our ride to the cities of Ceske Budejovice and Cesky Krumlov. Each day, while our two leaders, Wendy and Skye, provided longer and shorter route options, we packed lunches and did warm-up stretches.

The shorter route usually involved a van transfer to a starting point or a pickup for the ride back to our hotel. We rode at our own pace, while Wendy or Skye would "sweep," searching for riders in need of an assist or those who had gone astray.

The van carried our luggage from hotel to hotel. Accommodations were always clean. After one night at the Park Hotel Tosch in Kasperske Hory, we spent two nights at the Hotel Zvon in Ceske Budejovice and two at the Hotel Ruze in Cesky Krumlov.

We ate hearty Czech cuisine: goulash, organ meats, duck and goose, dumplings, and lots of gravy. Carp, pike-perch, and trout were also available, albeit usually fried. The Czech Republic is known for its beer, and the original Budweiser is brewed in Ceske Budejovice.

This city, established in 1265 by the King of Bohemia, served as a town for royalty. It was built on the salt trade route between Austria and Prague. We visited an old salt warehouse and the wagon train station before viewing the thirteenth-century Hluboka castle. The building had been renovated in the early 1800s by the Schwarzenberg family, who added Flemish tapestries, Venetian glass chandeliers, porcelain, and rare books.

During an evening walking tour through the central plaza of Ceske Budejovice, guide Helena Nechlebova pointed out thirteenth-century Gothic architecture, plus several buildings rebuilt in the sixteenth century in Renaissance and Baroque styles. On winding side streets, sgraffito facades with elaborate patterns and pictorial friezes were complimented by colorfully painted Bohemian homes. We toured the Cathedral of St. Nicholas, the sixteenth-century Black Watch Tower, City Hall with its Bohemia coat of arms, a Dominican monastery, and the Church of the Holy Virgin.

Our second day was spent in Ceske Budejovice riding a 36.8-mile loop through the countryside. Backroads had arranged for us to visit a "typical Czech Republic home" in the village of Holasovice, where we were hosted by Blazena AnderlovaIn, who had proudly set out tea and homemade cookies on tablecloth in her patio.

The next day, our ride took us from Ceske Budejovice to Cesky Krumlov, a 33.7-mile ride with a 2,000-foot gain in elevation. Cesky Krumlov is a preserved medieval town recognized as a UNESCO World Heritage Site. The Vltava River flows through this charming village of winding cobblestone streets and sgraffito buildings. While evidence of habitation dates back to the eighth century, the history of the village has been traced from A.D. 1253. The architecture embraces Gothic, Renaissance, and Baroque styles.

Exploring the region, some riders took a three-kilometer hike to the fourteenth-century Divci Kamen castle ruins, while others toured a twelfth-century medieval monastery built by King Otakar II in the small village of Zlata Koruna. The skyline of Cesky Krumlov is dominated by the immensity of the fortress, mansion, and tower of Schwarzenberg Castle, more grandiose than the castle at Hluboka. Magnificent treasures passed through the hands of its owners, including the Rozmberks and Jan Kristian of Eggenberg.

Helena Nechlebova, who lives near Ceske Budejovice, returned to give us a walking tour of Cesky Krumlov. She led us past the Hotel Ruze, an Italian Renaissance building designed as a Jesuit residence in 1586 and recently renovated. We walked through the village square, past a monument built to thank God for keeping the Black Plague from the town. Our last stop was St. Vitus' Church, where we saw the historic tombstones of abbots laid to rest along the side of the churchyard.

The final day of our bicycle trip brought some variety – a three-hour raft trip down the Vltava River. We enjoyed views of the Bohemian birch forest as we floated down the river. The current was mostly gentle, although two weirs and a few riffles provided an opportunity to get wet.

Saying our goodbyes, we boarded the bus for a three-hour return to Prague.

This elegant city, with magnificent architecture at every turn, is one of the few European capitals spared the devastation of both world wars. It features an architectural museum of building styles, include Romanesque, medieval, Renaissance, Baroque, Art Nouveau, and Art Deco. Prague is a perfect walking city.

Immersing ourselves in its wonders, joining the crowds taking the 15-minute walk across the pedestrian-only Charles Bridge, we wandered along cobblestone streets into the old village square with its Powder, Town Hall, and Bridge Towers.

We also took advantage of Prague's excellent public transportation. It's a good idea to buy the correct tokens at your hotel. We were "busted" in the metro station after David mistakenly bought children's tickets from a fare machine. The police picked us out of the crowd and, with a brusque explanation of "baby tickets," and made us pay a $13 fine.

One of the most fascinating tours in Prague is the old Jewish ghetto. The town's buildings, synagogues, and artifacts were preserved by Adolph Hitler, who intended to create an exhibit of an "extinct race." The ghetto, which was founded in the tenth century, contains six synagogues, a Holocaust museum, and a Jewish festival museum. Twelve thousand ancient tombstones, jumbled together crowd the town cemetery, where about 100,000 Jews, victims of the Holocaust are buried. The visit created strong emotions as I looked over the silent cemetery where so many Czech Jews were laid to rest.

After our daily excursions, we escaped the hordes of tourists visiting the city by retreating to the peace of our hotel, the Hoffmeister. The hotel is quiet and located near hundreds of steps leading up to the Hradcany Prague castle, which is flanked by the Gothic-style St. Vitus Cathedral and the Basilica and Convent of St. George, where we spent our final night listening to a symphonic Vivaldi concert, a perfect farewell to Prague, a city of beauty and history.

Part X.

Pumping Adrenaline Aerial Adventures

44. Skydiving in Marana and Bungee Jumping in Cairns

Mary Sky Diving in Marana, Photo: Patricia Gordon

The pickup truck door sign said, "The Bad Spot Cab Company—You Fall, We Haul, That's All, You All!" It's probably better that I didn't notice the sign when I climbed out of the cab and boarded a single-prop Cessna 182, about to climb to 11,000 feet.

The day was crisp and clear, visibility unlimited, with the winds light and variable, the kind of day pilots consider a beautiful flying day. Instead of flying the plane, I would be climbing onto its wing strut then plunging below into the wild blue yonder.

My friend Jeanie and I arrived at the Avra Valley airfield near Tucson, Arizona. After signing away all our rights to Marana Skydiving, we were advised about the life-threatening skydiving risks of falling 11,000 feet.

The legal stuff behind us, we climbed into the plane. As the altimeter climbed past 9,500 feet, Greg asked if I was nervous. I said no; flying in the small four-seat plane didn't bother me in the least. The image of me breaking both ankles on landing did, however, linger in my mind.

We reached altitude and I numbly followed his ground instructions. As the wind and prop blast hit me at 70 mph, Greg yelled "jump." I let go, and down we went, free falling for the first 5,000 feet at approximately 120 mph. I'm not sure of my feelings during the fall, but I do remember hoping the chute would open. When it did, the 3 to 4 G-force caused the harness to bruise my thighs. As we floated through the sky, Greg showed me how to direct the chute, read the wind sock, and flare for the landing.

Mary Sky Diving in Marana , Photo: Patricia Gordon

We had arranged to do tandem diving. Novice divers can fall to the earth attached to the chute of an instructor, without having to take a course. We started on the tarmac. Dressed in a flight suit complete with leather Amelia Earhart-type cap, Greg Behrens, instructor and owner of Marana Skydiving, showed us how to exit the single-engine Cessna. Jeanie and I took turns kneeling on the airplane floor with Greg behind us. His chute would be buckled to our harness.

Exiting requires reaching outside the airplane, grabbing the strut, placing the right foot next to the wheel and left foot on the side step of the door. I assumed the position, and Greg placed his feet next to mine. When he said "Ready," I lifted my head and feet as if I were jumping out of the plane; he was holding my entire weight below him in a parallel position. Yikes! There was one missing item. They had not asked me to bring or did they provide goggles. Damn, I couldn't see, the rush of air was making my eyes water. I missed the beauty of the descent.

Hanging inches from the ground, I came to a sudden realization: this instructor was not going to be my "cushion" on this tandem dive. He would not break my fall. No—I would be the first to hit the ground and cushion him. Things were not going as planned. I shook off the image of Greg telling me to keep my feet together and fall backwards onto my rear on top of him. That did not happen.

The landing came sooner rather than later (given the choice, I would have shortened the free fall so I could spend more time gliding through the sky). As we approached the ground, I braced my ankles tightly… then I fell flat on my face instead of my rear.

And then I saw it. The Bad Spot Cab Company pickup, with its appropriate placard-waiting to drive me back to the office. As promised, I fell, they hauled… and that's all.

Bungee Jumping

Bungee jumping in Cairns

Standing on a ten-story tower gazing over Australia's Great Barrier Reef, I was making every effort to contain my fear as I prepared to jump with my ankles tied together. Bungee jumping offers even the most daring, a new perspective on life. Was I scared… or, more to the point, how scared was I?

Echoing through my head was a continuous question from friends, "Mary, have you ever bungee jumped?" The question about it and sky diving were wearing thin. As a world traveler and adventurer, I had enjoyed scuba diving with sharks, hiking through developing (and less-developed) countries, flying single-engine turbo aircraft, and more. The bungee question was becoming irritating,

By chance, on my way to Papua New Guinea, I spent a few days in Cairns, Australia. I was unaware that the city was one of the world's most fun adult playgrounds, and home of A.J. Hackett's, founder of commercial bungee jumping. ◄

Each day had been its own adventure. I canoed the Mulgrave River, flew with the "postie" (mailman) 1,150 miles into the Outback, fished for marlin on the Great Barrier Reef, and caught barramundi in a nearby estuary. There was four-wheeling in the rain forest at Cape Tribulation, feeding kangaroos at the Cairns Zoo, and a historic train ride to the aboriginal town of Kuranda, with a return by bicycle.

The decision to bungee jump tantalized me. I decided to give it some serious thought on the twenty-mile bicycle ride down to A.J. Hackett's in Smithfield. I promised myself that it would be OK if I chickened out.

If you are guessing, my bicycle did head into A.J. Hackett's. Yikes! I had to weighed in, thankfully in kilos. The number was drawn on my hands for everyone to see and was taken so the bungee masters would know how far to adjust the rope based on my weight. The next challenge was forcing one leg after another up 132 feet of stairs to the top of the platform.

Feeling my knees wobbling, I stopped. I saw a huge spider, a golden orb, weaving her web on a tower strut. I tried to distract myself. Instead, I became determined to reach the top of the tower and jump—without taking time to consider the consequences.

The timing didn't work out as planned. At the top, an Australian television station was shooting a special on the bungee trend, which took about 15 minutes. My jump was then furthered delayed when the woman in front of me freaked out and decided to walk down the stairs.

The wait had "iced" me. My legs were now like rubber bands. The bungee masters took no notice, wrapping my ankles in towels and binding them with a cord.

Shuffling out on the platform, I knew if I looked down at the pool of water below me, I would never have the courage to jump. Instead, I kept my gaze on the beauty of the Great Barrier Reef.

5-4-3-2-1, jump! I balked—better than any major league pitcher. The second countdown seemed endless and, with a breath and a prayer, I took a swan dive off the tower.

After the second and third recoil of the rope, I started cheering. Nothing hurt! I had defied death! Finally, I stopped bouncing and the bungee crew lowered me into the raft that would take me from the pond to the dock. My knees were shaking so much, they had to help me out of the raft.

Would I do it again? Well… once was enough. But now, when people ask, "Mary, have you ever bungee-jumped?" I can smile and say yes, of course.

Many people have asked me how I compare bungee jumping to skydiving.

While both activities instill fear followed by a huge adrenaline rush, I found bungee jumping to be more frightening. Skydiving appears to have more safety factors built into it. In the end, I can't recommend that you try either activity, simply because I would never encourage others to take the risks that I do. However, if you are so inclined, be sure that you pursue either path with an expert. Your life is, literally, in their hands.

45. Ultralight Flying Over the Sonoran Desert in Avra Valley

Wind blows through my hair as H.L. Cooper and I fly in his open ultralight cockpit. Traveling at 45 mph, we are a mere 150 feet above the desert between the Waterman and Roskruge mountain ranges in Arizona's Avra Valley.

Animal tracks crisscross the scrubby desert. To the east lie recently harvested cotton fields. White cotton balls, missed by pickers, contrast with the green fields. From a distance, a cattle water tank appears to be covered with algae. As we move closer, we realize that we're really seeing small water lily pads.

In the heat of the day we do not see the deer, javelina, coyotes, or mountain lions that have been recently observed by ultralight pilots flying in the cool of a summer sunrise.

As we circle the area, airplane instructor Cooper zigzags around the occasional "dust-devil" wind funnel to avoid encountering turbulence. He cuts the engine to allow the ultralight to glide silently over the desert as we soar.

Spotting several hundred feet of flat desert, Cooper does a "touch and go" landing. He flares the ultralight, holding the nose gear up until touchdown, then restarts the engine using full throttle for takeoff. This is "low and slow" flying, unlike general aviation small-aircraft flying from point A to B. This is more like Wright Brothers' stuff, an airborne experience that takes you back to the open-cockpit, pioneer days of aviation.

When I had arrived at the Arizona Ultralight Association hangar, pilots Bill Breen of Tucson, Jim Arbore of Oro Valley, and Cooper had been watching a football game and talking "flying" during commercials. They were planning their next ultralight camping trips.

Some of their favorite camping sites are the tiny town of Cascabel in the San Pedro Valley and the Empire Ranch, north of Sonoita. Sometimes they attach floats to the wheel gear for landing on water to camp at Apache, Canyon, or Roosevelt lakes.

The sound of an engine interrupts the conversation. Tucsonan Tom Privett, is practicing touch-and-go landings on the dirt airstrip owned by the Arizona Ultralight Association. We walk outside to watch.

Ultralights are considered "experimental" by the Federal Aviation Administration. They are not recognized as certified aircraft. The FAA also does not recognize ultralight pilots because they are not required to have a license.

Safety is a primary concern for Cooper and the Arizona Ultralight Association. They have devised their own certification program, number of hours of flight instruction, cross country trips, plus flying and written test exams.

There is a difference between one and two seat aircraft, but basically flying techniques are similar to those used in general aviation. The panel includes an airspeed indicator, altimeter, ignition, magneto switch, and heading indicator. The ultralight is powered by a 66-horsepower engine with two cylinders, a two-stroke engine specifically built for ultralights.

This sport is a considerably less expensive way to get airborne. While ultralight flying is not a cheap hobby, general aviation airplanes cost considerably more for both training and purchase.

Flying with Cooper was a great adventure. I'm not sure he converted me, a longtime general aviation pilot, from the rush of the throttle's thrust of a single-engine Cessna Turbo 210, but it sure was fun seeing the desert up close, slow, and personal.

46. Soaring Planes and Hot Air Ballooning in Tucson

If aircraft could be considered sexy, the soaring plane would win. It has long-spanned wings and a narrow fuselage with a passenger seat behind the pilot. A car analogy might be a bright red Lamborghini.

In Marana, there is a soaring school, and I wanted to try soaring. Not to become a regular soarer, but to have a new taste of adventure.

Once the passenger is seated in the rear and all is ready, the glider is attached by a 200-foot rope to an airplane, which climbs to an altitude and distance calculated to allow the glider to return to the same landing strip.

Wind is the controlling factor in both direction and distance of flight. With the pilot seated in front of me, my vision was limited to side views. It was still beautiful to be aloft over the Sonora desert in total silence.

Twice I have flown in the same hot air balloon, and twice I have crash-landed. The jarring of the impact on earth then the carriage toppling over was not injurious. I've never seen other balloons crashing so maybe it was the pilot or her land crew being unable to tie-down the balloon.

Balloons are colorful, but it's just not appealing to me to be looking into residents' backyards, listening to the gas that controls ascent and depending on a ground crew to help you land.

There have been opportunities to take crack-of-dawn flights over both Victoria Falls, Tanzania, Kenya, South Africa, and in Turkey's Cappadocia. While all offer wonderful views, I prefer to pass the early morning aerial experience and skip a wake-up call.

I have parasailed from Mexican beaches. The thrill of flying behind a boat above the ocean is offset by the discomfort of a crotch-pinching harness, and women can expect many ground crews to catch them with arms around their breasts.

As for hang gliding off cliffs, I've tried twice off Southern California's famed Black's nude beach near Del Mar. It's another wind-dependent sport, and neither of my visits were windy enough to get a guide harnessed to me off the ground.

Part XI.

Grizzlies, Black, Kermode, and Polar Bears

47. Fortress of the Khutzeymateen Grizzlies

Khutzeymateen sow chewing sedge, Photo: Mary L Peachin

Lucy, matriarch of the Khutzeymateen Sanctuary, reigns supreme in a very exclusive wilderness. Along British Columbia's rocky Coastal mountain range between Portland Inlet and Work Channel, Lucy lives in a valley of ancient old growth rain forest. Unknown and unheralded, she is probably the most photographed grizzly in the world. The area has the highest density of healthy, grizzlies in British Columbia.

Some twenty plus years ago, Barney, the Valley's dominant male, sired Lucy's first offspring. According to Dan Wakeman, one of two guides licensed to operate in the Sanctuary, "Barney, one of the 'Barnacle Brothers' is a half-ton gentle giant." Barney's absent twin probably wandered away to another valley. Motley, a second dominate male, and Barney will typically mate each year with three females. Grizzlies are solitary animals the rest of the year.

Early fall is a "time of feasting" for wildlife, one that is determined by migration patterns of spawning pink and chum salmon who struggle through the final throes of death while fighting the upstream currents of Khutzeymateen or "Khutz" estuary.

Helen Blake, Lorna Butzs, my husband David and I have joined bear expert, Dan Wakeman, on a three-day grizzly viewing expedition. We are fortunate to join a privileged group of less than two hundred annual visitors who visit the sanctuary, one that is neither advertised nor considered much of a tourist attraction. In recent years, Prince Rupert has offered day boat tours to the Khutz, but they aren't license to go up the creek into the Sanctuary.

A grizzly sanctuary in its purest sense, it is located on Gitsi'is land, a tribe related to the Tsimshian First Nation people. They referred to the land as K'tzim-a-Deen, or "a long inlet in a steep valley."

This stunning landscape differs from Alaska or Yellowstone grizzly habitat because the area is not part of a national park. Hunting, fishing, camping, logging, and mining is prohibited. 200,000 acres exist solely for the protection of 50 grizzly bears. The Sanctuary is unique because the bears, which have not been hunted for more than 20 years, don't see humans as a threat.

Today, the Khutzeymateen is substantially larger than the original 100,000 acres explored and studied 20 years ago, by biologist Wayne McCrory and Dan Wakeman. The reserve was dedicated in 1984 by HRH Prince Philip, Duke of Edinburgh, who, at the time, was president of the World Wildlife Federation. The Prince donated $150,000 of seed money for McCrory to do his first independent study.

Dan waited for us dockside in Prince Rupert on his 40-foot sloop, the *Sunchaser*. Heading north to northeast for several hours, we motored along British Columbia's mainland before turning east into the interior Coastal mountain area of Khutzeymateen valley, a distance of 50 miles.

Sunchaser was hand built by Dan from teak wood. It has two forward twin beds, a small galley and dining table, and two aft bunks with privacy curtains. There is a single combined bath/shower. It's very cozy.

Dundas Island shielded us from gale winds and pounding waves of the open Pacific Ocean. We cruised through the waters of Chatham Sound passing Fort Simpson, the second largest (population 1,000) First Nation village along the coast.

Diving grebes, migrating from the Arctic to Mexico, "worked" the area consuming bait fish. Along the shore, a black bear peered curiously. In Work Channel, we trolled several fishing lines hoping to catch a salmon for dinner. Not a nibble.

We admired the sun setting over the mountain peaks of south Alaska's panhandle, five miles in the distance. The typical six to seven-hour trip had taken an additional three hours in the windy, choppy seas. We would later pass on an offer of a spaghetti dinner to quickly gobble a Caesar salad before collapsing into our bunks. It was close to midnight when Dan finally dropped anchor.

To Dan, "the putrid smell of rotting, dying salmon symbolizes the ending and beginning of another life cycle." He knows the bears well, and in their presence, he exercises caution. Dan packs bear spray, but has never used it. He approaches the bears by Zodiac, never on foot.

Sun Chaser sloop in Khutzeymateen, Photo: Mary L Peachin

Some bears are skittish, while Lucy and Blondie, 19-year-old females, will hang out eating or sleeping, giving viewers great photo ops. A third female, Gracie, who is approximately eight years old will probably have her first set of cubs next spring. Her mother, "Big Momma," a big muscular bear with the physique of a male, has not been seen in recent years. While these three females hang out in the same proximity, bears typically don't like one other. Constantly moving, each requires more than 1,000 acres of wilderness.

Sub adults are more inclined to make a bluff charge, either hissing or huffing to show their annoyance, a signal for the viewer to beat it. "Grizzlies are masters of intimidation."

We caught a brief glimpse of a bear crossing upstream. A sub-adult stood on his haunches eyeing us then continued tearing the skin off a salmon. As darkness descended, another sub-adult, one of the fifty bears roaming the valley fed along the shore. He searched for salmon then stopped to chomp on grass. Dan thought he might be a two-year old weaned by Lucy or Blondie. Both females gave birth last spring to three cubs by the same male.

A flock of mergansers skimmed the water. A territorial dipper chased another from its turf. Kingfishers flitted between the river banks. We watched the wake of harbor seals following the inbound tide. Seals swim upside down when fishing for salmon. They slap the lethargic salmon on the surface before consuming it.

Waterfalls plunged from cliffs, and the rise of the tide in the river created a fishing frenzy between gold and bald eagles. Viewing bears, as they gorge on salmon to bulk up for winter hibernation, varies from their springtime emergence with cubs and males eager to mate with females in estrus.

Khutzeymateen BC subadult, Photo: Mary L Peachin

The following summer we chose to fly into the Valley in a Beaver float plane from Prince Rupert. Joyce and Gary Follman, David Lovitt, Lori Mackstaller and I were welcomed by a vibrancy of life in the Khutzeymateen. Females were bringing their newborn cubs out of their hibernation dens, males searched for mates, and other males prowl the Sanctuary in hopes of becoming a dominant male.

The estuary was rich and fertile. Bears gorged on sedge grass and savored the tasty roots of the beautiful, but odiferous chocolate lily. The temperate rain forest was lush with Sitka spruce, hemlock, and cedar. Leafy alders, willows, and crabapple trees lined the water's edge. Khutzeymateen inlet, river, and estuary, approximately 10 miles long, steep cliffs rose to 6,500 feet. A few barren areas had been leveled by avalanches. Cow parsnips, skunk cabbage, huckleberries, and fireweed filled meadows. Sharing the Sanctuary were wolf, wolverine, mountain goat, porcupine, and river otter.

Glaciers were melting, waterfalls rushed over granite cliffs, lichen hung from trees. Whenever the tide exposed the muddy bottom of the stream, nitrogen nutrients form gas-like dollops of foam that floated like shampoo suds.

Blue and yellow lupine was in its prime. Cow parsnip, yellow and red Indian paintbrush line banks scattered with small chocolate lilies. Harbor seals nursed pups, while merganser ducks protected their newborn chicks. Harlequin ducks, their bodies a brilliant colored slate blue body, with brown flanks and bold white markings outlined in black, swam casually by us. A lone black and white loon seemed attracted to the sloop. The valley glistened.

A day on the inlet is dictated by "time and tide" determining the rise and fall of the estuary. Dan motors his guests in his Zodiac when the tide permits. This is usually for about four hours in the morning, and an hour after dinner. Before turning in, we listened to the weather forecast. Gale force winds and heavy rain were predicted, we were going to "experience the true rainforest." The "mood" of the mountain surrounded us, a low-lying fog-like mist tucked between and layered in curtains in the estuary. During the night, two spruces fell in the water. "Windfall, one tree fell and took down the other."

Barney, the dominate male of the Khutzemateen prowled the shoreline. Perhaps he was looking for Lucy, who had not yet appeared. Golden bear, a five-year-old, chewed on sedge between naps. Glaring at us when we invaded "her space", Dan quickly backed up the Zodiac. Suddenly Golden ran into the temperate Great Bear Rainforest. Twigs snapped and a bear that Dan had never seen rambled out of the woods. "He's not a dominant male, but at 800-900 pounds, he will become one in the next few years." He probably came over from the next valley to "check things out." That first afternoon we would observe eight bears.

A small movement in the sedge grass first appeared to be a tree stump. Taking a closer look, we discovered a rarely sighted grey timber wolf. Ravens squawk overhead. Dan commented "they must be protecting their nests." It's rare to sight a wolf and not have it run away. After pacing casually across the grass, the wolf ambled into the forest.

During those three early days of summer, the five of us observed 15 different bears, at least 25 to 30 close sightings. We observed what bears eat, see, their moods, the life of grizzly bears in the Khutzeymateen-this fortress of the grizzlies, where each can roam 1,000 acres.

By early fall, the chocolate lilies will be long gone, with only a few scattered purple asters remaining. Golden eagles, some boasting a six foot wing span, and bald eagles soar from tree to tree. Squawking flocks of Canada geese prepare for their southerly migration. Seagulls gathered on sand spits pick at the remains of pink salmon left by bears. Coho, unlike pink, flash like "silver bullets" to spawn further upstream.

The Khutzeymateen is the only place in the world where a grizzly can grow old. Lucy had three sets of cubs and her offspring now had cubs. She appeared late this summer with a pair of twins. When the time comes, and only in this sanctuary will Lucy wander off and die on her own terms.

48. Grizzlies Mating Around Knight Inlet, British Columbia

Siblings Mayhem and Mischief were acting a bit skittish. JFK, a dominant grizzly, had appeared in Knight Inlet valley with the intention of courting and siring their "mom," Marilyn (as in Monroe).

That morning, the stunning blond was suckling her cubs. A drama quickly unfolded as Marilyn, in a heartbeat, traded motherhood for romance. By that afternoon she had abandoned her two-year-old golden-colored cubs. As Marilyn and her partner wandered into the forest, a four-year-old sub-adult named Milton ran into the clearing. The frightened grizzly obviously wanted to get out of the path of Marilyn and JFK.

During the next three weeks, JFK will relentlessly pursue Marilyn mounting her to stimulate ovulation. After fertilization, he will depart leaving her to mate with other males. One theory suggests she does this for her own protection. Males remember their mates, but not the cubs, which they are likely to kill. Subsequently, if Marilyn gives birth to multiple cubs, they may not share the same father.

Protected from strong currents and the elements by its location in an elbow of the inlet, Knight Inlet Lodge, a floating resort anchored in Glendale Cove, is attached near the shore of the longest fiord in British Columbia, the 60-mile Knight Inlet watershed. Bear viewing in the valley is legendary. A population of 40 to 50 grizzlies are known to inhabit the area. During late spring, visitors come to view courting bears. Around late June, they observe sows emerging from hibernation with newborn cubs. Fall viewing is focused on bears bulking up for winter denning by gorging on spawning salmon.

Early in the morning, the lodge's capacity of 24 guests motored in six passenger 14-foot skiffs to search for bears along the banks of the cove. The two-hour excursion is repeated after lunch and again in the late afternoon.

This spring, there are fewer bears, but black bears, which instinctively keep their distance from grizzlies, have been sighted. The boat anchors offshore at a minimum distance of 150-feet. Camera shutters click as excited voyeurs observe two cubs hungrily nibbling on grass-like sedge, also known as bear grass.

Guide Corinne Wainwright explains how the grizzly identifying hump is actually a muscle used for digging. On a sunny afternoon, bear researchers, Barrie Gilbert and Owen Nevin scanned for bears from a blind perched high in a Sitka spruce.

After Milton's brief appearance, we turned our attention to bird watching. We aimed binoculars at bald eagles, a yellow-breasted blackbird roosted on a clump of sedge, osprey gliding on wind currents, a flitting red-breasted sapsucker, and a common merganser swimming with newborn chicks hopping a ride on her back. The hundred pair of nesting bald eagles in the area increases to more than a 1,000 during the salmon spawn. Their nests average about six feet in diameter, increasing in size each year that they re-build it.

In previous years, it's typical to observe approximately sixteen bears in Glendale Cove with three or more boars sparring for five sows. During the fall, occasionally a wolf or cougar join the bears as they fish the estuary for spawny salmon. Thorny wide leaf devil's club bush and pink rosehip flowers line the fir covered bank of the dark-tannic color crystal clear water of the estuary. Visitors view this amazing scene from one of Knight Inlet Lodge's four tree stands.

A solitary black bear grazed along the bank. He stopped eating to look at us. A bear taking notice of us is considered a "strike one." This bear determined that we were not a threat. The three-strike lodge policy includes any change in the grizzly's behavior, feeding habit, turning their head, yawning. Behavioral changes require the boat to leave the bear.

If guests choose, they can plan other activities including a rainforest hike, kayaking, fishing, jet boating, or in summer months, whale watching.

On a windy day, the water of the inlet churned as we departed for a day long boat tour through Broughton archipelago. Pacific white-side dolphin gracefully rode the bow waves of the boat. Heading north through Sargeaunt Passage, we passed several salmon farms before entering Tribune Channel.

We stopped for a picnic lunch on Burdwood island beach. Enjoying the tranquility of old growth forest behind us and snow-covered mountain peaks in the distance, we packed up for the ride to Echo Bay where old-timer Billy Proctor has built a small museum of personally beach-combed First Nation, Chinese, and Japanese artifacts. The final stop of the day was an ancient tribal island where ancient totems lay decaying on the floor of the rainforest.

Guide Wendy invited us on a bear tracking tour. Motoring across the bay, we spent time overturning algae-covered rocks to look at bear morsels: tasty worms, barnacles, mussels, and clams. Loudly announcing our presence to ward off any bears, we boarded a Knight's Inlet bus.

Along the road we passed other bear delicacies: crabapple, huckleberry, elderberries, lingonberries, salmonberries, and salal. We noted flattened grass where several bears had bedded. Wendy stopped the bus to examine fresh scat filled with fibrous matter created by sedge grass.

The bears we've been viewing had healthy coats, a result of a mild winter which determines the length of hibernation. In fall, during the pink salmon spawn (mid-August to mid-October) bear eat caught salmon gorging first on the protein-rich brain followed by egg roe and skin. They may or may not eat the meat and leave the guts for the seagulls. They will gain 100 pounds during this feasting season by consuming dozens of fish daily.

Stopping by a bear trail, Wendy pointed out paw prints in a boggy wallow. A western hemlock near the road had signs that it was used as a "rub" tree. A portion of the bark was smooth; other areas were stripped so the bears could start the tasty flow of sap. After a good upright back rub, the bears spray urine on the tree to leave their scent.

Another lodge boat tour followed the 1,500-foot deep fiord of Knight Inlet westerly for 25-miles. Towering granite walls spilled glacial waterfalls into the green water. Pacific white-sided dolphin frolicked in an inlet teeming with an oolichan spawn. Jamie guided the boat under the spray of a waterfall before turning the boat around at the Ahnuhati River, a native word "the place where the humpback whale meets the salmon."

Activities literally consume daylight hours. When guests are in camp, they either sleeping in one of the rustic dockside cabins or eating in the large dining room. Chefs Paul, Shauna and Edward keep everyone well fed with hearty, bountiful buffets.

A rainbow of colorful kayaks lines the dock. Paddling in the cove to observe the bears is as close to nature as you can get. Milton, a teenage sub adult, sunned himself on a waterfront boulder.

Don't expect any "down time" at Knight Inlet Lodge. The day begins at 6:30 am and ends around 10 pm, that is, if you choose stay around to listen to guide lectures about subjects that include bears, Arctic adventures, and salmon.

49. Lords of the Arctic: The Polar Bears of Churchill

Hudson Bay's frigid, turbulent waters solidify in late fall, allowing starving polar bears to migrate northward over the ice packs toward their seal-hunting grounds. They are eager to leave their summer home on the barren tundra surrounding Manitoba's frontier town of Churchill. Since last spring's thaw, they've eaten little but berries. Their resulting lethargy is evident. At a distance, when the monstrous canine incisors and claws are hidden, these great animals look like oversized creamy-white teddy bears — a far cry from their reputation as ferocious, sometimes cannibalistic carnivores.

Photographers, naturalists, and wildlife lovers from around the world come to Churchill, hoping to observe one of nature's great wonders. The town itself defines the word "frontier." Located in northern Manitoba, it can be accessed only by air or train, and it's the last stop on the railroad. During my visit, the main drag Kelsey Boulevard had no stoplights or paving, and the town's 1,000 residents were outnumbered by an estimated 1,200 polar bears. Global climate change has made the freeze later, and it has permitted visitors to view and snorkel with belugas in addition to being on the tundra searching for polar bears.

It's no surprise that Churchill has some strict bear-management policies. Patrols track bears, hoping to prevent bear confrontations with humans. Bright-green bear alert signs (call 675-BEAR) are posted everywhere. Around the outskirts of town lie trailer-size traps of galvanized steel pipe, baited with rancid seal meat. Any bear sighted within city limits, goes to jail. And no one walks outside town without a rifle.

Guide Paul Ratson — who showed us the nearby Prince of Wales Fort, built by the Hudson's Bay Company to protect British interest in the fur trade — brought his Marlin 4570 rifle on our brief walk. On our return he emptied the shells, explaining, "It's better to have and not need than to need and not have."

I visited Churchill in late October to view polar bears, joining a group of 20 other animal lovers from the United States, Australia, and Japan who'd signed on for a five-day, including time spent in Winnipeg, International Wildlife Adventures tour. Wasting no time after our arrival at the airport, we board a somewhat decrepit school bus that took us to Churchill's "polar-bear jail." Any bear that wanders into town or chooses to dine at the town dump (known colloquially as the "Polar Bear Dining Room") is tranquilized and taken to the jail — a corrugated-steel Quonset hut, formerly a military garage, that has been divided into 25 "cells." Captured bears are kept in solitary confinement until the autumn freeze, at which time they're released to head eagerly to their hunting grounds. On average, 100 bears "do time" each year. No food is served; the captors don't want bears conditioned to show up for the meals. If the cells are filled, a few bears are flown out to an ice floe, making room for new "incorrigibles."

Polar Bear, Photo: Rocky LaRose

Unlike grizzly and black bears, which hibernate during winter months, the polar bear is active throughout the year. Paul jokes, "All these bears are Capricorns," born in December or January. Adult bears breed every two years, in April or May; pregnant females are an exception to the migration, heading inland to den for the winter.

The rest of the first day is spent touring Churchill. The next day, we show up at eight, excited about our first up-close view of the bears in the wild. We board one of 18 "tundra buggies," each of which is a converted fire engine holding between 26 and 52 people, warmed by a portable propane heater. The single-gear buggies lurch across the tundra on their 600-pound, 52-inch Goodyear tires. We wipe steamy windows with paper towels.

Rocking and rolling, the buggy travels between 12 and 14 miles a day towards Gordon Point, about a 45-minute drive from the buggy depot. We scour glaciated rocky terrain in search of bears. The tundra is barren except for a few willows and white spruce, all bent toward the southeast by blasts of crystalline snow. "The direction of the tree is true; the compass can lie," says Paul. He points out the minimal vegetation – the few species that can survive at below-zero temperatures. A thin film of grease ice covers the many ponds leading out to Hudson Bay, the gateway for the polar bear migration.

The first bear is sighted, and we hurriedly open windows, craning our necks for a look. Serious photographers rush to claim a spot on the open rear deck. Our driver approaches cautiously so as not to frighten the bears, but that seems unnecessary. Several curious bears stand on two feet to paw the sides of the vehicle, while others nibble at the tires. The photographers go crazy, eating up the photogenic antics.

During the next two days, our buggy will encounter more than two dozen bears. They're unafraid; a stopped buggy frequently attracts a "bear jam," with other vehicles in the vicinity heading over to see which way cameras are pointing, or to follow up on driver-radioed sightings. Even with the traffic, there are enough bears to go around, and everyone returns to Churchill visually satiated.

In those two days, we see several subadult males playfully sparring. Our guide describes them as "testosterone with teeth." One adult bear enthusiastically gobbles seaweed along the shore of Hudson Bay, while a mother with a yearling cub snuggles in a snowbank in front of a lone spruce. Some bears laze along the four-wheel track, while others ramble up to the tundra buggy. After cautiously testing the strength of an ice pond, another bear shuffles across.

Each day offers something new to see. The buggy ride is long and somewhat jarring, but time passes quickly when you are gazing and gasping at the magnificence of these bears. And though feeding the bears is not allowed, humans are served a daily lunch of soup, sandwiches, and sweets. Each evening at 4:30, the buggies return to the depot in the encroaching dark. After the half-hour bus ride back to town, we have dinner and roll early into bed, looking forward to warm and furry dreams about our bear encounters.

50. Kermode Spirit Bears and Grizzlies, Great Bear Rainforest

Kermode Spirit Bear, Photo: Joyce Follman

Along the banks of a river stream, we had a great view, from a First Nations' wooden stand, of spawning pink salmon. A black bear was feeding her two cubs, when lumbering along the opposite side of the creek, a rarely sighted Kermode, referred to as the white "spirit bear." approached. Expecting a typically protective sow with cubs to charge the Kermode, we waited for the action to begin. The cubs apparently didn't have much confidence in Mom. Like a flash, they scrambled up the trunk of a red alder.

Most people have never heard of or seen a Kermode, a recessive gene subspecies of the black bear. An estimated 80 of them inhabit British Columbia's Great Bear Rainforest. The area is so remote, accessible only by boat or floatplane, that it gets few visitors.

When eight of us touched down in a Dehavilland Beaver, Tom Ellison, expedition leader, skipper and owner of the ketch *Ocean Light II*, was feeling ecstatic. During his 16 years of licensed bear viewing and 30 years of coastal sailing experience, he had seen a total of 18 Kermode. The previous day he had experienced his best day of viewing, his first sighting of a Kermode cub.

Eight of us had overnighted at gateway Prince Rupert's Eagle Bluff Lighthouse Bed and Breakfast. We took several cabs to the floatplane dock. After a long fog delay, we made the hour flight over the Coastal peaks and glacial lakes. The pilot glided the aircraft pontoons onto the water near the First Nations village of Hartley Bay, where Tom met us.

Black bear with kermode twins, Photo: King Pacific Lodge

After a short Zodiac transfer to *Ocean Light II*, listening to a brief safety talk, we weighed anchor to search for bears. An hour later, we motored close to an island. As we neared the shore, we were astonished to see a creamy vanilla Kermode standing on his haunches eating crabapples. After a brief retreat into the forest, he came out and we ogled him again. I had made four previous trips to the Great Bear Rainforest without success so for me the experience was instant gratification. Searching the rest of the afternoon, a large Steller sea lion had to suffice.

Tom boasted that his chef Susan Cohen was the best cook around. And, he wasn't wrong. Dinner included fresh salmon, spaghetti squash, salad with a miso dressing, and boiled potatoes. After dessert, we motored to nearby Bishop Bay in the Inside Passage to relax our bodies in a natural hot spring.

Ocean Light II's remodeled interior includes five double berth cabins that share two heads and one shower. There are no hotel-type amenities. This is an adventure requiring good physical shape and a "go with the flow" attitude for its flexible itinerary. Days are long and filled with activity.

Other than a BC Ferries boat making its 18-hour run between Port Hardy and Prince Rupert, we had the Inside Passage to ourselves. Crawling into sleeping bags in our bunks, we drifted off listening to the blow and tail slapping of humpback whales.

The next morning, we took a hard-bottom Zodiac to a rocky landing on Gribbell Island. We hiked a half-mile through old growth and alder rainforest to one of two Gitga'at cedar-hewn bear stands along Riordan Inlet. Soon after our arrival, two black bears ambled down the stream. Lazily, they fished for spawning pink salmon. Richard, our Gitga'at guide, explained that an abundant crop of salal provided the bears a choice of feeding on berries or salmon. For the next four hours, we had to be content watching Steller jays, dippers, and salmon dying as they struggled their way upstream to spawn.

Then the bear viewing action picked up. Across the stream, a hungry black bear aggressively chased salmon in the stream. After several unsuccessful lunges, he scored. Gripping the struggling salmon, he waded to the bank to consume every scrap and morsel.

A less adept subadult clumsily belly flopped into the water. After grasping a salmon, he retreated into the forest to enjoy his catch. We had a quick, faraway glimpse of a Kermode and several additional black bears.

Two Kermodes inhabit the area. Our Giga'at guide noted that this three-year-old Kermode was making his first appearance near the viewing stand. When we wondered why the bears didn't react to one another, he explained that black bears tolerate one another better than grizzlies. He said, "If two males are going to fight, they wait until nightfall." The second Kermode appeared briefly as we were leaving.

Nature's spectacular show wasn't over. As we saluted our day, a humpback, one of many feeding in Bishop Bay, breached and finned continually. Three harbor seals watched both us and the whale until it gave a final tailing. Around the dinner table, accompanied by opera and classical music, we relived the day's excitement.

Traveling six hours south to explore some of British Columbia's grizzly habitat, *Ocean Light II's, a* 71-foot mahogany and Douglas fir sailing ketch navigated the Inside Passage, the same waterway used by large cruise ships heading to Alaska. It wasn't just another "day at sea." Booming waterfalls spilled over granite cliffs. We caught a view of Buteland's abandoned salmon cannery, now a ghost town in disrepair. Migrating humpbacks and elephant seals shared this landscape, while Dall's porpoises rode in the wake of our boat.

Tom gave us a briefing on grizzlies: "These bears are unpredictable." He asked three members of the group to carry bear spray and reminded us to always stay close together. Unlike on Gribbell Island, we would eat only in the inflatable and relieve ourselves in the water.

Wayne McCory, a noted bear biologist and a wildlife photographer, was in Mussel Inlet when we arrived during midafternoon. McCory had observed 16 bears during the day and had experienced a false charge that morning by a sow protecting her cub.

The area is spectacularly beautiful. The valley has steep granite cliffs lined with rainforest. The inlet flows about three miles. Harbor seals fed in the bay, while enormous flocks of gulls, gorging on salmon eggs, lined the beaches at the mouth of the river. Discovered by explorer George Vancouver, Mussel Inlet was named for one of his men who became ill after eating mussels. He died in nearby Poison Cove. Today, the area is managed by the Kitasoo Nation, who live in the village of Klemtu.

Wasting little time, we spent the afternoon observing four grizzlies, including a pair of blond-faced twin subadults. When one of the males swam across the river, a black bear high-tailed it as he saw the grizzly approaching.

Tom announced that anyone wanting the opportunity to view a sow with a spring-born cub should be prepared to depart the *Ocean Light II* at first light.

His inflatable pulled up to a shore where we scrambled over clumps of sedge grass, dodging decaying salmon carcasses in the tidal flat. We waded across slippery algae-covered rocks and used a hollowed log as our viewing stand.

The cub was hungry for crabapple, and he leaped like a chimpanzee from one tree to another. When Mom wandered back to the stream to catch salmon, the cub cried at her disappearance. Eventually, the sow responded to her baby's cry and returned. Being downwind, the cub couldn't smell Mom's approach until she stood on her hind legs nibbling crabapples. Tom considered this viewing opportunity unique because sows typically do not expose their first-year cubs.

At low tide, bears dug under rocks for salmon roe while others feasted on salmon or crabapples. Two subadults wrestled playfully. A dominant bear joined forces with two siblings, chasing two bears up the side of a cliff. Trapped, one of the bears gave another a slobbery kiss, not the fight we had anticipated. During the day, we viewed 18 grizzlies, at one time we were surrounded by seven. We stood huddled together as some bears approached within several dozen feet. Looming large and still, we didn't seem to attract notice by these bears. They were well fed and females were playful with their cubs.

Four days of beautiful, sunny weather was an unexpected surprise. Brad Hill, a Calgary photographer, noted, when we awoke to rain our last day, that it would be a "monochromatic" day. And so, we experienced grizzlies in the mist. Only when a bear approached slowly, Tom might say, "It's OK Mom, stay gentle." We backed away.

51. Black Bears of Tofino, Vancouver Island

Gorging on salmon, the alpha black bear fed in Thornton Creek's prime catching location. Perched on a boulder, she eyed schools of spawning coho migrating upstream. Patiently, she scanned the ripples. When the tide rose, exhausted fish would be a paw's length away. Feasting to bulk up for winter, her hibernation would be easier.

Off the tourist beat, the creek side boardwalk surrounding Thornton Creek Hatchery is a "Do it yourself" bear viewing experience. Posted on a barb-wired chain link fence a sign cautioned, "If you encounter a bear on the trail, enter our gate quickly, but do not let the dogs out! Yikes! Fortunately, we did not have any unwelcomed encounters.

Thornton Creek Hatchery is one of those "word of mouth" destinations. Driving between Vancouver Island's cities of Nanaimo and Ucluelet, we paused briefly at a road side rest stop. An enthusiastic visitor raved about his recent bear viewing experience at Thornton Creek hatchery. He gave us his map with directions and told us, "Don't miss it."

Not far off our path, we made a detour to see the bears near Ucluelet, approximately 25 miles south of our destination in Tofino, the renowned western Vancouver Island beach town. Ucluelet's rugged shoreline, while lacking sandy beaches, is very scenic.

In 2000, Jim Martin, then known as "Oyster Jim," a man noted for farming over-sized oysters, hand built the two-kilometer Wild Pacific Trail, a groomed path winding along the Ucluelet coastline. The trail now has a second expansion. Every turn offers Pacific Ocean views. Hikers can stop for lunch on strategically placed cedar benches overlooking bays and coves. Many turnouts, offering peaceful vistas, have memorial benches, some paying tribute to young fishermen.

Black bear fishing, Photo: Mary L Peachin

At low tide, Clayoquot Sound, on the east side of the village of Tofino attracts black bears, sea lions, and eagles. They share the shoreline during low tide as they hunt for crustaceans tangled in bull kelp seaweed. In the fall, when salmon head upriver to spawn, the bears turn their attention to fishing.

Salmon also draw fishermen to the region. Serious anglers time their fishing around the slack hours of the tide's flood and ebb.

A pod of resident orca killer whales competed for the same feed, rolling, breaching, and "sky hopping" in circles, to the delight of whale watchers. Gray and the occasional humpbacks can also be sighted.

Pacific Rim National Park Reserve ends a few miles outside of Tofino. Established in 1970 as Canada's first national park on the Pacific coast, there are campsites along its beach front. Long Beach is a popular place for surfing, particularly during winter's high surf.

On the beach, folks dig for clams or search for oysters and sea urchins in tidal pools left by the outgoing waves. Kids hop from pool to pool, looking for brightly colored starfish and anemones.

Tofino is known for its beaches, surfing, salmon fishing, whale watching, winter storm watching, and seasonal bear viewing. Surfing competitions are held year-round in water averaging 45-50 degrees.

Known as the "Surfing Capital of Canada" six-star professionals travel from around the world to compete in October's tourney. They hope to win $150,000 in prize money.

Seasonal black bear viewing is another popular Tofino activity. There are no grizzlies on Vancouver Island. *Browning Pass*, a 37-foot yacht, is operated by lifetime resident Mike White. Cruising an hour to reach Gunner Inlet, west of Tofino Inlet, we searched the shoreline for black bears. Within minutes, a sow with two cubs lumbered out of the rainforest onto the rocks.

Adept at rolling boulders, the bears heartily ate the underside covered with mussels and barnacles. The bear's long tongues scooped up scampering crabs. Idling next to the shoreline, we could hear the crunching of shells. Undisturbed by our presence, after an hour and dozens of photo images, we left the bears to their foraging.

Browning Pass, a two-story boat, is also available for whale watching, touring, or dinner cruises. Tofino is known for its rain and ferocious winter storms. This time we lucked out and found Tofino better than ever, with mild and sunny weather to boot.

52. The Grizzlies of Smith Inlet

"Grizzlies headed our way – watch out!" Two bears chasing a sow and her cub were separated from us by a 75-foot stream. "Bear master" Tom Rivest, a biologist and owner of British Columbia's Great Bear Lodge, quietly stood from his perch on a riverside log. Tall and lanky, his body language backed up with a double-barrel 12-gauge shotgun, he quietly and firmly said, "Hey, bears." The bears, successful in chasing off the sow and cub, resumed their banquet of salmon. Casually he asked, "How was that for excitement?"

In six years of operating Great Bear Nature tours on Smith Inlet, Tom had never been in a similar potentially dangerous charging situation, Close-up photographs were a requirement for Paris nature videographers Jehanne and Didier LaCoste. That is why the four of us happened to be sitting on the rain-sodden bank of the Nekite River instead of in a blind or in Great Bear's bus. Tom stood guard with his shotgun and a flashlight-size can of pepper spray, protection that he has never had to use.

Two subadults, or "teenagers," catching a ride on the river's current floated by us. We eyed one another carefully. They drifted to a willow-covered island, then splashed through to the other side of the river before scrambling into the woods. When we wondered if our clicking cameras had frightened them, Tom reminded us that grizzlies are afraid of humans. Maybe we outglared them. He recalled a time when a sow, weary of mating, used his group as a shield. She ran past them, leaving them to deal with the aroused male chasing her. "In that situation," he advised, "you simply step aside, and let them pass. Right…

"Can you smell the pungent odor of the bear?" he asked. No, actually, decomposed fish along the shore overwhelmed any bear scent. But Rivest's nose alerted him to the presence of another grizzly. This time, we weren't stared down by a floating bear. It stopped to fish on the island's sandy beach. On the far bank, another bear growled. Tom anticipated our question: "She can't find her cub."

We heard a yelp. A mother had bitten one of the cubs on the bum. My heart continued to pound. This was more like Grand Central for grizzlies. Tom told us, "If this river wasn't separating us from the bears, we wouldn't be safe here."

Tom suggested that if a bear swam across the river toward us, we could nosily get their attention and they would likely retreat. "I don't want them using this bank as their exit path. Bear will chase each other, but one usually outruns the other without a confrontation. Older, slower bears are the ones that tend to fight and claw one another.

Tom's sensitivity to their rank odor allows him to know of a grizzly's presence before he sees or hears them. (The sound of a snapping twig is plenty of confirmation.) When he suspects a bear has stayed in the vicinity, hidden by dense temperate rainforest, standing, he turns in their direction and calmly says, "Hey bear, hey bear." If he doesn't think they've moved on, he'll continue, "Go around us, bear." Rivest has identified 35 bears in Smith Inlet and has named about ten of them. He thinks about 50 bears inhabit the Nekite Valley.

During a three-day visit, our 6 a.m. wakeup "call" was a gentle knock on the door. After a quick cup of coffee and a muffin, we hurried to board the bus before dawn. Eight of us (two each from Italy, France, Canada, and the U.S.) piled into a yellow 1992 Bluebird coach with eager anticipation.

The fourteen-passenger school bus windows open, allowing for clearer photography. Slowly we bumped through ruts and potholes on the abandoned logging road in the predawn. The six-mile road winds through a forest of red alders, western hemlock, red cedar, and ferns. It is almost an hour before we stop at a wide spot in the river. The willow-covered island divides the river, giving the bears more room to fish.

Before leaving the lodge, he had emphatically told us to always remain calm, stay together, and keep him between us and any approaching bears. "When you spot a bear, they can see you." Grizzlies are well behaved, he explained: "If you behave predictably, they're happy. It's all a question of bluffing. They don't know our strength, so as long as we don't act afraid, they won't bother us."

He also warned: No camera flashes.

Great Bear's cedar-bark blinds provide stable conditions that keep bears unaware and viewers feeling secure. The blinds and bus are the typical method to observe bears with Great Bear Nature Tours.

Current in the Nekite River churned with thrashing, spawning chum salmon, many dead and decomposing along the bank. "Get used to that putrid 'road kill' smell," Tom said. "It will be our aroma of the next three days." Squawking seagulls, oblivious to several grizzlies feasting nearby, scooped the river bottom for salmon eggs. The first grizzly we saw appeared from behind the willows on the bank, a mere 75 feet from us. My heart leaped into my throat.

Great Bear's floating lodge is 100 miles from civilization. It sleeps eight guests in five rooms, each with a private bathroom. Two shared showers are located downstairs. Margaret and Tom, along with helper/biologist Suzanna Ritchie, always carry bear spray slung around their waist. The ambience is family style. Help yourself to water, coffee, fresh fruit or cookies. After a mid-morning breakfast of cereal, yoghurt, toast, fresh fruit, and hard-boiled eggs, we had time to kayak, take a boat tour, check the lodge's Dungeness crab trap, or just hang out. Dinner is served family-style at a table.

Another day, Margaret was our guide. A bear walked down the road, then scrambled down the riverbank. She stopped by the side by the side of the road and pointed to several scooped-out areas. "This is where a bear and cub having been sleeping. They cleared the brush to flatten the ground. Like humans, they like to sleep comfortably."

Though we saw a dozen bears in one three-hour outing, one sunny afternoon there were no bears in sight for more than two hours. Other than sitting comfortably on lawn chairs in a cozy cedar blind above the river, admiring beautiful scenery, the highlight was seeing a flock of mergansers ducks and a Steller's jay.

Finally, after brief lull of two and a half hours, we were rewarded. A sow with three spring cubs lumbered out of the willows to fish in the river. Occasionally, the two cubs would snarl and fight over a salmon. The next moment they would playfully lick one another. By day's end, we had seen sixteen bears.

One morning we watched bears from the bus. Away from the high density of bears, Tom took us for a walk along the road, pointing out bear tracks and introducing us to Freebee. The four-year-old sow appeared to be more accustomed to humans than other bears were. Unfortunately, she stayed on the far side of the river.

During a visit to second blind, also built by Margaret and Tom, at the confluence of the Piper and Nekite rivers, we saw another sow with two spring cubs, plus a shy male that would grab a salmon and dart back into the forest. Vincent is past his studly prime. Missing his left ear (and named after Van Gogh), he has a scarred rump and a tumor on his foot. Watching his progress, Tom estimated that he was 20 years old. Life expectancy tops out about 30 years.

During spring, Great Bear clients view bears along the Nekite estuary by boat. When they first come out of winter hibernation, days are spend gorging on carcasses caught by winter avalanches, protein-rich Lyngye's sedge and skunk cabbage.

The Smith Inlet grizzly is darker than those in BC's interior because of rainforest habitat and lack of sun bleaching. It is similar in size to the larger Alaska bear. Grizzlies have a fierce reputation, and Tom shows a healthy respect for them. As for those of us who had the thrill of his guidance and expertise, well, we always stayed behind him. Along any future paths in bear habitat, we'll be saying like he did, "Hey, bear."

As we finished dinner on the last day, Suzanna interrupted to say, "The wolves are howling." We walk onto the deck, where a full moon cast a reflection of mountain shadows on the flat water of Smith Inlet. As a bank of fog drifted low overhead, echoes of a pack of Coastal grey wolves reverberated in the forest. It was magical.

Part XII.

A Serendipitous Career

I have worked since I was a teenager. Memories of being promoted from a Levy's stock girl at 15 to sales associate in junior girls reminds me of the day when a woman was buying her daughter's her first bra. I could only find a nursing bra. When the woman told me that the cup was too large, I said, "Don't worry, she'll grow into it."

My profession as an adoption caseworker was short lived because when I became pregnant, I was forced to quit. I couldn't convince them that I could better relate to my unmarried mother clients when I was having the same experience. I don't know if that was their policy or a city or state law.

I was a stay-at-home mom following the birth of my children in 1966 and 1969. I then worked as a sales rep, on my own schedule, selling a product name Balm Barr, a hand cream that I still use. It was sold to Mennen shortly after we moved to Tucson.

Temporarily jobless, when I joined David to take flying lessons, I convinced Arizona Frontier Aviation that I could increase their business by selling charters. They'd also get a return on their investment, because I would use their instruction to get my commercial and instrument ratings. My first pay check was ten dollars. A year and a half later, I was making more than the flight instructors. They told me, "Mary, we'd like to put you on a salary." Without a second thought, I said adios!

I rented an executive suite, and called some of my clients telling them that I had left Arizona Frontier. It didn't matter to them. They wanted to work with me, and now I had access to many aviation companies and all types of aircraft. The University of Arizona was one of my bigger clients. I coordinated air ambulance for the hospital's perinatal and neonatal departments, also the Native American, primarily Navajos, who flew their mothers-to-be to University Medical Center.

After a year, the University asked me if I would come to work for them, and open a transportation office. When I agreed, I had no idea the fury it would cause with local travel agents. The office was continually in the news. Travel agent were afraid they would lose University business, and didn't want what they considered competition. I made other suggestions like a Tucson-Phoenix shuttle as well as one around the campus. I was ahead of my time for those now functioning programs.

As the fiscal year ended, perched in my 4th floor office of the Administration Building, I was told by my boss (a Vice President,) "Mary, we don't have funding to continue this office." They couldn't fire me, but they didn't have the funds to pay me.

A friend Vance Campbell called me to tell me he was moving his ski store. He thought the space would make a great art gallery. "Mary, what do you know about art?" I had served six year on the Tucson Museum of Art board, but that wasn't a qualification, and my knowledge of art was minimal. I told him that I would start the business for him.

The Art Company opened in the former Ski Haus in the late '70s. It was a gallery selling primarily commercial poster and print art. I didn't sit behind a desk. I went everywhere in Tucson drumming up business. Three months later, I arrived at the gallery and found the door locked.

All the inventory had been moved to the basement of Vance's new Ski Haus in El Rancho Center, about a mile away. No sign, no visibility for the gallery. Who would visit a gallery in the basement of a ski store? I didn't worry for long. A few months later, the ski store went into bankruptcy and closed—with my inventory in the basement.

I went to the judge and explained the situation. I had a separate corporation with good credit. I rented a space about a mile north with great visibility and up went a bright red sign saying "Mary Peachin's Art Company." And the business grew, and we used "We hang out in all the best places" as our advertising tag.

Always hustling business, I sent a large apartment builder an offer for prices based on quantities of art purchased for his units. When he ordered more than 1,000 framed posters, I had quoted him a price that was less than my cost. Yikes!

I flew to Art Expo in New York City with his letter in hand. I needed distributor prices. Now I was in the wholesale business. Los Angeles was my next stop where I went to a production framer "sweatshop-type" operation.

Employing the best framers, they would design the matting and frame. The artwork was shipped directly to Los Angeles, our specifications were used, then drop-shipped to the client. My profit was about 5 to 10 percent.

During the fifteen years that I owned the gallery, we had three locations, and seven framers. They all took a new exam to become certified.

I had good landlords, and some not so good. Former Arizona governor Fife Symington gave me a rent reduction during the late '80s recession. Sheraton Hotels was the best landlord. They negotiated a lease from Boston in three days and I opened in the new Sheraton El Conquistador Hotel. When I didn't like the sales there, they offered to have their concierges sell the artwork. I was working on Easter Sunday *on my birthday* when I started asking myself, why am I still in this business? The staff all had declared a religious objection to working that day.

I can't say the same about my last landlord. My lease was ending, and I had planned to move back to El Rancho Center. I had talked about moving there for years with owner Al Kivel.

Several months prior to moving, another gallery approached Al to rent the space. He said, "I'm sorry, I'm saving that space for Mary Peachin." She replied, "In that case, I'll go buy Mary Peachin."

Sold! I couldn't sell my name and inventory fast enough. Fifteen years in the gallery business was about 14 years too many. The new owner didn't last long, and when she moved away the next year, she lost the use of my name. The gallery name reverted back to The Art Company.

There were two or three additional sales, and I have no idea what eventually happen to the gallery.

And so, I became a freelance travel writer and photographer. I went to an annual teaching conference in San Francisco until I established myself (thanks to the shark diving.) Getting mentored at one of the conferences, I was told I should get a photo agent.

Ted Streshinsky, owner of Photo 2020 in San Francisco, and a noted photojournalist, not only accepted me, he also mentored me. Before he died in 2003, he sold his business and my contract to Lonely Planet. They were purchased by Getty Images, who has never canceled my contract. I don't submit images after being paid $2.00 by Lonely Planet for images sold to Yahoo in Japan.

The days of publications being able to afford freelance writers has faded. In 1986, I started my own adventure publication on the Web, *Peachin and Peachin Leaders in World Adventure*. In those days, adventure companies paid to be on my site. Now everyone has their own website.

I was smart enough to get mary@peachin.com for my email, but not to register *adventure travel*. That was a domain I could have sold for a lot of money. Millions of readers around the world have read my adventures which I now publish bi-monthly. As long as it's fun, that's my pleasure.

Part XIII.

Jungle, Rainforest, Desert, and other Remote Journeys

53. Fishing then Swimming with Amazon Piranha and Bird Watching

The piranha chomped on a chunk of meat hooked to my native fishing handline. The sides of the dugout canoe tipped precariously close to the water as the fish tugged at the line. An avid angler, I was curious to catch the small fish with razor-sharp teeth, a species known to devour cattle in minutes.

Paddling on a twilight excursion on Lake Garzacocha to observe monkeys, caiman, and exotic birds like the hoatzin and greater ani, I had requested some fishing time just to satisfy my curiosity about the piranhas living in the Lake.

Cautiously retrieving the tugging fish, I passed the line to Carlos, our Napo Quichua Indian guide. Skillfully, he grasped the fish behind the head to remove the hook from its mouth. The anxiety of not having a fishing rod separating the piranha from the line and my hands was unfounded. Pulling in the piranha was similar to catching a blue gill or a perch.

Its razor-sharp teeth snapped as Carlos laid the 6 to 8-inch fish in the bow of the canoe. We planned to eat the boney fried ribs of the piranha for dinner at La Selva Jungle Lodge, located deep in the Amazon Basin of Ecuador.

At the time I didn't realize the challenge of visiting La Selva Jungle Lodge, or the circuitous journey to get there. Located in eastern Ecuador, near the disputed and previously hostile border of Peru, travel to the Lodge requires taking an overnight bus ride from Quito or flying a military transport plane to the dusty oil town of Coca, an Ecuadorian military post on the Napo River.

Arriving in Coca by air, a walk through the village took us to a primitive pier on the Napo River, a tributary of the Amazon River. Climbing into a motorized dugout canoe, while trying not to hit my head on its thatch palm cover, was just the beginning of a scenic journey down the Napo River. In order to avoid being grounded on one of the Napo's many sand bars, the driver guided the canoe from one side of the river to the other

Three hours later, bottom sore and bladder bursting, the canoe stopped at a dock edging the rainforest. After we disembarked, the four of us traveling downriver learned that we hadn't yet arrived at La Selva Lodge.

After a quick "pit-stop" at a thatch roof hut near the dock, we walked a mile through the rainforest on a hand-made walk way. The planks, made from chonta palm wood, were covered with moss and, occasionally, a board was missing or broken.

Reaching the end of the walk way, we climbed into a smaller, unmotorized dugout canoe. Two guides, in the front and back of the canoe, paddled us 30 minutes on a stream edged by the jungle to Lake Garzacocha, the beautiful setting of La Selva Jungle Lodge.

The Lodge's thatched roof open air bar and dining room is nestled high above the jungle floor. Yellow-rumped caciques in swinging pendulum nests distracted us during the welcome orientation. Serious bird watchers travel from all over the world to view its more than 400 species of exotic birds.

La Selva's 100 acres includes more than 1,500 flowering plant species, 750 trees, 100 reptiles, 120 mammals, and more than 42,000 insects including 50 different species of ants.

My son, Jeffrey, and I stayed in a thatched roofed hut. We had two comfortable beds covered with mosquito nets, and a bath with a toilet, sink and cold-water shower. Our front porch looked out over the rainforest. There was no electricity, two propane lanterns were provided in the evening. After dinner, I would crawl under the mosquito netting to escape the nightly invasion of ants, mosquitoes, and other crawling "critters".

The first order of business at the lodge was fitting knee-high rubber boots for our daily hikes in the muddy rain forest. The guides assured us that these hot boots would become "our best friend" and were preferable to our own comfy waterproof hiking boots. They were right!

Each day's hike was scheduled so that we could observe the many species of the jungle. While the terrain was mostly level, the challenge was crossing muddy bogs by balancing on strategically placed logs. When there were no logs to use for fording, we would wade, sometimes up to our knees, through suction-type mud to cross streams. Long sleeve shirts and pants were recommended to avoid stinging insects or plants. During a portion of each day's outing, there would be a canoe banked wherever it was necessary for us to paddle across a lake or down a river stream.

The lodge was casual, but the meal service was "Amazon chic." The homemade soup and main entree were always creatively garnished with native flowers and vegetables. Freshly squeezed exotic juices were served at each meal.

As we hiked each day in the jungle, we listened to the familiar screaming piha bird or the "throaty heavy breathing" call of the primitive hoatzin. Our English-speaking guide, Nikki shared her expertise about the jungle animals, insects, birds, plants and trees at each sighting. We also had a native guide, Carlos, whose keen eyes and machete broke trail through the jungle.

Trips were varied and included an outing to Yasuni National Park. Inaccessible to most people, by virtue of the journey required to reach it, the Park is reached by crossing the Napo River. Carlos stopped the canoe so that we could observe a variety of species of parrots: yellow crown, blue headed, mealy, plus dusty head parakeets.

Some birds were having a "Maalox moment" on clay cliffs along the River's edge. They congregate in this unique location to eat clay which aids in their digestion.

Our canoe trip across the Napo River to Yasuni introduced us to a different ecosystem from that surrounding the Lodge. We saw different varieties of vegetation, more bog-type bird species including the rare tiger heron. We found a bufo toad, one that is hallucinogenic when licked, large millipedes, and small tarantulas. Other hikes included a visit to the 140 foot "observation tower" near La Selva.

We climbed wooden steps encircling a tall kapok tree. Its spiny trunk protrusions were formerly used for pillow stuffing. The view over the ceiling of the rain forest provided a great opportunity for bird watching. We visited the "Butterfly Hilton" green house. La Selva raises and exports exotic butterflies to zoos around the world.

After observing the wonderful birds, insects, flora and fauna each day, we would return to the lodge for lunch or dinner. Hot, steamy, and dirty after a fascinating jungle outing, we jumped into Lake Garzacocha for a cool swim. We were assured that we were not part of the "food chain" for the resident piranhas.

I took a careful look of the piranha teeth in the jar I kept. Before jumping into the lake, I let a gentleman go first. When he survived, Jeffrey and I took a brief swim. When I returned to the United States, I took the piranha jaw to my dentist. I told him that I wanted my teeth to look the same. He immediately knew they belonged to the meat-eating fish.

Our three-day visit included the observation of the following:
- Ants--Leaf cutting (some that had stripped a large area of jungle vegetation), Army,
- Conga (large, black, with a nasty bite), plus a toilet covered with red ants in our hut.
- Caterpillars-- several false head species
- Bufo Toad, Dendrodates (poison dart) frog
- Walking sticks, Tarantulas
- Monkeys-- Squirrels, Red Howlers, White- front Capuchin
- Butterflies--Morph, Owl's eye (eggs, caterpillars, pupae, and adult stages)
- Birds: White- throated Toucan, Hoatzins (most prehistoric bird), Screaming Paha, Yellow-rumped Caciques, Greater Kinkade, White- wing Swallows, Greater Egrets, Greater Anis, Black Crown Heron, Amigas, Yellow Ridged Toucan, Smooth Billed Ani, Yellow-billed Nunbird, Red- bellied Macaws, Mealy parrots, Yellow Crown parrots, Blue headed parrots, Violaceous Jay, Spangled Continua, Crested Oropendola, Sand- colored Night Hawks (rare), common Piping Guan, Bats insectivores, osprey, Rufescent Tiger Heron, Cocoa Heron, Ruddy Pigeon, Dusty Head Parakeets, Red Cap Cardinal, Masked crimson Tanager, Ringed Kingfisher, Striated Ant Thrush, Blackmail Trojan

54. Among the Former Head-Hunting Tribes of Papua New Guinea

"Traveling alone, ma'am?" Gold miners, returning from a few days of vacation in Cairns, Australia, to their jobs in Papua New Guinea, were curious about a solo woman boarding an Air Niugini flight.

Two hours later, the plane landed in Port Moresby. The miners transferred to another flight to return to work. I wandered through the airport, which was teeming with locals just watching airplanes land, to the nearby domestic terminal to catch a connecting flight on a Fokker 28 to Hoskins, the largest town on the island of New Britain.

In the village of Hoskins, I took a cab for an hour's ride across the island to Walindi Plantation Resort. The *Febrina* liveaboard scuba diving boat anchors at the Kimbe Bay dock on the Bismarck Sea, which is located in front of the resort.

After several nights at the Plantation, we boarded the *Febrina* for a five- day liveaboard dive trip. Captain Alan Raabe motored for nine hours to Fathers Reef near the island of Lolobau, an active volcano. Deep wall drop-offs were landscaped with hard and soft corals. Whitetip, silver-tip and whaler sharks cruised the reef along with turtles, jacks, and barracuda. In spite of huge ocean swells, this was fabulous diving.

A giant stride off the back deck was easier than the challenge of re-entry. The divemaster would grab hold of our arms to pull us onto the deck waiting for the next incoming wave.

During the six-day trip, we went night diving, seeing fifty-pound-ish dogtooth tuna, cuttlefish and octopus. At a site named Reasons, the wall was covered with black, staghorn, table, brain, and leather coral plus velvet sea whips, fans, gorgonians, and sponges.

Sepik Spirit houseboat, Photo: Mary L Peachin (1)

One dive along the reef passed underwater caves between two sand chutes, appearing like a sand waterfall. At dawn there appeared to be a rush hour on the reef. Small colorful reef fish were swimming up, down and over the wall and coral trout lazed while being cleaned of para-sites by small fish.

Walindi Plantation Resort had also offered the same quality of diving in Kimbe Bay. Rough seas made for an hour of body-slamming travel in a speedboat to reach its reef walls. Kimbe Bay and the Bismarck Sea have 4,000 species of coral and 400 species of fish.

The late Max Benjamin, an ex-pat Australian, owns the resort. Arriving in New Britain in the 1960s, Benjamin started the Palm Oil Plantation, followed by the resort in 1988. There are six burres or bungalows with dining (family style) in a room adjacent to the bar and pool area. Walindi is a relaxing setting where diving is the focal point.

New Britain Island is a paradox. The locals have satellite television and Walindi has a telephone and fax machine, yet the shower water is heated by burning coconut husks. The guards at Walindi stand watch using a burning branch for light.

The island K-Mart is not a discount store. Its provisions are sparse and expensive. At the time, a box of Kellogg's cereal sold for $6. The vegetable market is the gathering place where locals come to sell their crops – betel nut, yams, coconut squash, and a variety of bitter-tasting greens.

As we returned to Hoskins for an early morning flight to Port Moresby, a nearby village appeared to be on fire. It was breakfast time and folks were using firewood to cook in their huts. My taxi driver slowed in the village as pigs crossed the road – pigs have the right of way in Papua New Guinea. The ownership of pigs represents one's wealth, and pigs are the focal point of ceremonial tradition.

Returning to Port Moresby, I met my son, Jeffrey, to join a Trans Niugini tour for two weeks. I had seen some of the best of the underwater world of Papua New Guinea. Now I was going to explore its countryside.

Papua New Guinea Land Adventure

Huli warriors wearing hornbill and Bird of Paradise, Papua New Guinea, Photo: Mary L. Peachin

Papua New Guinea is the largest tropical island in the world. Four million Papuans, Melanesians, and Micronesians/Polynesians speak more than 700 distinct languages. Located north of Australia across the Torres Strait of the Coral Sea, Papua New Guinea is a country of rugged mountains and thick jungles. The economy is based primarily on the production of gold, copper, coffee, cocoa, and sugar.

Our group, led by Papua New Guinea expert Greg Stathakis, gathered the first night in the capital city of Port Moresby. The Highlander Hotel was protected from rampant crime in a compound secured with fences, barbed wire, and guards. The following morning, we flew in a small plane to a grass strip in Timbunke village on the Sepik River. We boarded the *Sepik Spirit* houseboat using jet boats to tour the Blackwater area.

In native villages, we had a chance to buy artifacts and watch women grind sago palm starch for pancakes (a staple of their diet). We visited a palm-leave hut covered with a thatched roof. The family slept on straw mats covered with mosquito nets. They built fires next to their mats for both warmth and cooking. Many huts burn down or are destroyed by termites in three to four years.

Seventh-day Adventist missionaries had converted the villagers of Angriman and Mindimbit. Schoolchildren welcomed us into the classroom in the village of Mumeri. They proudly sat at their hand-carved desks and benches, sang a welcome song, then placed a crown of woven palm leaves with flowers on our heads. The artifacts made by children are primarily penis gourds. In the past these gourds, called horim, were the sole item of clothing worn by the men.

In some villages, natives would perform a "sing-sing" for us. Dressed in ceremonial costume, the men and women danced to the music of handmade flutes.

The Karawari region of the Sepik River is surrounded by rainforest, a change from the wild cane bordering the middle Sepik. Delayed by boat mechanical problems, we had time to only visit the village of Kundamin.

When we arrived, women were cooking sago palm starch, extracted from the pith of palm trees. The gluey starch is hard to stir and tasteless. Leaf vegetables and the larvae of the Capricorn beetle, better known as grubs, provide some variety to the diet. The grub worm grows in the decaying sago palm and they consider it a tasty treat.

Karawari Lodge has the appearance of a Haus Tambaran, a Tok Pisin phrase describing a traditional ancestral worship house in the East Sepik region. A large gable mask hangs above its entrance, which overlooks a beautiful rainforest valley. Birds are abundant, along with geckos and colorful insects. The rooms at the lodge were thatched-roof huts. Beds were covered with mosquito netting.

After crawling out from our mosquito netting before daybreak, we learned by radio message that our chartered plane to Mount Hagen had been grounded by fog. Two hours later we climbed a ten-foot embankment along the Sepik River to reach a 2,400-foot grass runway, where we boarded the airplane.

Mudmen at Mt Hagen Sing Sing, Photo: Mary L Peachin

In Mount Hagen, women sold bilums (hand woven string bags), which were displayed on the airport's barbed wire fence. Once woven from palm bark, many bilums are now made from colorful Hong Kong yarn. They are tied around women's heads to create slings for carrying infants and other burden. Before leaving Mount Hagen for the coastal settlement of Madang, we visited the public market. While viewing a variety of fruits, vegetables and other wares, we spotted a man selling ceremonial headbands made from scarab beetles shells interwoven with orchid leaves.

Madang is known as the garden spot of Papua New Guinea. We spent two nights at Malololo Plantation, which overlooks the Bismarck Sea. Day trips included visits to the fishing villages of Marot and Lusik. We hiked a beach surrounded by betel nut palms, breadfruit, boxwood, pandanus, and other exotic nut and flower trees. The hands and feet of Didol, the "big man" or village chief of Lusik, had been ravaged by leprosy.

While we were in Madang, Jeffrey got a bad case of food poisoning. Not having any choice, I told him he would have to travel sick. Before we boarded our airplane, he threw up on the tarmac. "Mom, I sure hope the upcoming pope's visit doesn't stop here," he said. A bit of humor from a kid who was worse for wear.

Departing Madang, we flew to Tari in the Southern Highlands. The Huli tribes inhabit this region. The men wear colorful headdresses of cuscus (possum) fur with bird of paradise feathers, or headpieces made from their own hair. A hornbill beak necklace is worn with ornaments hanging down their back. The Huli continue to have battles and remain one of the most primitive of Papua New Guinea tribes.

Huli battles or "paybacks" carry certain rules of conflict. The warring clans may determine a day to fight, maybe a time to stop for lunch. Women and children are seldom killed. According to our guide Greg, the tribal members do not seem to care when tourists watch them fight. While we did not see any fighting, on several occasions we saw warriors guarding clan borders. Some warriors held bows and arrows while others carried homemade guns. Some wore plastic helmets, some a leafy headdress.

We stayed at Ambua Lodge. Along the dirt road, forty-five minutes from the airport, we observed another Huli tradition. Pigs were staked along the road for a bride-price negotiation. The ceremony can take several hours or days depending on the value of the bride, her age and the wealth of her family. Wealth is measured by the number of pigs owned by the family. The pig is so revered in Papua, its image is on the ten-kina bill.

Another day, we passed a man preparing to take the painted skull of his father into his hut. Women are buried when they die, while men rest above ground for five years. When the skin has dried and dropped from the bones, the skull is painted, and placed in the hut of the son.

We had been told that two weeks prior to our arrival, a warrior named Andrew had been killed. Payback or another battle was expected in the next several days. Ambua Lodge is located between two warring Huli clans, the Jawali who lived in the valley, and the Huwale Pu, who lived in the adjacent highlands.

At the crack of dawn, I awoke to the cry of a warrior in the valley. Was he calling his pigs or was this a battle cry? We visited the village of Wapia, where we observed a sing-sing. In Boronapa village, the Huli demonstrated the making of fire by rubbing two pieces of cane with a cord. After an impressive bow and arrow shooting demonstration, we visited the women's side of the village, where they were tending a hut of pigs.

Men and women do not sleep together, but for the purpose of reproduction, they have sex in the household's garden. The role of women is to tend gardens, raise children, and carry burden in their bilums. Men do the hunting and cooking. Men believe that women are capable of casting spells and that they sometimes carry evil spirits. They are especially afraid of seeing women during their menstrual cycles. During this period, women stay in a specified hut.

One afternoon, we had the opportunity to go birdwatching. Papua New Guinea is known for its spectacular birds of paradise. We saw five species: King of Saxony, crested bird of paradise, several Princess Stephanie astrapia, a ribbon-tail astrapia with long white tailfeathers and a sicklebill, along with a king parrot. The twenty-four-inch tail feather of the King of Saxony is often worn in the Huli headdress.

There is also a huge variety of beetles and other insects. Species thriving in the jungle include the large rhinoceros beetle with its distinctive beak. Visitors are forbidden to purchase any bird of paradise feathers; there is a hefty fine for doing so.

On our final day in Tari, we visited the bachelor village of Kaka. Huli boys enter the village at sixteen to learn the traditions of their tribe.

During their eighteen-month stay, they grow their hair to use as their "wigman" headdress. The wig is then adorned with daisies and bird of paradise feathers. While they are learning Huli rituals and traditions, the young men cannot leave the compound or look at a woman. Their role is to maintain the grounds and tend the gardens. They are presented a carved diploma when they graduate, one they will be displayed with pride next to the door of their hut.

The opportunity to meet with Pajia, a witch doctor, was an experience shared by only a few visitors. Pajia hid from Christian missionaries for twenty years to avoid conversion from his religious practices attempts to convert him. When we saw him, he had not received foreign visitors for three years. With the help of an interpreter, Pajia showed us how he made knives from bamboo. He demonstrated his use of axes, bows and arrows. He took us to his garden where he showed us his medicinal powers. Rubbing Jeffrey's hands with a nettle leaf, he created a painful burning sensation. He then rubbed Jeffrey's hand with a ginger leaf. The pain subsided in about 10 minutes.

The nettle leaf is used prior to the scarring ritual to prepare young men for the pain they will endure during the ceremony. A mixture of clay, burnt lime and tigaso tree oil is put into self-induced wounds to create scars that look like tattoos.

Pajia also took us to his graveyard. Indicating great respect, his eyes were cast downward as he showed us the skull of his father. We walked through the graveyard to his "magic place," the burial site of his witch doctor ancestors. Located in a sexually symbolic rock outcropping were the painted skulls of his male ancestors dating back nine generations. Pajia's stones used in rituals also rested in this outcropping.

The remoteness of the region has resulted in fewer missionary conversions than elsewhere in New Guinea. The Huli tribe is frequently seen wearing traditional dress. Their faces are painted, and they wear bird of paradise feathers or fern headdresses and a loincloth. Some pierce their noses with bones. Sometimes they giggle when they see you and they may want to touch your hands.

The culmination of our visit was two days spent at the Mount Hagen Sing-Sing Festival. About fifty tribes danced and sang, wearing ceremonial costumes. A hundred and fifty tourists joined 30,000 to 40,000 natives to watch festivities held in the soccer field. The prize money for the best costume and dancing was 50,000 kina shared among winners. The New Guineans watched the dancing and singing from behind a barbed wire fenced surrounding the field, while tourists sat in a concrete grandstand. The more recognizable of the tribes were the Huli, Mudmen, and the Morabe.

Twelve of us had shared a two-week adventure of a lifetime. We said farewell to Papua New Guinea in Tok Pisin pidgin: "Lookim yu behind."

55. Alone at Dawn in Magical Petra, Jordan

The narrow winding chasm of the 10 feet wide slot canyon, or *Siq*, enveloped me as I wandered along its cobbled limestone path. Most slot canyons are formed by water erosion, this three-quarter-mile long narrow gorge is a geological fault, rising 300 to 600 foot, was split apart by tectonic forces that was smoothed by water. It leads visitors to *Al Khazneh*, or The Treasury, Petra's most elaborate ruin.

Nearing Petra, the path turned to gravel. I peered into many crevices of the deep rust-colored walls, sometimes catching glimpses of blue sky through open slots. The ancient capital of the Nabataeans, Petra once protected Arab traders, traveling the Silk Road, who came through the region with precious cargoes of spices.

56. *El Alumbrado*, Medellín, Colombia's Glorious Christmas Celebration

Medellin Xmas lights over River, Photo: Mary L Peachin

Medellín was not exactly on our path. I had come to Colombia to write an *Undercurrent* review on scuba diving along the west coast in Santa Marta. After a brief visit to gateway Bogotá, followed by diving, David and I heard such great things about the city of Medellín, we hopped a flight to take a look. A friend of a Facebook friend recommended a hotel. As a bonus, he gave us a grand tour of his city.

Medellín is sometimes called the "city of the eternal spring." Christmas is considered one of its most celebrated festivals. Throughout December, two and a half million residents revel nightly as they admire more than twenty-seven million Christmas lights. Street vendors line roads, musicians provide free nightly concerts, and kid-friendly exhibits and events can draw in the whole family. We became particularly fond of grilled corn on the cob. Plus, there are plenty of photographic opportunities.

Christmas lights line and skim the surface of the Medellín River. Lighted decorations encompass a total of 472 miles through ninety locations. The celebration began in 1955, when public utility company Empresas Públicas de Medellín (EPM) adorned the city with twelve and a half million lights.

Each year more tourists are attracted, with an attendance reaching 60,000 visitors in 2013. The celebration, known as *El Alumbrado*, or "the Lighting," is more than a simple government-supported celebration. It enlists thousands of volunteers who hang or float millions of colorful lights

Medellín, Colombia's second-largest city, is in the Aburrá Valley amid the Andes Mountains. Founded in 1616 by Spaniard Francisco Herrera Campuzano, it was originally called Poblado de San Lorenzo. In 1675, the queen consort Mariana of Austria renamed it Villa de Nuestra Señora de la Candelaria de Medellín, or Town of Our Lady of Medellín. When Colombia won independence from Spain in 1886, Medellín became the capital of the Federal State of Antioquia. During the 19th century, Medellín became a commercial center, first exporting gold, then producing and exporting coffee.

The construction of Medellín's Metro commuter rail, which runs the length of the valley, liberalized development policies, improved security and education, and brought both industrial stature and tourism to Medellín. As we rode up the mountain in the gondola, we could see numerous shanties housing lower income families. They previously had a steep commute in both directions if they worked in the city. The commuter rail offered them easy transportation and new opportunities.

Medellín is recognized for its universities, academies, commerce, health services, flower-growing, and nightlife. Each August, the nine-day 63-year old *Feria de Las Flores* (Flower Festival) is considered one of the year's most important social events. There is a beauty pageant, automobile and Paso Fino horse parade, and musical concerts. Metropolitan Cathedral even has its own display of floral arrangements.

In February 2013, Medellín was named one of the best places to live by travel magazines as well as the most innovative city in the world by the Wall Street Journal and banking group Citi. Its Museum of Antioquia houses a large collection of works by Medellín native Fernando Botero and Pedro Nel Gómez. Facing Botero Plaza near the Berrío Park metro station, twenty-three of

Botero's life-sized sculptures are displayed. He adds either humor or a political message to his artwork, which is primarily recognized by his voluminous figures.

Taking the Metro light rail from Santo Domingo station, then connecting with the Metro cable up to the small outdoor market at Parque Arfi is worth the eighty-seven-cent fee. Parque Arví's lush green fauna forms an important watershed as well as serving as a biological nature reserve for native plants and animals.

Down in the city, Carabobo's, which translates to "dumb face," is an eight-block pedestrian walkway, connecting Parque Bolívar to Plaza Botero and La Apujarra. Filled with shops, places to eat, and a wide selection of street vendors, it also offers interesting architecture, sculpture and historic sites. Carabobos, considered unsavory in the past, is part of the transformation that gives Medellín a new and friendly face. The city has been reinventing itself since the 1990s, after becoming infamous in the late 1980s as a home base for drug-running gangsters.

In addition to its festivals of *El Alumbrado* and *Feria de Las Flores*, the city offers upscale boutique hotels, fine dining, great public transportation, a temperate climate, and a beautiful location in a scenic valley between the Andes. If you visit Colombia, don't miss a visit to Medellín.

57. Haboob in Morocco's Sahara then Stranded by Icelandic Volcanic Ash

Morocco Sahara Berber boy and girl, Photo: Mary L Peachin

Tentatively reaching for my offer of a navel orange, she realized that her head was uncovered. Quickly she grasped her brother's hand as she pulled a veil across her youthful face. Curious about us, the two teenage Berbers had wandered from their goat herd to peer into our Land Rover.

As we would discover, today's Berbers are not fictionalized nomadic people pictured crossing the Sahara Desert in camel caravans. Most of them are sedentary farmers or herders who tend flocks of sheep and goats. We may call them Berbers, but they refer to themselves as Amazigh, a generic name that includes many ethnic groups sharing a similar culture.

Departing from Marrakech, our eight-hour drive would climb over Morocco's High Atlas Mountains before descending from Tichka Pass into Ouarzazate's Province of Draa Valley and our destination in the Sahara Desert. Thousands of years ago, this trade route traversing the iconic Desert was used to transport slaves from sub-Sahara Africa to Timbuktu, Mali.

Lined with prickly pear cactus and olive trees, the steep two-lane road passed numerous red clay hillside Berber villages. Fertile valleys were an oasis of date palms and bamboo trees. Olive groves were highlighted by clusters of red poppies. Women washed clothes in gently flowing rivers, men tended to their flocks.

Sahara tented camp, Photo: Mary L Peachin

After a long day on the road, we spent the night in a basic, but comfortable Kasbah in the Draa Valley village of Zagora. Originally named Tazagourt, Berber for "twin peaks," the city was named for its surrounding mountains. Ruins of an Almoravid (a 12th century Berber Dynasty) fortress could be seen on one of the peaks. Approximately 60,000 Berbers inhabit the area. The wealthier built many of the areas' prominent Kasbahs or castles.

Not far from Zagora, the village of Tamegroute, known for its green pottery, houses a 15th century library. More than 4,000 manuscript collections date back between the 11th and 17th centuries. Scripted in indigo, gold leaf, and natural dyes, the collection includes copies of the Koran, mathematic and astronomy documents, a Turkish dictionary, and the history of Fez, a city founded by Fatima.

A second Berber village, located a short distance from Tamegroute's antiquities library, featured maze-like passages that wound between thick walls of clay and straw. A series of dark windowless rooms, lined with carpets, packed in as many as twenty-five residents.

Erg Chigaga Morocco Sahara, Photo: Mary L Peachin

Finally, we reach the road to M'Hamid village, gateway to the Sahara, which narrowed to a single lane. It was obvious that we were literally coming to the end of Morocco's road.

Little did we know that we were headed into a haboob, a whirling sand storm that would even ground the camels. As the dunes became higher, sand blew across the disappearing road.

Suddenly our four-wheel cruiser glissaded over slippery sand. We slalomed between date palms as we crossed the road-less Desert. The sand storm, making visibility minimal, had been raging for days. My lips were caked with sand. We were grateful that our driver Hassan, born in the nearby village of Tagounet, knew the area well.

The Sahara is considered the world's largest non-arctic desert. Covering most of North Africa, its size is comparable to that of the United States. It spans the Red Sea and areas of the Mediterranean almost to the Atlantic Ocean. Its history dates back more than three million years.

Riparian areas, green with pockets of rocket or arugula grass, indicate an occasional oasis with a perennial source of water. An oasis usually leads to Ait Atta Berber nomad sightings. The ground well creating the oasis provides food and water for livestock. Children help support their families by looking for a handout.

Erg Chigaga's famous red dunes, thirty-six miles, a two-hour drive, or four-day camel ride from M'hamid village, rose in the Desert wilderness. The only accommodation is a bivouac or permanent nomadic camp consisting of twenty goat and camel hair tents, with a shared bathroom facility. Staying in a bivouac camp is basic at best. Sand still managed to seep inside the tent coating our mattresses. The raging haboob dust storm obscured the magnificent red colored sand dunes. Blowing sand canceled the sunset camel ride into the dunes, a highlight of a Morocco visit. This was one night of *sleeping around* that was rejected. Without visibility, we drove eighty miles to spend the night in a hotel.

Driving through the iconic Sahara is a unique experience. Initially, swirling winds over hilly terrain created continually changing dunes which demand challenging steering, similar to that of driving on ice. As the desert levels, navigation becomes easier.

After a night at Bab Rimal Hôtel de Charme in Foum Zuid, we continued on to visit the UNESCO fortified village or ksar of *Ait Benhaddou*. Nearby, a Berber women's' cooperative welcomed visitors to observe their painstaking, finger-numbing weaving, knotting, and embroidering of carpets. There is, of course, the opportunity to buy a wide selection of finished carpets for "a very good price." Watching the women working tirelessly making rugs that sold in the thousands of dollars begged the question of how much they were paid to spend a year or so weaving them.

After a night at Kasbah Ellouse outside Tazaknt village, we picked up the camel route through the Qunila Valley. Along the road, women carried heavy loads of grain on their backs.

The turn off to Telout's salt mine was unmarked. Inside the cave, salt dripped from the ceiling formed stalactites. When the mine was operational, men used dynamite to blast salt crystals from the hard rock.

In the Berber village of Telout, Kasbah Glaoui, built by a Berber War Lord in the 1800s, was used as a Senegal and Mali slave trading post, a military outpost, and served for a time as the home for the Pasha or King of Morocco. Slaves were exchanged for salt and gold. As one of Morocco's largest castle, it is in the process of being restored. Mosaics blend with beautiful tile. Its ornately designed plaster is being salvaged.

Heading back to Marrakech, we reflected on a journey into history in a unique place that is basically off the tourist path. We had visited two vastly different places, the hustling city of Marrakech, which hosts much of Morocco's charm, and the emptiness of the arid Sahara Desert and its shy Berber people.

Our last night in Morocco we planned to stay in the Berber souk *Jemaa el-Fnaa* at Riad al Massarah, a traditional town house built around a courtyard. When we arrived, our host Michael told us that he had been trying to reach us.

He told us, "you aren't going anywhere tomorrow."

The 2010 Icelandic eruption of Eyjafjallajökull volcano disrupted air travel across western and northern Europe for what would be six days. David had a board meeting in Seville, Spain the following day.

As luck would have it, I took our guide Hassan's telephone number. I called him and asked if he would drive us to Tangiers to catch the ferry to Gibraltar the next day.

More than $500 later, a day long drive, and a bribe by Hassan to get us on a full ferry, we arrived late in the evening in Spain. Lucky again, David had brought Euros, the only money we could use to hire a cab for another two-hour ride. There was a comfy bed paid for and waiting for us in Seville.

58. "Riding the Winds" in Bridger Wilderness, Wyoming

Singewald, owner of Bridger Wilderness Outfitters and our trail boss for the week, was about to lead seven of us on a 125-mile horseback ride the length of the Wind River Range in the Bridger Wilderness of Wyoming. As we prepared to mount our horses, Tim called out, "Saddle up and head 'em out! We're burning daylight."

More than 100 years ago, Congress set aside land for what would become the country's first national forests. Straddling the Continental Divide, the Wind River Range has six of the largest glaciers in the continental United States. The range's 1,300 lakes are filled with cutthroat, brook, and a rare species of high-elevation golden trout.

Lighting his Cheroot cigar, Singewald signaled and we were off, our horses departing the Green River trailhead towards the Highline Trail. Tall and lean, the former banker exuded confidence that came from 14 years of guiding hunting, fishing, and horse pack trips in Wyoming.

Our group of eight, all horse owners except me, was supported by three wranglers who cared for the quarter horses and the eight pack mules that carried our camping gear and food. Many horseback trips have a base from which they ride each day. This eliminates the work of setting up and breaking camp daily.

I wasn't a new dude to horseback riding. Growing up I went riding almost weekly at the El Conquistador Hotel stables. This area was desert in those days. Now it is recognized as Tucson's first shopping mall.

David rode in Los Charros, a yearly "men only" five-day ride operating out of the Mountain Oyster Club. What the hell! I started a women's ride, The Aravaipas, that annually took day rides from the Elkhorn Ranch near Sasabe in southern Arizona. We loved our wrangler, Lloyd Wortman, and the Miller family, who owned the ranch and another spread in Ennis, Montana. We also rode in Aravaipa Canyon, a Bureau of Land Management park near Safford.

While we camped traditionally, we had our ride "catered" by Katherine, then one of Tucson's finer chefs. Another time, we switched it up and eight of us flew in my Cessna and Sherry Starr's Beechcraft for a weekend of Mexico diving in San Carlos. We had lots of fun in spite of Sherry scaring her passengers on the return by not fully closing the door of her Cherokee.

I didn't see any red flags warning me about a week-long pack trip in the Bridger Wilderness. I quickly ran to Walmart to buy myself a tent. I was ready to go.

Spring arrived late in Wyoming that year. When we saddled up in mid-July, there was still snow at higher elevations. Facing a solid snowpack, Singewald decided to reverse the direction of our trip, by first tackling the higher snow-covered passes in the north. He reasoned: If we departed, as originally planned, from the southern Big Sandy trailhead, we would have been five days into the ride before reaching the snow-packed passes near Green River. If the horses could not make it through the more treacherous terrain of the higher elevation, we would not have enough provisions to backtrack to the southern trailhead.

A few hours into the first day, we had a short but serious scare. A 10-year-old girl and the horse she was riding were briefly swept downstream as we forded the Green River's glacial waters during an afternoon shower. (She was the only child in our group). Although horse and rider righted themselves and were soon safe, Singewald's concern heightened when the peaks of the Green River Pass came into view. He viewed snow blanketing the mountain from top to bottom.

We kept going, though, moving slowly and leaning forward to make it easier for the horses to climb the rocky terrain. We crossed several patches of snow. Suddenly Singewald's horse, which led the group, fell through a patch of ice glazing the snowpack. Singewald got his horse up, but after that experience he decided to take a detour and "bushwhack," to avoid crusty snow on the slopes of the pass.

We rode on for another hour. Reaching an elevation of 11,200 feet near Elbow Peak, we saw that snow covered the entire mountain. We were no longer able to bushwhack around patches. In the next few hours, as we carefully worked our way onward, three more horses, including mine, Salmon, broke through the crust of the hard-packed snow. Sharp rocks buried under the snow cut the legs of the horses. After eight hours, the horses were hurting, the riders were weary, and everyone was more than a bit tense. I was beginning to question what I was doing on the pack trip. I couldn't reach high enough to unsaddle Salmon at the end of the day.

Finally, after eventually navigating the high passes, we began to feel more relaxed as we descended from the barren landscape of Hat Pass into the trees and flowering meadows flanked by views of mountains and lakes. We stopped to tend the horses, then camped that night in a beautiful glen near a waterfall.

Luckily, we got into our tents before a deluge began. Thunder and lightning boomed and crackled as hail and rain pounded our tents during the night. I had mistakenly bought a child-size tent so I was sleeping on the diagonal, my feet barely inside the tent. When the storm hit, my tent started leaking. I beg my friend Gail, an avid rider and horse owner, if I could crawl in her tent. I don't think she was too happy about that.

The wrangler's "yip" calling in the mules for packing came too early the next morning. We would spend the day riding seven hours through Lester and Baldy Passes, again at elevations exceeding 11,000 feet. As before, magnificent views continued to distract us from the hard riding and long hours in the saddle. The Wind's lakes and ridges are only seen by a few.

Two hours daily were spent making and breaking camp. Each night the wranglers rounded up the horses, corralling them inside a transportable solar-powered electric fence, which keep predators at bay and prevented the horses from straying. Some of them were hobbled for the night. Riders were responsible for saddling and unsaddling their own horse, and setting up their own tents at each campsite. Some folks were riding their own horses, while Gail and I used the outfitter's horses. She was well adept at caring for her horse, but I pretty much flunked those duties.

In a nearby stream we would rinse off our bodies and on one occasion, we jumped into a lake. While it felt great to remove the dust of the trail, the water was so icy, we never again fully submerged our bodies.

The cooking wasn't fancy, but there was plenty of food. After breakfast – bacon, eggs, or pancakes – we would each make a sandwich, packing them in our saddlebags for a picnic lunch at a scenic spot along the trail. I was good at that.

Each night, we hovered around a cozy campfire to eat our dinner. Nathan, our wrangler-cook, served up some mighty fine trail-fare that included hamburgers, pork chops, steak, and pasta.

In the evening, the wranglers recited cowboy poetry while we passed around a flask of Yukon Jack, pouring it into our Sierra tin cups. We spun a few yarns about past adventures as we sat around the campfire, before finding our tents and falling into a deep sleep.

On the third and fourth days we continued to descend, and the trail became scattered with rocks and lined with boulders. One horse slid on a rock, while another got his shoe wedged between rocks. Luckily, Singewald and the well-trained wranglers were able to pry the horse's hoof from the rocks without it panicking or breaking a leg. They gently nuzzled the horse as they freed his leg.

That night, as we rode into our campsite at North Fork Lake, the sky began to darken. We had just set up our tents when a severe storm erupted. Lightning, thunder, and high winds raged for about three hours. That night we ate standing up, shivering as we huddled under a tarp. The temperature dropped so low the water in our drinking bottles froze, and we fell asleep huddled under blankets in our tents. This was the worst weather of the trip. The storm passed by morning, leaving us with cold, crisp sunlight for the last two days of the journey.

We rode into lower elevations, the scenery growing lusher with every mile. The lakes and river streams ranged from glacial green to sapphire blue. Once we descended below the tree line, the landscape was filled with spring flowers: lupine, Indian paintbrush, monkey's hand, elephant head, daisies and dandelions bloomed in the late snow. There were beautiful vistas, including a view of the favorite of rock climbers, the Cirque of the Towers.

Near the trailhead to the Wind River Range, we began to see backpackers along the trail. Although the terrain was too rugged for most hikers to reach the interior of the wilderness, the closer parts of the range are popular for hiking. As the number of backpackers increased, we knew we were nearing our take-out trailhead.

In seven days, our 125-mile route had taken us from Green River Lake to Big Sandy trailhead. We had climbed five passes: Green River, Elbow, Lester, Baldy, and Hat. We had camped at campsites including Green River, Big Water Slide, Timico Lake, Prue Lake, Raid Lake, and the East Fork River. We had jumped into the icy waters of Timico Lake, and eased carefully into the waterfalls at Big Water Slide and the East Fork River to cleanse our bodies.

The ride was a true wilderness experience. We lived in the same blue jeans for a week and put mosquito netting over our heads at twilight. We ate and slept on the ground. We lived in dirty clothes, falling asleep to the scent of horse that permeated our tents. We listened to the sound of tinkling cowbells, worn by the mules at night. Our reliable horses carried us over a variety of terrain of snow, rock, and mossy bogs. We forded rivers, creeks, and one shallow lake.

Was it an adventure? You bet it was! Definitely not one for this novice, rather one for experienced riders, those comfortable with horses and long hours spent in the saddle.

There was no complaining on this trip. Despite the hardship, or perhaps in part because of it, our group grew close over our week in the wilderness. The bond grew to include not only the trip leaders and guests, but also the horses and even the mules-a small group that had together made a journey. As for me, when I finally dismounted Salmon, I put my arms around her neck, grateful that I had survived. Since then I have ridden on a camel and an elephant during my journeys, less comfortable that any horse. I've concluded that keeping my feet on the ground is more comfortable.

59. Trekking, Rafting, and Tigers in Nepal

Nepal has a reputation as a mecca for mountain climbers. It's true that the country features some of the world's highest and most majestic peaks – Everest, Llotse, Dhaulagiri, and Annapurna — but it offers more than technical climbing. There are trekking expeditions, river rafting, and elephant safaris as well as views into its fascinating cultures.

You won't want to sleep through the approach and landing in Katmandu. On a clear day the view of Himalayan peaks is spectacular through the airplane window.

Katmandu is crowded and congested, home to beauty and suffering. Nestled in a valley at an elevation of 4,500 feet, it is surrounded by green mountains. Temples, palaces, and city squares that are consecrated to Hindu or Buddhist deities. A walk through the city includes glimpses of temple architecture, deformed beggars, ritualistic cremations along the banks of the Vishnumati River near the Shobabhogwati Temple, and crowded streets filled with people, cats, dogs, goats, and cattle.

Arriving in Katmandu three days before our scheduled trek, my friend Sherry and I met up with our guide Molly and two male travelers. She led us through the cities of Katmandu, Patan, and Bhaktapur. We visited the Hindu temple of Pashupatinath, the Buddhist shrines of Bodhnath and Swayambunath, and Durbars (palaces). We took time to shop in the city's crowded bazaars.

The third morning, we departed for the city of Pokhara, a 2,000-foot drop in elevation in the valley of Annapurna's foothills. Pokhara is a gateway for trekking and rafting adventures. The bumpy 120-mile bus ride past terraced rice fields and rural villages leads to the small city on the banks of Phewa Lake, below the fishtail summit of Machhapuchhre.

Historically, Pokhara was a destination on the trade route between India and Tibet. Mule trains, bringing goods from remote regions in the Himalayas, camp on the outskirts of town. This region is inhabited by hardworking Magar farmers, and the Gurung people, known for producing valiant warriors, who once enjoyed fame as Gurkha soldiers.

We reached Pokhara in the afternoon and immediately headed for a field near the edge of town. Porters unloaded our belongings for our Annapurna trek. Starting at the trailhead of Bijayapur Khola, we began our trek along a ridgeline. After passing through the village of Kalika Thar, we climbed four hours to our first campsite.

Porters, who carried our baggage, set up the camp for our arrival. Waiting for dinner to be served, we admired the peaks of Annapurna South and Machhapuchhare. The menu included hummus, dhal bat (lentils), and vegetables, all cooked on an open fire. Water carried from a nearby village was boiled and, for additional protection, purified with iodine. After eating in the camp's dining tent, exhausted, we drifted off to sleep in tents pitched next to a rhododendron forest.

The next morning, we were awakened by the lead Sherpa guide who, with a soothing "good morning," left a cup of hot tea and a washing bowl outside each of our tents.

Daily, we hiked for four to six hours, over gradual rises and descents. We covered between six and eight miles a day at a steady pace, always staying below 6,000 feet. While elevation did make the hike more strenuous, a steady pace and lack of baggage made it doable.

We passed terraced rice and mustard fields, citrus and oak groves, and more rhododendron. These sights had backdrop views of Annapurna, Dhaulagiri, Gangapurna, and Machhapuchhare. The next two nights we camped near the village of Shyaklung on the Chisapani Danda ridge.

Each day we would rise early and trek until noon. Children eagerly stopped to greet us. Some of their parents carried household goods on their heads. Frequently the trail was stair-stepped near villages, but the majority of the trek was along dirt trails.

After four days of hiking, we had made a circular trek back to the Pokhara Valley. A road opened up into a clearing, and there — like a mirage of the modern world — was a taxi. The driver loaded our bags and delivered us to the edge of Phewa Lake, in Pokhara.

Our luggage was loaded on a raft. After we were aboard, a pulley contraption took us across the lake to a small island and Fishtail Lodge. That night, we luxuriated with hot showers, real beds, and a tasty dinner.

The next day we set off on a two-day rafting trip down the Trishuli River. After a four-hour bus ride, we put-in the village of Charaudi. Soon we were floating through a subtropical jungle landscape. Hanging gardens lined the banks, periodically we passed under fragile-looking rope-and-plank bridges, used by locals.

The rapids were rated at Level 2-3, gentle enough that we could jump in the water and be safely swept along. That afternoon, we descended through Ladies' Delight, Upset, Surprise, and Bijili rapids before camping near Kuringhat. The next day featured a few more similar rapids before we arrived at our take-out site, Rocky II.

Once again, there was a taxi waiting at our take-out. (How did Nature Expeditions, our tour company, arrange the timing of the taxi with our arrival?) This time our journey took us south into the inner terai, or flat river plain, of the Ganges River, which runs through the south-central hill region of Nepal. We were headed to the famous Tiger Tops tented camp, in Royal Chitwan National Park.

Chitwan is best known as the habitat of the Indian one-horned rhinoceros and Royal Bengal tiger. After the taxi ride, we traveled by canoe, then hiked through the jungle to a tented camp. Along the trail, we observed a rhinoceros wading in the river with her young, as well as hog deer, hornbills, and signs of tiger tree-scratching both sharpening their claws and leaving a scent. After one more night of camping and a short hike, we reached Tiger Tops lodge.

Our group enjoyed the amenities at Tiger Tops, but eagerly awaited the next day's elephant ride to search for white rhino and tigers.

After "bathing" the elephants and feeding them a lunch of grass and grain "sandwiches," the mahouts, or elephant caretakers, climbed up the trunks of their elephants to help us mount. Stepping from a platform on the second story of the lodge, we lowered ourselves into a four-person boxlike seat roped to the elephant's back. On our ride, we sighted rhinos, deer, and even a python. The mahout used his prodder to pull the python out of the brush. Swaying back and forth in a boxy contraption was not very comfortable. I'd rate it more or less like riding a camel.

Our final night at Tiger Tops, as we sipped cocktails, we heard a bell. It was the signal from the nearby jungle that an endangered Royal Bengal tiger, baited by a tied goat, had been sighted.

Abandoning our drinks, we followed our guide's advice, hopped the lodge bus to the trail and ran through the forest into a blind, where we were each allowed 10-minute view. The tiger gnawed on the now dead goat for only a few minutes. I was glad I had hurried to be first. I was one of the few to see the tiger who ran from the noise of people approaching.

With our Nepalese journey winding down, we headed back to Katmandu, flew to Bangkok, then home to the U.S. We may not have summited Everest or Annapurna, but the Nepalese land, culture, and nature was a wonderful experience.

60. Detained and Deported from Hanoi

As I prepared to board a flight in Bangkok to fly to Hanoi, the ticket agent handed back my passport. "Where is your Vietnam visa? You can't fly to Hanoi without one."

It not like this was my first departure. I had been diving in Thailand's Adaman Sea, and my flight itinerary had taken me to Singapore from Los Angeles. Not one airline agent noticed that I didn't have a Vietnam visa. I knew that having a visa was a requirement; it was my second trip to Vietnam. It was one of those matters that both the Chicken Divers' travel agent and I had overlooked.

I had enjoyed a previous Vietnam visit so much I was returning – when this issue arose. Vietnam Airlines finally decided that I could get a visa at the Hanoi airport. I boarded the plane and arrived to discover that getting a visa in Hanoi was not possible. I knew that I was in real trouble.

Suddenly I was surrounded by Communist guards who didn't speak English. I used hand signals to try to tell them that my guide was waiting for me in the baggage area. At least 40 minutes had passed, and I wondered if he was still waiting for me holding high a "Peachin" sign.

He was, but that didn't help. I was detained for 22 sleepless hours in a shabby airport "transit" room. I received a message that my Hanoi tour agency would try to get me a visa. It didn't work. They simply didn't have enough time or the capability to work through Vietnam's bureaucracy.

I asked my guards to contact the American Embassy. Months later, I asked former U.S. Rep. Jim Kolbe why the embassy didn't help. He learned that they had been told that I was detained, but since I wasn't in Vietnam on "official business," they couldn't help me.

My small threadbare room had two twin beds with heart-shaped pillows that ironically said in English, "I love you." The windows were sealed, yet mosquitoes buzzed around the room. I had read on the airplane that Hanoi was experiencing a West Nile virus epidemic. I swatted mosquitoes most of the night. Exhausted, I covered the dirty bedspreads with my clothes, and lay down.

The bathroom's window and shower door were cracked, and the toilet was dirty. Yuck!

The guards had allowed my guide to come and take me into the airport for dinner. I shouldn't have asked what I was eating. They told me that it was carp, a "bottom feeding" fish.

Evidently, I had arrived on the day's last flight into Hanoi, so they put me on the first flight to Singapore the next day. When I reached customs, the officer looked at my passport and said, "Happy Birthday." I burst into tears.

He asked if he could get me a visa to return to Hanoi. I thanked him and said, "Could you please get me on the first flight to Los Angeles?"

I was never so happy to see that sign, "Welcome to the United States."

61. Secrets of Seoul, South Korea

Visiting Seoul, South Korea was a serendipitous surprise. The previous year, an expedition ship David and I were meeting in Nome, Alaska, gateway to the Aleutian Islands, was blocked in the Northwest Passage by ice packs. The following year, not wanting to risk icy conditions, the ship changed its meeting point to Seoul, South Korea. We would then fly four hours to Petropavlovsk-Kamchatka, Russia, a port less than 600 miles from the Aleutians.

Seoul had grown significantly in the past decade, and there were many choices of neighborhoods to stay, each offering a different attraction. A large city, Seoul covers some three hundred square miles, split by the Han River.

Ten million people live in the city, about a quarter of the country's population. The northern Gangbuk area is known for culture and history, while Gangnam is the business district. Westerners might be familiar with Gangnam style, a popular dance.

Asking around, I learned everyone I knew had visited Seoul on a cruise ship. They didn't have to worry about finding their way or the basic lack of communication. David and I are not cruisers so that wasn't a consideration. We chose to fend for ourselves.

Seoul is considered a safe city. I wanted a centrally located hotel as a base for exploring. No tours, no guides, just a quick four days before our flight to Russia.

We stayed at a local favorite, The Shilla. It was a two-hour drive from Inchon International Airport. The hotel was packed with families with many young children, drawn to the hotel's indoor and outdoor pools. Swimming is very popular in Seoul and the hotel's multiple pools offered nifty swim caps and private lanes for their "swim members." I wish that we had arrived during quieter school days rather than in jam-packed summer time.

The Shilla's three restaurants were fully reserved, so we had to eat on the early side. Not a problem since we were also dealing with jet lag.

We didn't stray far the first day, and with more time, the DMZ (demilitarized zone) would have been on our must-see list. I figured it was just another border crossing but later learned that there was much to see.

The DMZ buffer zone, about two-plus miles wide, was built in 1953 during the armistice agreement among the United Nations, North Korea, China, and the Soviet Union. With minimal development along the border, over the years, nature has created a varied landscape of forest and grasslands that includes rivers and estuaries.

The endangered Asiatic black bear, along with moose, leopard, Eurasian lynx, and goral sheep are found in the zone. Birdwatchers can observe black-faced spoonbills and red- and white-crowned cranes migrating from Siberia.

There were several other places that I would have enjoyed spending more time. Deoksugung Palace, which protected the king until 1910, is one of Seoul's five Grand Palaces, with a twice-daily "changing of the guard" reenactment. Since 1996, guards in colorful silk costumes, wearing samurai swords and tall top hats, have performed the ceremony. The finale is the beating of a large colorful drum. The ritual is similar to that at London's Buckingham Palace, although less formal and more colorful.

Deoksugung Palace was occupied by the Joseon Dynasty for five centuries between 1392 until 1910. In the 16th and 19th centuries, the Japanese invaded. Under Japan's colonial rule, the palace was converted into a public park.

While selecting a place to stay, I remembered the extraordinary experience, while bicycling in Hokkaido, Japan of sleeping on the floor in traditional ryokans. Namsangol Hanok Village, near Namsan Mountain, offers five traditional hanok houses as well as Gugakdang theater, all within its traditional gardens.

While this would have been a more authentic Korean experience, Seoul's Hanok Village was too isolated for our short stay. I must also admit that my creaky body preferred a Western bed over a tatami floor mat.

During our Japanese bicycle tour, we didn't get up at 4 a.m. to visit Tokyo's famous Tsukiji Fish Market. I would have enjoyed watching bluefin tuna being auctioned for tens of thousands of dollars. It's a missed experience I have always regretted. Having dived much of the world, on multiple occasions I saw jet aircraft waiting to fly outrageously expensive tuna to Japan. Tokyo's Tsukiji Fish auction has now moved, and tourists are not welcomed during the auction.

Discovering Noryangin Fisheries Wholesale Market, our thoughts turned to fresh sushi. The Seoul market is open year-round, 24 hours a day. The "high class" live fish auction is held between 1 and 3 a.m. We slept past that early auction time

Missing the "high class," the finest quality tuna quickly sold, we wandered past vendors selling tuna, king crabs, and other shellfish. We had to try the tuna. Using hand signals, we asked for a small slice compared to the big slices that we saw others buying. Out of nowhere, a waiter appeared with a tray and led us to a very informal dining area, where dining with other Koreans, we picked up chopsticks to dunk our tuna slices in wasabi and soy sauce. We watched as the kitchen prepared a live king crab for another customer.

After filling our stomachs, we realized that we were lost. How did we get out of the market? We finally found an English-speaking gentleman who told us to walk around the building to the street and hail a cab. This market is not yet on the tourist circuit.

We also visited Namdaemun, Seoul's largest traditional market dating back to the '60s. While this is not necessarily a place to visit for the finest fabrics and latest fashions, the low-cost market is a great place to pick up casual attire and accessories. Best of all, Namdaemun shopping was a cultural experience. We bargained, saw what was popular in Korea, and spent the time almost exclusively with Koreans.

I'm sure we could have spent days exploring Seoul, but we had to meet our group the next day at 4:30 a.m. at Incheon International Airport. Avoiding the two-hour early morning trip, we spent the night in a very ordinary airport hotel. It was a sleepy ending to a great experience in a fascinating city.

62. Traveling Though Croatia Without an Itinerary

Dubronik, Croatia, Photo: Mary L Peachin

Admiring a stunning view of steep, jagged dolomite and limestone karst cliffs towering above the Adriatic's malachite waters, we listened to the melodic chiming of Dubrovnik's cathedral bells. During our swim, we were unaware that a rising tide had carried us 100 yards from the ladder leading to our hotel's pool. The hotel was covered by vegetation on the cliff so we had to make our way back to the ladder.

While the chill of the Adriatic Sea was invigorating, we were eager to stroll into the ancient, walled city of Dubrovnik. After a brisk swim against the current, we dressed and made our way down to its cobblestone streets.

Croatia's 7th century captivating city of Dubrovnik was severely damaged during the 1990s civil war. Now, fully restored, terracotta tiled roof tops and smooth marble passageways weave between white limestone buildings.

Cruise ships shuttle passengers to a landing near Pile Gate, a 16th century drawbridge. Couples stroll the Placa promenade and patrons spend hours at outdoor cafés, lingering over espresso or gelato. Others tour historic attractions, browse in small shops, or haggle with sidewalk vendors for embroidery, jewelry, and souvenirs.

Our plan was to explore the serpentine Dalmatian coastline by bus and ferry. We quickly learned that Croatia's tourist season abruptly ends on October 1st. Ferries connecting many of Croatia's 1,000 or so islands would now determine the schedule of our 16-day northerly odyssey to Zagreb.

Our journey was now dependent on semi-weekly rather than twice daily ferry departures. Many hotels and restaurants were closed, cultural events and festivals were over. We required some flexibility, so we rented a car. Our trip reminded me of our self-contained bicycle trip to Japan: no reservations or itinerary. This time we were spared the challenge of peddling.

We left Dubrovnik on a two-lane, cove-hugging road overlooking the Adriatic. Stately 400-hundred-year-old cypress, trees of ripening fruit, grape-laden vineyards and olive groves lined the highway. Families tended fields or harvested grapes. The landscape and air seemed to glitter. Roadside litter was nonexistent.

Thirty-seven miles northwest, the Mali Ston area, once an important salt-producing area, is renowned for its locally farmed oysters and mussels. The Kralj family serves up the freshest in their family restaurant, Kapetanova Kuca. It was a delicious lunch break.

Boarding a typical Jadrolina ferry between islands is like a drill. There are no reservations. A few minutes before departure, the ticket office opens. After tickets are purchased, a queue of vehicles, at precisely the scheduled departure time, rolls to the end of the dock, then up a narrow ramp. Cars and trucks are wedged on the boat like sardines. Larger ferries have salons, and perhaps Croatia's best coffee.

Most Dalmatian coast touring is highlighted by ferry hopping to islands such as Mljet, Korcula, Viz, Brac, and Hvar, to name a few of the more popular inhabited islands.

Korcula is one of the larger islands. Its architecture is similar to that of Dubrovnik, though the city is unwalled. Korcula claims to be the birthplace of Marco Polo. Ordinary hotels near the old town are expensive. Throughout the countryside, families rent rooms, which is where we spent the night.

Not only is Croatia stunning, its people are warm and friendly. Men are tall, women are sophisticated and stylish. It's always possible to find someone who speaks English. The country, accommodations, restaurants, and restrooms are clean. The majority of independent travelers we encountered were Brits, Germans, and Aussies.

After ferrying from the mainland village of Drvenik to Sucuraj, on Hvar Island, we took a 48-mile hairpin road to Hvar city at a snail's pace. Cliffs towering high above the Adriatic do not permit an inch of room for error. There are no guard rails, not even a shoulder. In Croatia, road signs are infrequent, with even fewer distance markers. With only one road up the coast and the need to cross to and from islands, you arrive when you arrive. On the western tip of the island, in the city of Hvar, marble streets and stone buildings surround a small harbor. Visitors come to kayak, scuba dive, sail, raft or explore historic attractions.

Hvar's history dates back to its 4th century B.C. founding by the Illyrians. Two centuries later, Hvar was conquered by the Romans. Slavic tribes settled the island during the 7th century. Today, most surviving architecture is Gothic. Hvar's city fathers welcomed the sisters of St. Benedictine. Cloistered, today they support themselves by patiently stripping the spines of agave to weave delicate lace.

Croatia white truffles, Photo: Mary L Peachin

Octopus and truffles. It's hard to get a bad meal in Croatia. Both seafood and meat lovers will rejoice. Fish are classified as first (wild) and second (farmed) class. Many meals are preceded by an amuse-bouche, a bite-sized hors d'oeuvre. and conclude with a glass of grappa. McDonald's and a few other international chains exist only in several large cities, like Opatjia and Zagreb.

With the coffee not to our taste, we would have welcomed a cup of Starbucks. On the other hand, hot chocolate made with real syrup and a dollop of whipped cream was sinfully delicious. There are fast food hamburger stands or "slow food" typical restaurants. In most places, a frosty draft beer is a better choice than a glass of young wine.

On the road again, the ferry to Split returned us to the northern coast of the mainland. At the landing, women with available rooms flash "apartment for rent" signs as they walk between offloading cars.

Ravinj, Croatia, Photo: Mary L Peachin

Split, a major gateway and a geometric maze, is a booming metropolis complete with traffic jams and stoplights. Diocletian's Palace is an ancient palace built for the Roman emperor Diocletian at the turn of the fourth century until his death in 305 AD. Trogir, a charming village northeast of Split, attracts many tourists wanting to bypass the hectic pace of the city.

Zadar is the largest city in upper Dalmatia. Built on a peninsula, it dates back to the 4th century B.C. Greeks, Romans, Turks, French, Austro-Hungarians, Venetians, and more recently, the Yugoslav army battled for it. World War II almost destroyed it.

Just east of Zadar is Croatia's oldest royal village, Nin. Until it was conquered by the Romans, it was a Liburnian settlement. Access to the pedestrian-only town, in the center of a shallow lagoon, is by footbridge.

If the city streets of Croatia are clean, the recently opened toll road between Split and Zagreb is spotless. Not a skid mark in sight. Miles-long, well-lit tunnels bypass Plitivice National Park, a forest of colorful fall foliage ascending, literally, into the clouds. Exiting onto a local road to Senj, we found women under bright umbrellas selling honey and homemade goat and cow cheese. Others sold olive oil and wine in home style bottles. Roadside restaurants grilled lamb and suckling pig on spits.

Picturesque Rabac, a fishing village about halfway down the eastern coastline of Istria, hugs a snug cove. "Ah, Istria, this land is about olive oil, wine and truffles," Persic Vladimir, owner of Villa Annette, proudly stated as he embraced a plate of three locally harvested white truffles, valued at 500 euros. Yikes!

During WWII, Italian dictator Benito Mussolini drained a lake in the village of Plonin to plant trees. Istria may have lost a beautiful resource, but Mussolini's destruction resulted in the cultivation of truffles, a delicate fungus that sells for 2,500 euros a kilo. Truffles grow on tree roots. Dogs are trained to find them and dig them out.

At the southern tip of Istria, the city of Pula's primary attraction is a 1st century Roman amphitheater. Centuries ago, gladiators battled as 20,000 spectators watched from two tiers of seats. A smaller version of Rome's Coliseum, most of its 95-foot-high wall is intact. During the Middle Ages, many of the seats were removed for use as building materials.

Northeast of Pula, the 7th century port village of Rovinj has maintained its medieval appearance. Each daybreak, fishermen arrive with their daily catch. Locals scurry to the open market to buy fresh fish and produce.

Rovinj's steeply worn marbled streets are too narrow for vehicular traffic, except for a few vans shuttling hotel guests from parking lots outside the old town.

For more than a hundred years, exactly at noon, an explosion is fired from the Lotrscak Tower in Zagreb. The capital city is the political and economic hub of Croatia. Istria and the Dalmatian coast dazzle. It is disappointing to see garbage and walls tagged on Zagreb streets. The cultural hub, while moving at a frenetic pace, appears like an unsightly "graffiti city."

If you can look beyond this graffiti, while dodging nonstop electric trolleys barreling curbside in both directions, Zagreb offers hidden charm and colorful Baroque architecture.

Little is known about the city's early history. Mongols destroyed Zagreb in 1242. In the 15th century, it emerged as Croatia's capital after Turks captured most of the country. Ban J. Jelacic Square is the gateway to the Upper Town's outdoor markets of Dolac. Flower vendors steal the show amid fruit and vegetable sellers. There's also an indoor fish market."

"Ah," as Persic Vladimir said, "Istria is about olive oil, wine and truffles." He could easily have been talking about the entire country. Croatia is a beautiful landscape with a fascinating history. It offers wonderful cuisine. The Croats are friendly and honest hosts. Watch out, Croatia! Americans will be coming in mass to visit.

63. Farm Friendly Slovenia and WWII's Fanja Partisan Hospital

Croatia's offseason ferry schedule hastened our tour by several days. We were hearing good reviews about neighboring Slovenia, but we had no idea if we would be permitted to enter the country. As we circumnavigated the heart-shape peninsula of Istria, we decided to give a visit to Slovenia a try. The border guard simply waved us through the international gate.

Bled Monastery Slovenia , Photo: Mary L Peachin

Spanning the fertile valleys of southeastern Slovenia are a number of farms who have opened their gates to visitors, welcoming them to share in the lifestyle of Slovenia's countryside. Many of these truck farmers harvest crops, churn cheese, age sausage, smoke meat, and ferment wine for family consumption. Any crop abundance is trucked to a nearby local market.

Sharing life on the farm is a unique experience for visitors. Farm stays, costing considerably less than a hotel, are rated by apple symbols, not unlike hotels being rated by a star system. Slovenia's Tourist Board qualifies, rates, and inspects each farm, and they provide an easy process for making reservations.

Slovenia's southeast wine country is a place where vineyards grow on hillsides above the valley's farmland. Sixty kilometers southeast of the capital city of Ljubljana, the Seruga family offers a 4-apple farm stay.

Their dining area, warmed by a stone hearth, is the usual place to get acquainted. Lili Seruga was baking a rum and walnut cake for afternoon visitors so we followed her into the cozy kitchen. We sipped homemade apple juice while we talked about farm life near the village of Ratez.

The Serugas store apple juice in barrels for up to a year. They also distill blueberry and green walnut brandy along with apple and pear grappa.

Organic vegetables grown on the farm for cooking include potatoes, cucumbers, lettuce, beans, herbs, cabbage, carrots. Fields of corn are raised to feed the animals.

Lily can host 50 people in her dining room, and in a separate building, she has 11 guest rooms. Lily's husband, Salvako, when not doing farm chores, works as a German interpreter in local villages.

Breakfast is typically bread, meat, and cheeses. Dinner is a fixed menu of homemade soup followed by an entrée of meat, rabbit, chicken, pork, or veal, and dessert. Trout, from a stream rippling through the farm, is served on special occasions.

To earn a four-apple rating, the farm must meet Slovenia's high standards. Each room must be a specific size and nicely furnished. It must include a private hallway and bathroom. The family must serve breakfast and dinner in a restaurant-type setting.

Staying at a farm gave us the opportunity to explore rural countryside. In the nearby village of Sentjerneje, we stopped to look at another 2-apple farm stay, Turisticna kmetia Pr Martinovh, a long word for Martin's farm. Two basic rooms offer the opportunity of staying on a more serious working farm. Owners Marta and Zan Krhin did not speak English so their daughter Urska showed us around. She welcomed us by inviting us into the wine cellar for some homemade cveček wine served with a plate of salami.

While the rooms were not on the same scale as Seruga, the hospitality was equivalent. When the Krhin's are not taking care of guests, they are tending to their pigs, cattle, and horses. They harvest cveček grapes, and make their own cheese and salami. Guests can ride on horseback or in a horse-drawn carriage. Nearby excursions include visiting the Carthusian monastery in Pleterje, the Smarjske Toplice Health spa, or the Slovenska Konjjeniska Lipizzaner stud farm.

Passing the stud farm, we observed yearlings being carefully scrutinized by prospective buyers. Body definition and gait were examined before payment was made and the colt branded.

Along the road, taverns were grilling suckling pigs on barbecues. In the village of Ratez, we stopped at Gostilna Pod Klanckom restaurant to join locals eating this tasty treat of crispy pork.

Farm stays might be comparable to staying in a bed and breakfast. The difference is enjoying the country environment, and not having to share the same house with the family. At the same time, sharing the family meal provides camaraderie. Staying on a farm gives a taste of local color and a unique experience especially for city dwellers.

WWII's Slovenia Fanja Partisan Hospital

Franja Hospital bunk, Photo: Mary L Peachin

Gravely wounded, World War II Slovenia armed forces, U.S. pilots, and soldiers of other nationalities were carried blindfolded through rushing waters of the barely accessible and narrow Pasice gorge. Hidden at the summit, was a simple hospital. A facility that saved more than 500 lives between 1943 and 1945.

The hospital primarily treated soldiers from the 9th Corps of the Slovene Partisan Army engaged in warfare with the Nazi German Army in the Primorsko and Gorenjska region. After suffering severe causalities in the field, the idea of building a hidden partisan hospital to care for these dying men began to take root.

Janez Peternelj, a local resident of Cerkno, proposed the location for a clandestine partisan hospital to Dr. Viktor Volcjak. Its first cabin was built high in the almost inaccessible Pasice gorge, and on December 23, 1943, the first wounded soldiers began arriving.

Between 1943 to 1945, Dr. Franja Bojc Bidovec, ran the lifesaving facility, one that has maintained and preserved its authentic appearance as a symbol of the partisan medical service. It is an emotionally moving testimony to the humanity and resourcefulness of its physicians, and other medical staff.

The hospital had the capacity to care for 120 patients at one time. 522 of the 1,000 wounded soldiers were severely wounded. Soldiers carried to the hospital included Slovenes, citizens of Yugoslav nations, Italians, Frenchmen, Russian, Poles, Americans and an Austrian. A captured German soldier joined the hospital staff after his recovery remaining there until the end of the war.

Sixty-one patients died during the hospital's two-year operation. They were buried in unmarked graves along a trail above the hospital. A small bottle with personal identification and information was enclosed in their graves.

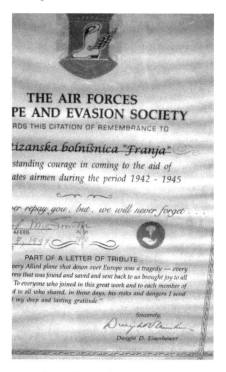

Eisenhower letter, Photo: Mary L Peachin

Admitted near a checkpoint near Pasice village, the wounded were blindfolded before being carried into the gorge. This was done as a measure of secrecy. If they were ever captured by the Germans, they would be unable to identify the location of the hospital. To hide the trail, the wounded were carried through the streambed in handmade stretchers. For their safety, bunkers and hidden shelters were built on steep rocky slopes.

Despite operating in challenging terrain, with the frequent need to perform delicate surgical operations, most of the wounded were treated successfully. Hospital workshops made orthopedic accessories like casts and crutches. A new method was developed for sterilizing instruments and dressings. Other necessities of life were provided, and hospital patients never experienced hunger.

For Franja and the other clandestine hospitals of Slovenia, security were crucial. If a hospital was discovered by the Germans, it lacked any effective ability to defend itself.

The success of the Franja Partisan hospital was attributed to the gushing stream flowing through the gorge. The trail of the wounded could not be traced. Those carried to the hospital by staff, were typically transported at night. Minefields and machine-gun nests were place in the surrounding area so that access to the hospital could only be made through the stream, footbridges and drawbridges hidden in the steep Pasice gorge.

Still preserved in the steep walls rising above the stream are several fortified bunkers and natural caves, additional hiding places for the wounded. Although enemy forces launched several searches for the hospital, it was never discovered.

Today, small street signs direct visitors to the well-preserved hospital. A mile-long dirt path then a steel catwalk crisscrosses the gorge leading up to the thirteen wooden cabins. Some of the cabins include hospital wards, an orthopedic workshop, a surgical ward, doctors' offices, a wood-burning stove kitchen, wards, and a simple office with a desk.

On it, lays a wrinkled letter, in a simple frame, from General Dwight D. Eisenhower. It is a thank you note to the Slovenians for saving the lives of American pilots shot down during the war.

In spite of an enormous avalanche in January 1989, the hospital, its access buried and three cabins destroyed, was rebuilt and restored as a museum. More than 500 lives were saved by Dr. Franja. Devoted to her mission, she humbly declined any honors for her war heroism.

64. Turkey, Living in a Historic Muslim Neighborhood

Our "penthouse" apartment was on a narrow cobblestone street built into a hillside. The neighborhood, formerly the Greek Orthodox area of Istanbul, was now inhabited by Turkish and Arab working-class neighbors.

On the street, lined by attached apartment buildings, women bought food from passing vendors. Responding to the call of their sales pitch, the women would lower by rope a plastic bucket filled with Turkish lira from the window. The vendor placed the goods in the bucket to be retrieved. It was convenient shopping.

Our third-floor apartment was called a penthouse because it was on the top floor of the building. It had a great view of Istanbul's Golden Horn and Marmara Sea.

Penthouse in Instanbul, Photo: Mary L Peachin

Our three-week accommodation was in a six-apartment building. Motion-activated lights illuminated circular, un-railed stairs up three flights to our "home." We would become culturally immersed in this working-class Muslim area of Istanbul.

After a lot of research, we decided on this apartment because of the excellent comments about the helpfulness of the owner. He was knowledgeable and friendly. He told us, "You will not need a guide." Baris and Nasan An made our immersion into an unfamiliar culture possible.

The apartment had one bedroom with two small windows. Furnished with Ikea furniture, apartment amenities included a washer, kitchen with a microwave, dishwasher, refrigerator, and a hot plate for cooking. A spacious bathroom had heated towel racks.

The queen-size bedroom loft-type vaulted wood ceiling had skylights. Steeply pitched, its ceiling had a few low head-knocking areas.

Each morning, we were awakened by the melodious sunrise call to prayer drifting through our skylight. David headed to the local baker to buy simit, a sesame-covered bagel-like roll, which we ate for breakfast along with yoghurt and honey, and a slice of an unfamiliar yellowish/ green melon.

We would then look through our guidebooks to decide our plan for the day: an attraction or a market. We could spend years exploring Istanbul, with its 20-million population, and not cover it all. Densely packed Istanbul's wall-to-wall colorful buildings rise along undulating hills and create a rainbow landscape edging the waterways of the Golden Horn, Marmara Sea, Bosporus Strait and Black Sea dividing Europe and Asia.

Totally independent, without an itinerary, we experienced Turkey by immersing ourselves in its culture at our own pace. There would be no tourist circuit for us.

Turkish Simit, Photo: Selin Rozanes

That's easier said than done in a place where communication is almost impossible. In Istanbul, signs have no English translation, and virtually no one understood us.

First, we explored our neighborhood by walking down the hill to a side street that led to a major road. In an empty lot, we saw a lamb being butchered. Along the way, we passed small job shops or cellar factory-type businesses, a smoked-filled men's gambling hall, and an always-busy manual car wash. If we continued straight to Mustanik Street, there was a small market, bakery, fruit stall, other small businesses, and a watchmaker who replaced a battery for my husband David.

Most women walking the street covered their heads. While we never felt uncomfortable, no one ever greeted us. They were neither friendly nor unfriendly. An exception was a boy in the grocery store who tried to teach David some Turkish words.

One of the most interesting tours I took was *Culinary Backstreet's Beyond the Bazaar*. Istanbul's Grand Bazaar is one of the world's largest and oldest covered markets. It spans 61 streets with more than 4,000 shops. While attracting between 250,000 and 400,000 visitors daily, on our tour, we didn't see a single tourist.

Our trip climbed up multiple stairs, with uneven steps, to visit the workshops of the Bazaars' many artisans. We stopped to sip Turkish coffee with workmen at a nameless place, and other "hole in the wall" food vendors. There were no names or menus, and sometimes I had no idea of the name of the dish I was eating. We even went on the rooftop to see a view of the city. It was a stuffed from eating, strenuous climb work-out, but an experience ranking at the top of my list.

A non-smoker, throughout the middle East, I had seen smokers sitting on carpets using flavored tobacco filtered through a water-filled hookah. I couldn't resist that opportunity. Smoking hookah, according to the culture is a time to relax and talk with friends. While it was a unique experience, it was not something I would not try again. I didn't inhale.

Istanbul's traffic was jammed and chaotic. We took a taxi only as far as the Spice Bazaar, where we could take a tram to a Sultanahmet attraction or the ferry to Istanbul's Asian markets. We always returned to our apartment by bus. It was a decision based more on time than money. A single prepaid card can be swiped for all public transportation. Being caught in a traffic jam for an hour or more was not an unusual experience. The bus, with its own lane, was faster than a taxi.

While it was nice to be able to have dinner at home, we frequently went to a restaurant. After dark, we took a cab. Our congenial and helpful hosts, Baris and Nasan, wrote directions in Turkish to the nearest familiar attraction to the restaurant where he had made a reservation. Returning Baris' directions were a well-known neighborhood restaurant, one any driver would know. We then walked back to the apartment.

Returning by taxi was a different story. It always cost substantially more. Cabbies working in tourist areas seem to have the habit of running up the meter.

Kidnapped by a Taxi

His taxi number is 577 055 07. If you happen to hail this yellow cab, don't get in. After giving the cabbie explicit Turkish written directions, when he did not cross a bridge familiar to us, we realized that we were going for a "ride." The trip to a restaurant had cost us seven lira the meter was now passing twenty lira. We pointed in a different direction than where we were currently headed. As the shouting match escalated, the cabbie sped down narrow roads until guards stopped him at gated community. None of the various guards had any idea of the location of our destination. We couldn't get out of the car because we were too remote to find another cab. We were being "kidnapped."

We would have to jump out of the cab near a major road with enough traffic to find another taxi. Seeing two security guards in an isolated park, we made our escape. We asked the guards to call the police. The taxi driver became even more irate, yelling, waving his arms, and asking for money. The guards recommended that we get back into the cab. I called our Turkish-speaking landlord, told him our problem, handed the phone to the guard, as the battery died.

When the police arrived, we were prepared for the worst. Out of the darkness, a man with a tray of tea arrived. The taxi driver hastily grabbed one as did the police and security guards. We didn't feel like it was teatime.

The upshot was that the police asked us to give the cabbie ten bucks, and he begrudgingly left. They called another cab, asked us for another $10. They gave the money to the new driver, and told him he could not charge us one cent more.

Living in Istanbul was a unique experience. During our three-week stay, we made brief visits to the cities of Bodrum and Cappadocia. We briefly gave up the hustle-bustle of the city, but not our immersion.

While we visited many attractions on our own, we also out of necessity joined several organized tours.

Turkish Flavors owner Selin Rozanes offered us an in-depth tour of the Spice Market combined with a ferry trip, tour of the Asian street markets, and lunch at the acclaimed Ciya Restaurant. We were offered samples at many shops. We later returned to our favorite vendors to buy ingredients, and frequently returned to eat at Ciya.

Another day we took a city tour that gave us the opportunity to avoid long entrance lines, see highlights and learn more specific information.

A trip to Istanbul would not have been complete without the experience of visiting a hammam. Built in 1741, Cagaloglu Hammam, in Sultan Ahmet Square, is a Turkish spa-version visited primarily by locals. The cleansing rituals in the Turkish steam bath took place in a domed Ottoman marble edifice. After using a copper bowl to pour water over my body, an attendant exfoliated then soaped and massaged my body. Certainly not as comfortable as Western spas, the experience was very unique.

A tour of Istanbul's Jewish heritage sites required advance permission, a passport, and a guide. It was enlightening to learn how Muslims, Christians and Jews have lived together for centuries.

Back in our neighborhood, when it was time for our departure, David wanted to say good-bye to shopkeepers, his baker and grocer. We wrote a note of thanks to those who took such good care of us at the municipally-run Soysal restaurant, where we frequently ate.

Five times daily we had listened to the call to prayer. We began to notice the variations between the voices of the muezzins. From sunrise to sundown, we felt that we had been immersed in the Muslim culture.

What we learned:

- Outside of popular Istanbul tourist destinations almost no English is spoken. This includes menus and all signage. Our efforts to communicate were rarely understood.
- Taxis are not regulated. Insist that the meter is used and watch it to see that the correct flag drop amount is displayed. Some drivers will turn off the meter before you can see the final charge. There may be additional night and cab-calling charges. Always give the driver a written destination, and carry a map. Many drivers will say they know a destination, then use their cell to ask other cabbies.

- Don't let street hawkers at tourist attractions like the boat/ferry dock or bridges get a cab for you. They appear helpful, but obviously get a commission from a higher cab charge.
- Avoid using 100 Turkish lira bills. We had some new, acquired directly from the bank, bills refused as being counterfeit.
- There are many circular and high, uneven staircases. Be prepared to climb many stairs and walk on poorly maintained streets.
- Turks love sweets: baklava and Turkish Delight, a powdered Chuckle-like candy. There is virtually no ice cream, but lots of sweet desserts. Condiments like butter, catsup, or salad dressing are not routinely served. Ask for them.
- Muslim prayers are recited in Arabic, a language not known to many Turks. They have to memorize the prayers.
- The traffic is horrendous. Don't ever expect a vehicle to stop for a pedestrian. There is a prepaid swipe card good for all public transportation including ferries. People who have spent the total amount on their card have to pay someone to swipe for them. Conveyance operators do not accept cash.
- The history and diversity of the country is fascinating, its early historic architecture amazing. Istanbul is a crowded, exhilarating city where Muslims and members of other religions appear to interact without problems in spite of their differences.

65. Sea Kayaking with Orcas (Killer Whales) in Johnstone Strait, British Columbia

We looked like a colorful rainbow paddling red-and-turquoise two-person kayaks past banks of forest. Under our red spray skirts, which kept us dry, we wore yellow PFDs (personal floatation devices) covered by green, yellow, or red rain jackets. The area — the Inside Passage between Vancouver Island and Alaska, specifically the Johnstone Strait, a 68 mile channel along Vancouver Island — is colorful, but we stood out in our clearly manmade finery, alerting passing boats and cruise ships to our presence.

In the strait, cedar, hemlock, and shore pine were edged by berry-laden salal shrub (a delicacy for the local bears). The crystalline waters flowing past bull kelp and eelgrass revealed bright red blood starfish and sea stars, anemones, sea cucumbers, and an occasional river otter or harbor seal. Schools of juvenile pink salmon and herring darted past our paddles. Bald eagles perched on tall firs, sighting for fish, while great blue herons and black oystercatchers waded on rocky shores. On the shore, deer peeked from the trees and a mother raccoon eyed us warily, protecting her fuzzy cubs from the intruders.

Johnstone Strait Baby orca, Photo: Mary L Peachin

My family —husband David, daughter Suzie, son Jeffrey and his girlfriend, Kristin — had chartered a floatplane to fly us into Farewell Harbour, two hours south of Port McNeill, British Columbia. There we met the kayak-laden forty-foot *Spirit Bear*, operated by Northern Lights Expeditions, for three days of cruising and kayaking.

The *Spirit Bear*, a former fish trawler, was totally renovated, with a loving touch, by Northern Lights Expeditions owner David Arcese. The boat is designed for a maximum of four guests, but our family of five scrunched in: David and I slept (lying like pencils) on the kitchen table, which converted into a bed, with the kids distributed between the bed in the wheelhouse and a master stateroom with a shower. Skipper Alvin Sewid had a cabin and head (which we could use) in the fo'c'sle, and there was a pumping head next to the dining table/bed. The top deck could be used for sleeping, although it was too cold during our trip. Despite the close quarters, we were cozy and happy to be family.

On the boat, Northern Lights guide Jenny MacPhee led us through safety instructions for the boat and the fiberglass kayaks. We then got underway. Alvin, a member of the local Mamaliligula tribe, heading the boat south to Cracraft Island.

The following three days unfolded in much the same way: Each day we paddled for several hours, exploring the strait and coming in close contact with local marine life. Jenny, at mealtime acted as chef, worked in the small galley, and sometimes it seemed as if we paddled from meal to delicious meal — one night, we feasted on pizza, choosing from a menu of toppings that included artichoke hearts, olives, avocados, grilled or raw onion, yellow, green, or red peppers, garlic, pesto, and marinara sauce. Pastas were equally varied, as were fresh salads topped with tomatoes, olives, blue cheese, and walnuts. Desserts varied, ranging from cakes made with fresh fruit and granola to rich chocolate brownies. Breakfast was fresh fruit and Tasmanian toast (cream cheese between two pieces of grilled buttered toast).

But food was far from the only draw. We had also come to these waters for some whale watching, hoping to see orca (more commonly known as killer whales). But the more traveled strait is subject to a "whale jam," boat gridlock wherever orca are sighted. We decided to forgo kayaking in the heavy boat traffic of the strait, opting instead for wilderness paddling. We were lucky to sight whales several times, each time climbing back into *Spirit Bear* and cruising closer for a good look. Away from the crunch of traffic, they swam around and under the boat, giving us clear and beautiful views.

Our kayaking route took us to anchorages at Klaoitisis Island, Mound Island, and Codfish Pass in the Pearce Islands. One afternoon, Suzie and I fished for dinner while David, Jeffrey, and Kristin tried a "rope-and-ladder" technical climb on Little Kai Island. Each night we lowered a prawn trap, but succeeded in catching only one prawn, which we released.

The culture of the region was also much in evidence, and here Alvin, with his native heritage and lifetime of experience in local waters, added greatly to the trip experience. Early on, we stopped to admire some pictographs and a "chief's bath," both carved into the granite rocks of Crease Island.

Another day we visited a 10,000-year-old abandoned village. Alvin's son, Tom, has assumed the role of guardian of the village's 14 fluted-beam dwellings, once inhabited by the Kwakiutl people. We sat at the beachfront for an hour as Tom told us the legends of his ancestors, finishing up with more recent tales featuring the exploits of his late grandfather, a Kwakiutl chief.

The day after our visit, Alvin received a radio call from Tom, who'd heard of our prawn-trapping failures. He was bringing us "gomies," fresh Dungeness crab, which we ate that night as an appetizer for the rock cod we'd caught earlier that afternoon.

Most Northern Lights trips are seven days, but the kids' work schedules kept ours to three. On the fourth day, we reluctantly left the *Spirit Bear* and headed north to Port McNeill, where the kids would head back to work and David and I would take a floatplane over to the luxurious Wickaninnish Inn on the west coast of Vancouver Island in Tofino. After a wonderful family adventure and great kayaking, we could hardly wait for a roomy bed and a long, hot shower.

Part XIV.

Antarctica, Arctic, and Circumnavigation of Iceland

66. Antarctica's Penguin Highway

Gentoo penguin, Photo: Mary L Peachin

"There are two kinds of penguins in the Antarctic, the white ones coming towards you (from the ocean) and the dirty ones going away from you."-Anonymous

Antarctica's penguin highway is one of nature's great two-lane, gridlocked non-stop traffic rush hours. Unfortunately, this incredible sight is not readily accessible. Icy penguin trails curve, meander, detour, then disconnect through treacherous terrain following a path frequently obscured by snow or cloud cover.

Penguins inhabit an environment so inhospitable that there is an only a three month—December through February—window when daylight hours or "summer" conditions melt enough of the ice pack to allow ship navigation. But, for many, the 600 miles of open rough ocean of the Drake Passage, deters them from visiting the penguin highway of the Southern Continent.

Making the Passage in 30-foot seas, we tightly gripped the sides of our beds for security. Unsecured objects flew across the cabin. By morning, the majority of 110 passengers were so seasick they wished they were dead or someone would mercifully shoot them. Ropes were placed along hallways for walking while straps were tied to beds, like seat belts, keeping you from falling out of bed. A woman, toting a handful of barf bags into the sparsely occupied dining room, projectally erupted. She cleared the room as if she was spreading a contagious disease.

Finally, at mid-afternoon on the second day –landfall! We made the first of many wet beach landings. Sliding from the pontoon of the zodiac onto the beach, our legs were protected from the frigid water by rain pants and rubber boots.

The penguin highway traverses steep, snowy terrain or sometimes simply follows an easy walk on a beach. Shivering in below freezing cold became irrelevant. Following a web-footed path surrounded by penguins, our eyes were glued to binoculars, our camera shutters clicking,

At Aitcho Island in the South Shetland Archipelago of the Weddell Sea, colonies of chinstrap penguins hunkered on the beach. A distinctive narrow band of black feathers artistically extends from ear to ear under their chin. Rocks were covered with the ammonia-like, fishy stench of guano, and skeletal whale bones littered the beach. It is thought that white guano indicates that penguins have dined on fish or squid. If it's pink, they've gorged on krill. Three or more days without food, it turns greenish in color.

Penguins shared the beach with three ton 12-foot lazing elephant seals. The bull, known as the "beach master," can mate with as many as 100 females, but he must fight other bulls for domination, to earn the right to service his harem. Occasionally, a whiskered head would rise to yawn or snarl at another. In the 1800s, these creatures were almost wiped to extinction for their oil.

Many of the brush-tailed chinstrap penguins had week old chicks. Penguins lay two eggs, but in many cases, only one chick will survive. Sleek and fast underwater swimmers, they waddle clumsily on land. Squawking exchanges between males and females appear related to taking turns nesting and nurturing the chicks.

It's difficult to distinguish between sexes. Males diligently pick pebbles on the beach or attempt to steal some from another nest to compulsively tidy their nest. Gentoo's might gather 3,000 pebbles, while the Adelie (named for a French explorer's wife) may collect a mere 300 stones. Like any nursing infant, the chick, fluffy rump sticking out with its head snuggled under the warmth of the parent's breast, will emerge to nibble the parent's orange beak for a regurgitated meal.

Brown Bluff, at the northern tip of the Antarctic Peninsula, has a colony of approximately 25,000 black-headed Adelie and gentoo penguins. The size of these chicks and their growing appetites required both parents to hunt. In groups, they waddled to the edge of the water then spontaneously, as if on cue, synchronically plunged into the ocean.

Allegedly, the penguin in the front is pushed, and if a leopard seal doesn't attack it, the other penguins feel safe to enter the water.

For the novice, it's difficult to differentiate between gentoo and Adelie species. Gentoo have a subtle white spot on their crown, while Adelie have small white rings around their eyes. Expedition leader, Tom Ritchie compares penguins to tubby little people in formal attire. They walk upright, as they stumble and slip on ice, just like people.

The "Devil", discovered by Swedish explorer Otto Nordenskjold in 1901, has a breeding colony of 10,000 Adelies. These penguins waddled up a cliff leaving a pattern in the snow like the etched icy trail of a skier.

Most of us were asleep when Tom Ritchie announced the rare sighting of Emperor penguins. The ship edged slowly along a tall, tabular glacier cracked with deep crevasses as it approached the taller three-foot penguins. Crunching ice rattled the re-enforced hull as we excitedly huddled on the bow watching two Emperors followed by an Adelie plunge into the frigid water. Shy and eager to get away from us, they slid or "tobogganed" on their chest carving a trail to the water's edge.

Throughout the morning, we continued to have Emperor sightings. We had the unique experience of observing two fluffy and one molted chick.

Sighting an Emperor penguin chick seldom happens because mating occurs deep in the ice pack during the dark, intolerable Antarctic winter. Nesting males endure harsh conditions by almost starving for three months, while females hunt food at sea. During this time frame, the ice continues to pack making the distance to water as far as 100 miles. Females return when the chicks are born. They feed their newborn as the famished males toboggan and waddle to water's edge to satiate their hunger.

Naturalists believed their first sighting of three chicks, old enough to have been abandoned by their parents, occurred because the edge of their ice flow broke away. Nearby, a 12-foot spotted leopard seal, a ferocious predator, lay in wait on another iceberg. Hopefully, the fluffy chicks would mature by molting in the next week, enabling them to swim to safety.

At Madder Cliffs on Joinville island, 50,000 Adelie, gentoo, and chinstrap penguins nested on snowy patches, offshore rocks, and high on the steep slopes of the red rock island. Surrounding the colony were snow white pigeon-sized sheathbills, the only Antarctic bird without webbed feet. This bird is the "hyena" of the continent scavenging everything from guano to corpses. Sheathbills and brown skuas prey on both eggs and newborn chicks.

Humpbacks, attracted to the same dense krill plankton diet of the penguin spy-hop to peek at us, fin as if waving, then tailed as they sound.

Kayaking Cuverville Island, Antarctica, Photo: Mary L Peachin

Bailey Head on Deception Island is a composite of volcanic calderas. It features a natural amphi-theater with a unique "penguin highway." Spotless birds returning from the sea walk on the right side of the path, while dirty penguins heading to the sea, pass on the left in this 100,000 pair gentoos colony.

Swimming in the Antarctic? If the penguins are so adept, well, why not give it a try? First, the expedition pitched in to build a "swimming hole" on the beach in Whalers Bay. A better de-scription might be a muddy hole heated by fumaroles or sulphuric-smelling steam rising from the flooded center of the crater.

Whalers Bay or Port Foster was a Norwegian whaling station in 1900. The beach is scattered with whale skeletons, rusted metal shelters, and broken remnants of wooden boats used to car-ry water. Hiking the steep saddle of Neptune's Window gave us a feeling of appreciation of the challenging climbs made by penguins.

A 40-knot katabatic winds swirled clouds of snow down the glacier in Neko Harbor. No big deal for the penguins. They turn their layer of blubber and feathers against a wind strong enough to knock us off our feet.

The penguin's black and white counter shading provides camouflage and also helps control their temperature. Like mammals, they are warm blooded birds who spend many hours preening them-selves. From a gland just above their stiff tail feathers, preening replenishes a warm layer of oil on their coat. Nasal glands at the base of their bills allow them to excrete excess salt from sea water.

Kayaking in the Antarctica offers the unique opportunity for an eye level view of the sleek swimming penguin. At Cuverville Island, located in the middle of the Errera Channel between

Ronge Island and the Arctowski Peninsula on the mainland, we admired the compact, stream-lined, short bodies of the penguins from kayaks.

Their stiff wings attached to strong muscles are used for propulsion. Feet and stubby tails serve like a rudder. Like a flipper, it thrusts them forward with an upward stroke of their wing.

The penguins, totally unconcerned about us on land, were afraid of our yellow kayaks. Water is the one place where they are vulnerable to predation. Porpoising out to sea, they left trails of guano floating in the water.

We watched Adelie's jump in the water and occasionally glimpsed one gracefully speeding under the kayak, white feathers gleaming in the clear visibility of the water. Pack ice crackled like rice crispies, air escaping through its density.

The low positioned legs of the penguin may minimize drag in the water, but force them to waddle in an upright stance on land. Appearing clumsy and awkward, they are really quite agile. Three yellow hooked webbed toes grip slippery rocks and ice. For an additional hold, they will occasionally use their beaks.

Antarctica ice Lemaire Channel, Photo: Mary L Peachin

Returning north, the mile-wide Lemaire Channel, located between the mainland and Booth Island, is considered one of the most beautiful places in the Antarctic. Its seven miles are hemmed by high, steep, glaciated snow-covered mountains. Grounded and floating icebergs were shaped and colored with different shades of deep blue glacial ice. The experience was magical.

Antarctic expeditions offer the adventurer onshore, up close opportunities to observe three or four of the seventeen species of flightless birds. Here, in an icy wonderland in magnificent scenery are footprints in the snow, those of the penguin highway.

67. Arctic's Baffin Island, A Barren Land of Eternal Sun

Arctic iceberg, Photo: Mary L Peachin

Arctic ice sustains life on the spongy tundra. Sparsely vegetated by dwarf-size flowers, large-flowered wintergreen, fireweed, Arctic poppy and willow, berries, and fungi, cover a barren land. Where sea and land clash, ice packs flow, and pressure ridges drift in the current with the occasional iceberg.

These large freshwater ice formations are thought to have calved from glaciers on Greenland's ice shelf. Polar bears, the region's apex predator stalk bearded seals who build lairs beneath the ice to protect their pups. Others prowl beaches below high cliffs waiting for thick-billed murre chicks to fall from their nests. When hunger and ferocity prevail, a polar bear might even be willing to risk injury battling a tusked walrus.

Huddled pairs float on ice flows, while herds sprawl on tidal washed rocks. Belugas, narwhals and other sea mammals migrate with the flow and breakup of the ice. Unlike Antarctic's snow-covered landscape of glaciated icebergs, Arctic's Baffin Island, home to 30,000 people in 18 communities, looks like a frigid desert.

Wildlife includes brown and collared lemmings, short-tailed weasels, Arctic fox and hare, caribou, and wolves. The more frequently sighted bird life, in addition to the cliff dwelling murres, include red-footed black guillemots, snow bunting, common and king eider, Canada and snow goose, glaucous gull, red-throated loon, rock ptarmigan, plus numerous fulmar.

Baffin Island is a gateway to the Arctic Ocean's village of Iqaluit, an Inukitut translation for "Place of Fishing." Established as a Canadian military base in 1941, the city now serves as capital of Nunavut territory. During wintry blizzards, its brightly painted yellow airport serves like a beacon to aircraft.

Tides in shallow Iqaluit's bay dictate ship passage, which is provided by Zodiacs from a rocky beach. Varying in depth between 30 to 40 feet, during low tide, the bay is a muddy wetland. While waiting for high tide, we toured Iqaluit, home to almost 1,300 residents. A red roofed museum was formerly the Hudson Bay Company. Snowmobiles, rather than cars, sit idle under stilt-built homes. One of the longest streets is the 3.7-mile *Road to Nowhere*.

When Captain Andrey Rudenko weighed anchor on the 328-foot *M/V Lyubov Orlova*, a glowing red sun hovered above Canada's Northern horizon. Built in 1976 in the former Yugoslavia, our expedition itinerary was a 1,400-mile voyage. From Igaluit, we would journey to destinations around Baffin Island ending in Kuujuag, Nunavik, a new self-governed region of Quebec.

Throughout the night, we motored 75 miles southeast to exit Frobisher Bay. The Russian ice breaking ship, crewed by a staff of 52, then turned north into Davis Strait. The lengthy Bay was named for Martin Frobisher, an explorer for Queen Elizabeth I. In 1578, he sailed, with 15 ships and 300 Cornish miners, in search of gold. Instead, Frobisher and his men returned to England with 1,100 tons of ore that was determined to be iron pyrite or fool's gold.

Arctic itineraries, dictated by 30 to 40-foot tides and violent storms, can change momentarily. The calm water in Frobisher Bay turned nasty when the ship reached the open sea in Davis Strait. Fifteen-foot swells and six force winds quickly scuttled an excursion to view walrus on Monumental Island. The *M/V Lyubov Orlova* pounded north past the Lemieux Islands before arriving late the second evening in the calm, protected waters of Cumberland Sound.

In order to expeditiously alternate offshore zodiac departures, expedition leader, Julio Prellor, divided the 78 passengers into two groups.

Pangnirtung or "Pang" is located 31 miles south of the Arctic circle. Harp seals and a minke whale greet our arrival at Baffin Island's second largest community. A tour of the small hillside village included Parc Canada's Auyuittuq National Park visitor Centre, the Uqqurmut Center for Arts and Craft, and Angmarlik Visitor Centre.

The Centre's manager described tools and artifacts found in an early Inuit tent-like seal skin hummock, one supported by whale bone and covered with seal skin. Arctic wildlife provided clothing, food, and warmth and was a key to early Inuit survival. Adjacent to the hummock, a seal bone game, played like monopoly, was displayed. The Centre also included a whaling museum. In the adjacent Recreation Centre, Inuit youth demonstrated their popular game of high kicking, and women provided a throat singing demonstration.

Looping southward, the ship made another attempt to explore Monumental Island. Successful this time, we found a large colony of walrus lazing on an outcropping. Approaching downwind, we could smell the pinnipeds before we saw them. "Foul areas" listed on early navigational charts were thought to be named for their putrid odor. Atop the summit of an adjacent rock, a polar bear, perhaps curious about our four 16-foot Zodiac "armada" surveyed the walrus colony as its next meal. Nearby, a towering 100-foot iceberg was estimated to be 10,000 years old.

Stellar Sea Lions, Photo: Mary L Peachin

Kekerten island, designated a historic site, is located about 30 miles from Pangnirtung. It was used by Scots and Americans in the late 1800s and early 1900s as a whaling station.

Snow buntings and sandpipers fished near the shore. Propped on a rock, the skull and upper jaw of a bowhead served as a reminder of how whalers almost single-handedly wiped out the species. Strewn among the Arctic blue grass tundra, was an occasional patch of dwarf flowers and fungi, rusting vats used to render blubber into oil, tangles of wire, pulleys, and barrel hoops. The grim sight of skeletons deteriorating in wooden coffins told the story of how remnants of the past fade slowly in the Arctic.

Whenever we went ashore, the ship's bridge first scanned the area for polar bears. Several of the crew, armed with rifles, stood watched on nearby hillsides. The air temperature was a moderate 50 degrees. Julio didn't need to remind us twice to use insect repellant and mosquito jackets for protection against the "Inuit Air Force" of mosquitoes and black flies.

Hoare Bay was a sculpture garden of ice flows mixed with an occasional iceberg. As our zodiacs slalomed around various sizes and formations, two walruses, a mother with cub, were spotted on a flow. In order not to stress them, the zodiacs remained at a distance.

Akpatok Island's steep limestone plateau rises between 500 and 800 feet. Twenty-eight miles long by 14 miles wide, cliff crevices are summer nesting sites for approximately 600,000 black and white thick billed murres. Polar bears, several with cubs, patrolled the beach waiting for chicks to fall or an opportune time to plunge into the water to snatch a murre distracted while fishing.

Designated by the Canadian Wildlife Service, Akpatok is considered a special protection site. Its western coastline has an abandoned drilling site that offers the opportunity to hike or beach comb for fossils.

As our journey came to a close, an announcement through cabin intercoms asked us to hurry to the upper deck—there we observed the magic of the Northern Lights.

Once again, the tides of the Koksoak River dictated ship disembarkation for our departure from Nunavik's city of Kuujjuag or "Great River."

68. Circumnavigating Iceland and Siglufjörður Herring Girls

Orcas surrounded the ship: starboard, port and forward of the ship. As we circled them, the killer whale pod swam, breeched, and frolicked. The scene was an example of a food chain feeding frenzy. Diving white gannets bombed the water for fish leftovers. What a fitting finale to our journey circumnavigating Iceland. The beginning twelve days was equally exciting.

Less than three hours after departing the port of capital city Reykjavík, the *Explorer* sighted humpbacks. Spouting air as they surfaced, they feasted on herring scraps left by diving Arctic terns.

Overnight we motored to Iceland's southwest peninsula. The steep, basalt cliffs of Látrabjarg are home to many species of seabirds: puffins, guillemots, cormorants, northern gannets, fulmars, gulls, kittiwakes, and 40 percent of the world's population of razorbills. Europe's largest bird cliff, it is more than two miles long, rising to almost three hundred feet tall.

Iceland Mývatn geothermal activity, Photo: Mary L Peachin

A wet landing by Zodiac on Flatey Island's volcanic topography provided our first hiking opportunity. After departing Breidafiord landing, we explored a hilltop cemetery, then a historic Lutheran church. Less than two miles long, the trail along Lundaberg cliffs provided views of puffins, more swooping Arctic terns, and kittiwakes.

Boarding the Zodiac to return to the ship, we stopped for a closer view of nesting kittiwakes, many with chicks, fulmars, puffins, eider ducks, famous for their down, and Arctic terns. The latter are known for migrating up to 44,000 miles a year, from the Arctic to the Antarctic and back, with significant east-west movement as well.

A second afternoon hike provided more bird species: skua, redwing, redshank, purple sandpiper, and colorful red-billed oystercatchers.

Dynjandi or Fjalifoss "Mountain Falls," in remote Westfiords, is a series of seven thunderous waterfalls. Calm waters in the surrounding fjord gave us the opportunity to kayak. We embraced the cool freshness and close-up water view.

Vigur Island, the second-largest island in Isafjordur Bay, is inhabited by a farming family who earn their livelihood by fishing, collecting eggs, raising sheep and harvesting treasured eider down, a tedious and costly effort. A large colony of Arctic tern and puffin inhabit their island.

Eyjafjallajökull Glacier, north of Skógar and west of Mýrdalsjökull, is one of Iceland's smaller ice caps. The 5,417-foot ice cap covers the caldera of a volcano which has erupted frequently since the last glacial period.

In April, 2010, Eyjafjallajökull erupted from the top crater in the center of the glacier, causing jökulhlaup or meltwater floods, in nearby rivers. This required the evacuation of eight hundred residents. It was estimated to be as much as twenty times larger than previous ones. A second eruption scattered volcanic ash several miles into the atmosphere. This caused air travel disruption in Europe for more than a week – the same ash which disrupted our trip in Morocco.

Cruising by Ísafjörður, which translates to ice fjord, this northwest town, on a sand spit on the peninsula of Vestfirðir (Westfjords) is one of the country's largest fisheries. In recent years, the city has become a tourist destination serviced by ferries.

A tour on the mainland took us through a dark single-lane five-mile tunnel to Skrudur Directional rules of the road provide sporadic widenings for yielding the right of way to oncoming vehicles, their headlights mandatory.

In Flateyri, after visiting a bakery and a store where books were sold by the pound, we were serenaded by a young gal in a small church. Formerly a fishing village, Flateyri still exports dried cod heads to eastern Asia. Moving on, we had a choice of hiking to the Arctic Fox Center on the Valagil trail or taking a walking tour through the back streets of Isafjordur.

The northern city of Akureyri, about a six-iron south of the Arctic Circle, is on one of Iceland's longest fjords (36 miles). With a population of 18,000, it is Iceland's second-largest urban area and is home to quaint cafés and fine restaurants. Locals and visitors party late into the night. The seafood restaurant Rub23 features robata grilling, a method used by fishermen in Hokkaido, Japan. Lystigardurinn, the most northerly botanical garden, has a large display of high-latitude plants.

Around the year A.D. 1000, about 400 Icelandic Norse, considered pagans by the church, were converted to Christianity by missionaries. Pagan statues were tossed into the 24-foot-deep cascade now known as Goðafoss – Waterfall of the Gods. The falls is part of the 108-mile-long Skjálfandafljót, one of Iceland's longest glacial rivers.

Mývatn is a shallow lake surrounded by wetlands in an active area near Krafla volcano. There one finds a rich diversity of water birds including Barrow's goldeneye, red-breasted merganser, wigeon, gadwall, mallard, common scoter, long-tailed duck and Eurasian teal.

The area overlooks almost a dozen pseudo craters formed from ice erosion. Two major types of basaltic lava flow, known by their Hawaiian terms as a'a and pahoehoe, have created deep fissures, some of which still vent steam. When volcanoes erupt through snow, magma or molten rock create table rocks.

Locals smoke fish in small buildings over smoldering grass and sheep dung.

Grjótagjá was a popular steaming 140-degree (60 Celsius) bathing spot. Once owned by Vogar farm, separate pools for men and women were used for nude bathing. When the Vogars sold their property, the new owners discontinued the bathing. Stunted larch trees were surrounded by fields of blue lupine while barren soil areas, sterilized by toxic volcanic sulphur and iron, were a stark contrast.

Námafjall, a high-temperature geothermal area, is filled with steaming mudpots. When water is in short supply, the mud turns to clay, and steaming fumaroles.

Heading to the long northeast peninsula of Laganes near the steep sea cliffs of Skoruvíkurbjarg and Skalavikurbjarg, we cruised through the currents merging the Gulf Stream with East Greenland or Irminger North Atlantic current. Laganes, a narrow peninsula between Þistilfjordur to Thistilfjördur and Bakkaflói, is shaped like a goose head. This region is known for rich bird life, especially for viewing gannets and Brünnich's guillemot from land. Ocean conditions make for excellent fishing. The hamlet of Skalar has now been abandoned.

Visitors who enjoy fresh cod and salmon will love the fresh catch served in Iceland. Locals enjoy a different variety of food. Much of it is smoked with sheep dung or preserved. Icelandic food includes, reindeer, lamb or hangikjöt, dried cod and haddock, puffin, sheep's head, and fermented shark. These dishes are typically served with brennivín, known as Black Death, a high-alcohol spirit distilled from potatoes. At about 40 percent alcohol, it's similar to vodka.

Djúpivogur's small harbor is the oldest port in the East Fjords. Nearby Papey Island was thought to have been a hermitage for Irish monks until the arrival of the Norse. More recently used as a farm, its cliffs are covered with nesting birds. Burrowing puffins, members of the auk family, are becoming endangered. They do not have enough food to enable breeding. The Northern Hemisphere's version of a penguin, they share the cliffs with oystercatchers, razor-bills, and common and black guillemots. Neighboring fulmars are known to spit a greasy substance. Chubby spotted grey and harbor seals swam playfully.

Frequented by occasional campers, the island is home to Iceland's oldest and smallest church and the Hellisbjarg lighthouse. Cotton grass and sedge line an often-muddy track.

In 1963 the island of Surtsey was formed when a volcano erupted 430 feet beneath the ocean's surface. Undersea vents created a stark but now-vegetated basalt island that is considered part of the Mid-Atlantic Ridge. As the volcano continued erupting, Surtsey reached a maximum size of 2.7 square kilometers in 1965, but has since been eroded by wave erosion.

Our final stop was Heimaey, or Home Island. It is the largest island in the Vestmannaeyjar archipelago, and the largest and most populated island off the Icelandic coast. Its 4,500 inhabitants watched Mount Eldfell erupt in 1973. By continually spraying seawater on the lava flow, they saved their harbor, the most important part of their economy.

As our circumnavigation came to an end, the captain alerted us to "killer whales." Gannets, diving from all directions, surrounded the female orcas with calves, and males identifiable by their larger, fin. It was a fitting way to end the cruise: humpbacks as we set off, orcas on our return, with lots of bird watching and close looks at still-active volcanic areas.

It was a fitting way to end the cruise: humpbacks leaving, orcas on our return topped by lots of bird watching and admiring geothermal activity.

Siglufjörður Herring Girls

Her red babushka contrasting with a plaid shirt and yellow rubber apron, she inhaled a cigarette while scooping herring from a long tray. She quickly fileted, salted and tossed each herring into a barrel. Speed matters when you're being paid by the barrel.

Norwegians taught Icelanders the technique of fishing and salting herring at the start of the 20th century. During the brief summer fishing season, "herring girls" would work thirty-hour shifts to keep the fish relatively fresh. They were also paid by the pound. Men, who did the fishing, might have to wait anywhere from a few hours to several days to unload their catch. The fish were then separated by freshness and size to determine whether they would be used as food or made into meal or fish oil.

For each barrel, the girls tucked a token into their boots. At the end of the week, on payday, tokens were converted to kroner. When they took time off, the evenings were spent drinking and dancing with the fishermen. The gal showing us their technique shared, "It was a short season with no time to rest. We had all winter to catch up on our sleep."

The building behind them housed a dormitory where the girls shared multi- level bunks. They had a shared bath and small kitchen.

An adjacent building was used to process the fish while a third housed fishing boats during the winter. In spite of many warnings of overfishing, Iceland, Norway, and Russia continued to fish the herring until they eliminated the industry in 1968.

Many towns and villages along the north and east coast of Iceland were deeply affected by the arrival of herring fishing. Nowhere did the herring industry have an impact as large as Siglufjörður. During the summer of 1903, Norwegian fishermen arrived sailing on herring vessels. In four decades, the small village was transformed into a thriving town with more than three thousand inhabitants with twenty-three salting stations and five reduction factories.

As the herring industry grew, a gold rush-like atmosphere led to Siglufjörður being dubbed the "Atlantic Klondike." The town became a magnet for herring speculators who came and went, some making a lot of money during the boom. Siglufjörður became a mecca for tens of thousands of workers.

During storms, the fjord's sheltered waters contained a massed fleet of hundreds of herring ships. Siglufjörður's streets were crowded.

When Icelandic pioneers developed more-efficient fishing technology, the stability of the herring stock was strongly impacted. As early as 1950, the catch began to decline.

In 1989, local volunteers spent five years renovating the Róaldsbrakki factory to create a three-building museum to recognize Siglufjörður's herring industry.

Róaldsbrakki, the original 1907 Norwegian salting station, exhibits history of artifacts and photographs detailing Siglufjörður in 1940 when thousands of people arrived each herring season in search of a well-paid jobs. They included the herring girls, fishermen and other workers. Hundreds of herring girls, who arrived from around the country, were housed at the station. The upper-floor living quarters still remain untouched.

Grána, a herring factory built in the 1930s, displays the reduction of herring into meal and oil. Machinery gathered from old, abandoned herring factories, including Ingólfsfjörður and Hjalteyri, have made the exhibit appear like the original factory.

In 2004, The Boathouse, the newest building, was opened by Crown Prince Håkon of Norway. An example of the town's bustling harbour has been recreated.

Today's salting demonstrations provide visitors the opportunity to share a historic time. An accordion player adds to an atmosphere that prevailed when Siglufjörður served as the center of Iceland's herring fisheries.

Siglufjörður Herrings Girls, Photo: Mary L. Peachin

Part XV.

The Wonders of Africa

I spent twenty years diving around the world during my passionate search for whale sharks. I averaged three to four dive trips a year. As technology increased, a number of whales and sharks were tagged making their locations more reliable. During two summer trips to Holbox and La Paz, my passion was satisfied.

Surfacing, I went to Africa, one of everyone's most interesting destinations. I was fortunate to have a friend like Sally who had enjoy a longtime passion for Africa. She knew that she wanted to fly, the best guides, and the most interesting places that she hadn't visited. While our gateway was Nairobi, most of our visit was in Tanzania with a taste of Kenya at the end of a two-week trip.

69. Serengeti, Roaring Lions Outside My Tent, Charging Elephants, Wild Dogs, and the Chimps of Mahale National Park, Tanzania

South Africa Lion, Photo: Mary L Peachin

As our small plane landed on a dirt strip lined by red oat grass, what appeared from the air to be tiny specks transformed into full-size, grazing zebras, giraffes, and wildebeest. The sound of the prop did not disturb the grazing herds.

Two six-passenger open-roof, four-wheel-drive Land Rovers met us at the strip. Swarthy, English and Swahili-speaking guides Allan Earnshaw and Tim Melesi, offering a combined 30 years of experience as African safari guides, welcomed us to the plains of the Serengeti in Tanzania.

Our "airport transfer" to our campsite at Moru kopje was not the typical traveler's shuttle ride to a local motel. Along the dirt track, we frequently stopped to observe some of the 2 million wildebeest and Burchell's zebras who migrate north from Tanzania to the greener pastures of Kenya. We marveled at Thompson gazelles, topi and warthogs, running comically with upright tails.

Lilac-breasted rollers, superb starlings, and blacksmith and crowned glovers wowed the birdwatchers in our group of eight. We listened to the shrieking cry of the turaco, also known as the "black-faced go-away bird" because of its black face and the sound of its call. A marabou stork perched on a tree patiently waiting his turn as jackals and hyenas devoured a zebra.

The Moru campsite was at the base of a colorful rock outcropping or kopjes typical of the flat-topped acacia and grass savannah of the Serengeti. Our excited group tumbled out of the vehicles to explore the campsite we would call home for the next several days.

Each tent included an awning-covered "front porch" with a chair, a two-cot "bedroom" with dressing room, and a separate toilet-shower area. The "toilet" was a porta-potty with a pail of dirt and a trowel, a substitute for flushing water. For showers, water was heated by the campfire, then hoisted by a porter above the tent. We had three minutes of gravity-fed water to cleanse ourselves from the dust of the plains.

As we sat around the campfire watching the sunset, we were amused by Tim and Allan's tales from their experiences in Africa. Tim's enthusiasm and Allan's skills in tracking, smelling, and listening made these Kenya-born men perfect guiding partners.

Tim shared one of his previous adventures: "I went into the bush to take a leak and I stepped on this bloody, deadly puff adder snake. When I yelled for Allan's help, he said, 'Shut up, I'm listening on my shortwave radio to BBC's Dow Jones report." Apparently, this kind of experience was just another day in the bush for these guides. We soaked in their amusing banter before heading for our tents for the night.

The firm-mattress cot was covered with wool blankets and a colorful African bedspread. I pulled the covers over my head to keep warm from the chilly 50 degrees of the winter night. I could hear lions roaring, wildebeest grunting, zebra "chirping," and baboons babbling. Just as I began dozing, I was jolted awake by an unforgettable, raspy "sawing" call, vibrating much too close to my tent. The next morning, I learned that this unusual cry was that of an amorous leopard searching for his mate. The thin canvas of the tent was the only barrier separating me from the nocturnal animals roaming the surrounding bush.

After a wake-up call with a warm mug of coffee delivered to our tents, we ate a quick breakfast in the dining tent before our game drive began shortly after sunrise.

Meals were scheduled around game drives — although a sandwich might be quickly tossed aside for the chance to see an elusive African wild hunting dog or greater kudu. Typically, we returned for lunch and a rest period, then set out on a second game drive later in the afternoon.

Serengeti, Africa Cheetah, Photo: Mary L Peachin

Although the migration of the wildebeest was a spectacular sight in itself, it also afforded us the opportunity to see more than 100 lions in the Serengeti. One afternoon on the savannah, we discovered a majestic golden-maned male dragging his rear paw behind him. Allan and Tim surmised that the lion had been bitten by a venomous spitting cobra.

We saw prides of lions lounging on rocky kopjes, with cubs nursing and tumbling among the adults. We watched lion pair for mating, stalk prey, and eat their kill. We even observed one lion sleeping in a tree, his stomach bulging from a recent gorge.

And these weren't the only big cats we saw. Having heard the leopards' love songs during the night, Allan skillfully located the male leopard slinking through tall grass. Climbing the steep pitch of a nearby kopje, the leopard emerged on the opposite side of the outcropping. Seeking cover, he quickly crossed the track in front of us and disappeared into the thick bush of an adjacent kopje.

Our luck in finding the leopard was only the beginning. During the next 24 hours, we saw the rest of the "big five" (lion, leopard, rhinoceros, elephant, and Cape buffalo) on everyone's wish list of African animals. Another early morning game drive the next day took us across rugged terrain covered with herds of Thompson's gazelles, the favorite prey of cheetah. Later that day, we found four cheetahs openly sunning themselves next to a pond. A black rhinoceros stood in the distance while a lone Cape buffalo glared at us from nearby brush.

Serengeti, Africa Hippo, Photo: Mary Peachin

Returning to camp the second day, we saw a herd of elephants grazing near a stream. Oxpecker birds dined on ticks while perched on the backs of a variety of animals, including giraffes. Bat-eared foxes and honey badgers peeked at us as they scrambled into their burrows for cover. In the tall grass, a pink-legged male ostrich flapped his wings in a mating ritual. We saw the brown-black topi antelope, a male vervet monkey boasting a midnight-blue scrotum, and smaller antelopes such as the klipspringer and Kirk's dik-dik.

Red oat grass was mixed with thorny acacia and cloth-grabbing "wait a minute" bush. Magnificent euphorbia candelabra surrounded the crusty white soda banks near Lake Magadi. We knew that clouds of dust in the distance signaled animal migrations.

Petroglyphs carved into the boulders showed evidence of ancient civilizations, an unexplained archeological message. Shiny black obsidian fragments and remnants of a stone circumcision tool lying near the bed of a waterhole added to the mystery of this land's ancient inhabitants.

After a day of game driving, we enjoyed spectacular sunsets as we sat around a campfire while sipping "sundowners." The sky glowed with ribbons of red and gold while our group of adventurers gathered to relax, converse, and revel in a sense of camaraderie that comes from sharing an enthralling safari.

Dinner was more elaborate than a camper's standard freeze-dried meals. Every night, our nine-person crew produced gourmet dinners that might include an entrée of steak or pork chops cooked on grates over fires, or a pasta dish baked in Dutch ovens. Elegant meals, which also included soup, salad, vegetables, and dessert, were served on fine dinnerware atop a beautifully clothed, candlelit table. The hard-working crew cleaned our tents, washed our clothes, turned down our beds, and even zipped our tents securely each night.

We headed for our tents shortly after dinner. I would spend another night listening to the nocturnal calls of animals through my thin canvas tent, looking forward to our next game drive.

Chimps of Mahale National Park on Lake Tanganyika

The dirt strip landing approach at Lake Tanganyika was unforgiving. There was no go around or second chance. The end of the runway was a mountain. A single engine Cessna Caravan carried eight of us plus a pilot, and two guides. Heavily loaded, the plane landed safely on Kalolwa's short 2,500-foot runway in Mahale National Park. Following a rain storm, the wet clay runway "grabbed" tires, refusing to release them, thus making landing impossible. It reminded me of San Francisquito, the location of the cover photo of this book, where my dive buddies and I were stranded overnight by a rainstorm creating a short, muddy strip.

I marveled at the take-off distance, lift, and load capacity of this Cessna "beast of burden." With the exception of airspace near Nairobi, we flew alone in the skies over Africa. Many of our approaches or departures into dirt airstrips took us through scattered fluffy cumulous clouds. Checking and buzzing airstrips to clear them of animals was standard procedure.

Elephant with bullet hole in ear, Photo: Mary L Peachin

Our flight to Mahale had taken two hours. We boarded a wooden dhow for an hour-and-a-half boat ride north on Lake Tanganyika to Ronald Purcell's camp in Mahale National Park. It took a Zodiac several trips to transfer our group and baggage to the open-deck boat. The mahogany wood of the deck glistened from a recent oiling.

The dhow stopped to pick up two armed guards. We were told it was "standard procedure," as we eyed an AK-47 rifle and a Chinese equivalent. We assumed the guards would be leading us on a mountain hike in search of chimps. Later we would learn that the guards were protecting the camp from refugees fleeing from The Democratic Republic of Congo, thirty miles across the lake.

Purcell's camp is on a solitary beach on the east side of Lake Tanganyika, not far from one of the campsites used by Henry Morton Stanley during his search for Dr. David Livingstone.

The only indications of a campsite observable from the lake are a white canvas tent used for dining, a smaller white tent housing a library, and a beach umbrella. Guest tents with adjacent pit toilets and open showers are camouflaged in the dry, high-canopy forest. Luxury, here, is several hours of solar-powered light for reading.

Purcell's experiences in the bush are sometimes crazy. As we arrived, he was planning to make a thirty-mile Zodiac night crossing on Lake Tanganyika to The Democratic Republic of Congo to recover a stolen boat engine. His camp manager, Simon, was concerned that he might be killed in the politically unstable country, or at the very least jailed. Two days later he returned, without the stolen engine, telling tales of civil unrest and ten-year-old kids running through streets carrying guns.

While Jane Goodall was doing research on chimpanzees further north in Gombe, Kinji Imanishi and Junichiro Itani of Japan were doing similar work in the Mahale mountain range. The semi-deciduous, semi-evergreen high canopy is a natural habitat for the fruit-eating chimps. During their study, the Japanese carved primitive trails into the forest.

Loud, screeching cries of the chimps echoed through the forest as they hooted, hollered, and chattered. Their greeting is unforgettable.

After settling in, we were off for two and half hours of hiking steep hills, making treacherous descents, fording streams, and stumbling over roots and animal dens. A troop passed quickly into the forest, stopping to grab lemons from a tree using both their hands and feet.

We watched a second troop well known to our local guides. The grandmother chimp occasionally walked over to groom her daughter, Ruby. Two brothers and a baby rested nearby. Ruby, in esterase, continually "presented" her swollen tush to an alpha male named Banana. After mating with her twice, Banana became more preoccupied with eating lemons. Ruby would nuzzle him, spread her legs and appear to do anything to entice him to mate with her again. Banana, while displaying an erection, was so engrossed with eating that he dropped a lemon rind which comically looped over his penis.

After a strenuous day of hiking, I developed a blister on my toe. A member of our group was an orthopedic surgeon. I asked him how to heal it so I could hike the next day. "No problem, Mary." He gave me some tea-tree oil, which did the trick.

A second day of hiking brought more success in finding a troop of chimps. This time, the chimps were on the move and we had to leave the trail and trek through heavy bush to briefly sight and follow them.

Kasisha village, where Mahale park rangers are stationed, was home to about fifty natives. The trip was about thirty minutes south by boat. Our surgeon was eager to make balloon-animal hats for the children. At first, the kids were very wary. Harold and his wife, Nancy, showed the kids how balloons inflated and the sound they made when popped. Timid and scared, the kids were astounded. A small mirror was set up so they could see their hats. Soon, the entire village came to watch and participate. It was a fascinating interaction between two very different cultures.

The crystal-clear water of Lake Tanganyika (400 miles long by thirty miles wide) is home to many species of cichlids. After the chimp hike, wearing a borrowed mask and snorkel, I jumped in the lake to cool off and "wash my clothes."

The many cichlids I saw didn't look like the "Ziggy" I knew from my son's aquarium. Jeffrey's Ziggy had made the trip in a U-Haul from Los Angeles to Bozeman when Jeffrey attended graduate school at Montana State. He was given up for adoption when Jeffrey graduated andheaded to San Francisco for his job with Price Waterhouse.

As the water calmed near dusk, five of us took rods and hand lines and trolled in a small boat. A lone hippo gazed at us from the bank. I was glad not to have seen him while snorkeling. We caught four-pound blue-and-yellow striped Quye, another type of cichlid. The setting sun silhouetted the ridges of the Mahale Mountains as we returned to camp. The fish was thinly sliced and served as sashimi.

The next morning, we would have a daylong journey back to Kenya and the luxury of the real beds and hot showers of Borana Lodge.

Borana Lodge

As we photographed a white rhino with her calf, she charged the topless Land Rover. She ran huffing and puffing, but sounded like a buzzing bee. I asked our driver, Bobby, how he knew when to floor it. He replied, "When Wangesah, our Samburu game tracking guide, tells me." This charge in the Lewa Downs Rhinoceros Preserve was more unnerving than the elephant charge in the Ruaha.

Borana Lodge is at the base of Mount Kenya. Six manyattas, or thatched-roof rooms, are carved into the side of a mountain overlooking a waterhole in the valley. Each room blends into the contour of the land. The decor includes colorful materials, fine art and sculpture. Large bathrooms have baths or showers built into the rock. A fireplace provides warmth for each room. The grounds are manicured, and an infinity swimming pool is edged to a cliff.

Fluorescent-colored agama lizards sun around cattail lily ponds. The lodge is surrounded by 45,000 acres of ranch. Acacia and cedar trees frame the view of Slide Rock, the rock image used in the *The Lion King* movie. The wide expanse of country extends to Mount Kenya, its peak frequently obscured by cloud cover.

The gourmet cuisine included a full breakfast, buffet lunch, and four-course dinner bring dining guests from long distances. Cocktails or "sundowners" were served around the large stone fireplace in the living room.

One and half hours from Borana, the Ndorobo Laikipia, blood relatives of the better known Maasai and Samburu tribes, have a small village. The four-wheel-drive track is a roller-coaster ride through cedars and euphorbia candelabra. It is a long but beautiful drive.

The Ndorobo Laikipia were dancing when we arrived. Colorfully dressed, with bodies painted in red ochre, they jumped high in monotonous rhythm. They demonstrated the mixing of dung with mud to hold the sisal plant used to weave the low, dank, and smoky manyatta shelters. Their goats are protected nightly in a thorned acacia "boma" enclosure. Walking around the dusty, fly-infested ten-manyatta village, we saw a blacksmith heating steel over a wood fire to carve spears. We passed a trap that had been set with a spear in a tree and used as a killing missile for unwary prey. Women milked goats, while an elder, his nose destroyed in some past encounter, played a game of Bao on a board with stones.

As dusk approached, we ended our cultural exchange. As we made the long drive back to Borana, I thought about the handsome faces of these Ndorobo Laikipia, and I wished I knew more about their customs.

70. South Africa, the Garden Route, Sabi Sabi Safari, and After Apartheid

In October, 1993, South African Airways invited me as an American travel writer they would like to host for a three-week tour of their country. They planned the itinerary, reserved the hotels, and included a rental car. I was so happy when they included David. The following stories include some of our adventures. I did not include Victoria Falls, wedged between Zambia and Zimbabwe, as it was a brutal 100 degrees, we had no air conditioning, and a drought made the falls merely a stream. We overnighted in Durban, an interesting city on the coast, that we didn't get a chance to explore, and Johannesburg, where we visited Soweto, home to Nelson Mandela, and the interesting Apartheid Museum.

Cape Town

Cape Town's Table Mountain, Photo: Mary L. Peachin

Orographic clouds, created by moist air, frequently cover or create a "tablecloth" over all or part of the 3,500-foot flat-topped Table Mountain. Cape Town's stunning backdrop comprises almost 15,000 acres of sculpted shale, sandstone, and granite. The mountain is a landmark that dominates the landscape of a city wedged between it and Table Bay, which opens into the Atlantic Ocean.

Cape Town's setting makes it easy to understand the South African city's numerous accolades as a beautiful, livable and romantic city. To many visitors, the southern tip of the world may be a cruise ship port of call or a gateway to Kruger National Park safaris. Many travelers will agree that Cape Town is a city that can be considered a designated destination.

It is a long haul to get there, but Cape Town is well worth the jet lag. Touring the Cape of Good Hope or infamous Robben Island (of Nelson Mandela fame) is simply an amuse bouche, a small taste of what South Africa has to offer.

During our October visit, we experienced Cape Town's strong and relentless winds. Known as South-East winds, they atypically blow from land to the sea. Locally this phenomenon is referred to as the "Cape Doctor." The resulting clean air" makes the city glisten. While the wind may result in a canceled Table Mountain gondola ride or a visit to Robben Island, there is so much else to do that visitors can easily fill their schedules.

We did just that by enjoying a daylong drive to the Cape of Good Hope. The Atlantic coastline road connects the wide sandy beaches of Clifton, Camps Bay, Llandudno, and Sandy Bay.

Simon's Town, one of South Africa's oldest naval settlements, attracts visitors primarily to its nearby Boulders Beach. Sheltered by large, rounded rocks, the area is home to a protected colony of endangered African penguins.

At Hout Bay, ferries provide a chance to view a colony of Cape fur seals on Duiker Island. Aboard the 82-foot Calypso, a converted World War II air-sea rescue boat, we steamed beyond the jetty of Flora Bay to Duiker's seal island. Seals, prey to the great white shark, would attract divers, but Duiker does not have the dive facilities of Gansbaai's Dyer Island, along the western cape, a noted destination for shark divers.

The journey along Chapman's Peak Drive is a spectacular route. Within five miles, 114 curves follow a rocky coastline. Sheer drops make it a popular location for television car commercials.

In the Cape of Good Hope Nature Reserve, which dates back to 1939, visitors can see wild zebras, ostrich, and baboons. The area is uniquely landscaped with fynbos, a colorful, flowering collection of shrubbery.

Legend has it that the Cape of Good Hope, a rocky promontory, was discovered by Portuguese navigator Bartolomeu Dias in 1488. Dias supposedly named it the Cape of Storms. A superstitious King John II of Portugal renamed it the Cape of Good Hope. The king hoped that Dias' discovery was a good omen that India could be reached by sea from Portugal.

The signage at the cape, in English and Dutch, notes that it is always windy. Fortunately, it was not at its worse velocity of 150 mph.

Our return to Cape Town included a visit to the 1,300-acre Kirstenbosch National Botanical Gardens. The gardens originally belonged to the Cecil Rhodes estate. Kirstenbosch, named after J.F. Kirsten, a garden manager in the 1700s, has been owned by the government since 1913. The gardens are dedicated to indigenous plants of South Africa including traditional African medicinal plants and a perfumery garden signed in braille, as well as evergreen cone-producing cycads and proteas.

Since 1997, Robben Island Prison has been a museum and heritage site. South Africa's first democratic president, Nelson Mandela, and Robert Mangaliso Sobukwe, founder of the Pan Africanist Congress, were incarcerated there.

Robben Island has been inhabited for thousands of years, including a time when the ocean channel separating it from the cape mainland was dry. When the Dutch occupied the cape in the mid-1600s, isolated Robben Island became a prison. In the 1840s, Robben Island was converted into a leprosy colony. During WWII, it served as a training and military base before being converted back to a prison.

During our visit, high winds prevented cable cars to Table Mountain from operating. The two-mile-high sandstone plateau is edged by steep cliffs. It runs from eastern Devil's Peak to Lion's Head in the west. The table top mountain provides a dramatic backdrop to Cape Town. Its Signal Hill, also known as Lion's Rump, is a favorite place for sundowners or evening cocktails.

Our hotel, One & Only Cape Town, offered captivating views of Table Mountain from its location adjacent to the Victoria and Alfred waterfront, the town's working harbor. Two Oceans Aquarium and a shopping mall were nearby.

Looking back on our visit to Cape Town, we feel that we saw a small portion of what the city has to offer. It is a city worth a longer stay or even a destination visit.

Steenberg, the Mountain of Stone

After migrating from Germany to Constantia, South Africa in 1662, Catharina Ustings experienced a life of hardship. At the time, the area that would later become South Africa's noted winelands was total wilderness. It was a country where women had no rights. Catharina, a twenty-two-year-old widow, married Hans Ras, a soldier who had homesteaded along the Liesbeck River. The new bride was unaware that Hans lusted for women slaves.

Following their wedding celebration, he would be severely injured in a wagon collision. While Hans would live to father several children with Catharina, he had the misfortune of being devoured by a lion. Catharina's next husband would be killed by a Hottentot. Her fourth husband would be trampled by an elephant. Her fifth and final husband, Matthys Michelse, did not provide her financial security. Without rights, Catharina could not own land. She timidly approached Simon van der Stel to request a piece of his land to build a farm. He granted her wish. (Rumor has it that it might have been because she was also his mistress.)

Today, less than an hour from Cape Town, Steenberg's Farm hotel has manicured grounds and a stately lodge in the northern shadow of Table Mountain. It is surrounded by vineyards and a championship golf course.

Catharina's fine dining restaurant has been renovated into an avant-garde decor. Its entry includes a bubbly bar, Gorgeous, a nickname for the late Graham Beck. Executive Chef Garth Alamazan offers contemporary South African cuisine. Relatively new to Steenberg's culinary experience is Bistro Sixteen82. The Cellar Door bistro, with a glass-walled view of the winery, serves creative tapas.

Since Governor Simon van der Stel planted vines in 1685, the Western Cape has enjoyed a rich winemaking heritage with many vineyards and estates surrounding Constantia, Stellenbosch and Franschhoek, Paarl and Wellington, and Breede River Valley. It is an area of rolling vineyards and Cape Dutch homesteads.

Steenberg is the oldest farm in Constantia Valley in this premier winemaking region. Wouldn't Catharina be proud if she could see it now?

Garden Route to Hog Hollow

Lions, leopards, elephants, rhinos and Cape buffalo, known as the "Big Five," attract visitors to South Africa. The southernmost African country offers more than safaris if you can take time to explore.

My husband, David, and I rented a car and ventured northwest six hours by from Cape Town following the Garden Route. The road to Hog Hollow Country Lodge, modern highway N2, follows the Indian Ocean coastline. We meandered among secluded bays before heading inland at Plettenberg Bay, where the highway leaves the coastline and heads into ancient forests surrounded by fynbos (natural floral shrub gardens).

The private deck of our cabin at Hog Hollow Country Lodge was cantilevered over Matjies River Gorge, an immense wilderness that made us feel almost like we were clinging to the rim of the Grand Canyon. Covered by a forest-like growth of Australian wattle, the gorge was spectacular.

This fast-growing, invasive species, brought to South Africa 25 years ago to produce tannin for processing leather, overtook native vegetation. Farmers, who were encouraged to plant wattle, didn't realize they were about to ravage a rare, indigenous fynbos forest unique to the Tsitsikamma area.

After six years of traveling through England and Southeast Asia, Andy Fermor decided to return to post-apartheid South Africa. While he was building Hog Hollow, Debbie Reyneke was working as an executive in the hospitality industry.

An avid walker, Reyneke invited a friend to hike for five days along the Otter Trail on Tsitsikamma coast. Following their trek, her friend suggested they dine at a new lodge, a place called Hog Hollow. She didn't know when she invited him that he owned the lodge. The dinner would lead to a long-lasting partnership, one in which each used each using their expertise to add value to the lodge.

Each of the homey lodge's 16 cabins has a private deck overlooking the gorge. The main house features a large dining room table, where guests plan their daily activities over breakfast or unwind at day's end around a candlelight dinner served family-style.

But Hog Hollow is more than a remote lodge. The quality of its nearby attractions is what makes the journey fascinating.

Tenikwa Wildlife Awareness Centre offers a unique viewing experience of wild cats in captivity. Guides provide up-close encounters with cheetahs, a leopard and other indigenous species, servals and caracal among them.

Meerkats dig in and out of holes in their open-air enclosure near the visitors' center, while blue cranes and maribou storks stand nearly motionless near the side of a pond.

Not far from the adjacent village of Kurland, Monkeyland Primate Sanctuary has a suspended 300-foot-high canopy walk offering close-up views of monkeys and other wildlife. The sanctuary is home primates ranging from Asian gibbons to Madagascar lemurs. Knowledgeable rangers describe the habits of mammals roaming free in the forest.

Birds of Eden, Scarlet Ibis, Photo: Mary L. Peachin

Adjacent to Monkeyland is Birds of Eden Sanctuary. Its canopy walk weaves throughout a five-acre aviary. Some 220 species of birds range from African indigenous to the exotic.

The collection includes previously caged pets that go through a process of rehabilitation, which includes socializing with other birds as well as the strengthening of their flight muscles.

Prior to their arrival at the sanctuary, a number of cranes, flamingos and ducks have been subjected to cruel pinioning, the removal of a portion of a wing, leaving them forever earthbound.

Some of the species found in Birds of Eden are ground-living, or terrestrial. Among them are colorful golden pheasants; shy, minuscule, white-starred robins; terrestrial bulbuls, live thrush, bearded barbets and the colorful tauraco.

Sun lovers found higher in the canopy include the channel-billed toucan, black-necked and green aracaris (toucanettes), as well as white-tailed and Inca jays.

Along the forest deck area, blue, green wing and gold macaws mingle with 12 species of vocal conures, ringnecks, parakeets, and lorikeets.

In the grasslands, marsh and woodlands are scarlet ibis, flamingoes, spoonbills, blue and crowned cranes, egrets and moorhens. Smaller parrot species include budgies, lovebirds and cockatiels. Birds of Eden hosts 29 species of ducks including the rarely sighted hornbill.

If you prefer to interact with an elephant, that experience is available at The Elephant Sanctuary in The Crags, Plettenberg Bay. We held their trunks walking down a path, then fed them. We could have taken a ride, but I've been there and done that.

Near Plettenberg Bay, right and humpback whales, bottlenose and common dolphins, and killer whales frolic close to shore. Not as well known as Gansbaii, (Afrikaans for "bay of Geese") Plettenberg is an alternative destination for scuba divers looking for a caged encounter with a great white shark.

A relaxing, less-active break can be enjoyed at the Bramon Wine Farm near Plettenberg Bay. In addition to buying, there is the opportunity to enjoy tasty cheese, a unique sparkling Sauvignon Blanc, or a variety of tapas as you enjoy a view of the Tsitsikamma Mountains.

The Garden Route is not on many visitors' itineraries. It's off the tourist path and offers many unusual and unheralded attractions—and that is what makes it well worth the experience.

Sabi Sabi in Kruger National Park

Sabi Sabi, Kruger National Park leopard, Photo: Mary L. Peachin

Guide Andrew Viljoen loaded his 458-bolt action rifle as he got out of the Land Rover. My heart skipped a beat. Four of us were going to follow him on a hike through Sabi Sands bush. Located in South Africa's Kruger National Park, the area is home to the "Big Five": leopard, elephant, rhino, Cape buffalo, and lion.

The head guide of Sabi Sabi Earth Lodge doesn't mince words: "I've spent hundreds of hours in the bush and have only been charged several times. Walk single file, be quiet, listen to my commands, and whatever you do, don't run!" Bushwalking in the southern veld doesn't give you the same sense of security as riding in a Land Rover. Walking, would allow us to observe critters that we would not see from the vehicle. My adrenaline was flowing.

It was early fall, and the aerial roots of the leopard orchid hung between branches of an acacia tree. A poisonous apple's red bud was in bloom. While turning over rocks to look for scorpions, we only found millipedes and a lone frog. Euphorbia has a poisonous milky substance. Locals use it as an ingredient to kill fish and other animals. African wattle's softness makes it a handy plant that, in an emergency, can be used for toilet paper.

Signs of game were everywhere. Our eyes focused on our surroundings. We learned about animal behavior: Hippos scatter their excrement, elephants dig for roots, and rhinos mark their territory with urine.

As we exited Nelspruit's thatched-roof airport, the gateway to Kruger, to drive several hours to Sabi Sabi's Earth Lodge, a herd of impala pranced across the road, as if to whet our appetite. The road to the national park, designated in the 1890s, is lined by eucalyptus trees, fields of macadamia nuts, avocado, lychee, and citrus groves. Banana trees, living one year, shelter younger trees sprouting in their shadows. Purple flowers of the jacaranda tree stood tall next to the brilliant fuchsia blooms of massive bougainvillea trees.

We had entered Kruger at Sabi Sands River Shaw gate. Since the lodge is not protected by electric fencing, we were advised to call for an escort for our evening's dinner walk from our room to the main lodge.

Before sunrise, we were on safari the following day. Animals are most active early in the day. We spent three hours four wheeling in a fortified, six-passenger Land Rover with guide Andrew Viljoen. Louie Mkansi, known as one of the best trackers in the park, sat on the front right seat adjacent overlooking the hood. He used a stick to guide Andrew as he carefully looked for animal tracks along the road. In the first few hours, we saw a black belly bustard, kudu, impala, weaver nests hanging in acacia trees, and a common duiker displaying its curly horns. Stopping near an aramurela tree, which is used to make alcohol, Andrew held his rifle during our stop for tea and biscuits. A lone lioness lay in the bush with three cubs. We passed a white rhino, and saw the seldom-observed-in-the-open large-plated lizard sunning on a rock. That afternoon we saw two more white rhino, impala, a warthog, a dark brown Walberg nested eagle with her mate, and white-faced whistling ducks.

Sabi Sands' 50,000 acres was formerly the Eastern Transvaal/Lowveld. It is now called Mpumalanga, and over the years has been increased in size by the conversion of adjacent farms. In 1884, South African President Kruger made it a wildlife sanctuary.

Kruger is paved, so safaris vehicles are forbidden to go off road. We see wildebeest in the distance. A yellow hornbill covers her nest to feed the female with chicks through hole. The Land Rover encountered an adult leopard waking down road periodically spraying to mark. Down the track a hyena trotted in hopes of scavenging a kill. We saw a bachelor herd of half a dozen Cape buffalo, one with a bloody tail, had obviously escaped a kill the night before. Returning to the lodge, we saw a Nile crocodile in front of the lake.

The morning of our last safari, a pride of 20 lions were eating a recently killed buffalo. The first thing they eat are the eyes. We wondered if the buffalo was with the buffalo we had seen with the bloodied tail. A female lion crossed the valley with five cubs to join the pack as they roared and tore at the hide. A cub with the buffalo's tail crouched under a bush. Young adult males fought over choice bits. It was gruesome, but still an awesome sight.

Part XVI.

Culinary Adventures

Travelers are often warned, "Don't eat the street food, and don't drink tap water." I don't do the latter, and for the former, I rely on trustworthy guides who can vouch for a vendor's hygiene and cleanliness.

There was a time, when I was flying frequently to Mexico, that whenever I crossed the border it seemed that I would come down with a bout of *turista*." Fortunately, those days are over.

71. Street Eats of Old Quarter Hanoi

Hanoi culinary tour dried beef salad, Photo: Mary L. Peachin

Bluntly, I asked guide Windy Phong, "Are we going to get sick?" He explained "Not with me, I only go to places that are clean." We had to place our trust in Windy, an experienced guide, who serves as a consultant and culinary adviser for Chef Martin Yan, a Vietnam television host.

We arranged to meet Windy after viewing Hanoi's iconic Thang Long water puppet theater, probably the city's top tourist attraction. Popular folklore figures bob along in the theater's small pond, the bars that control them hidden underwater while the operators stay behind a screen.

Our eight tastings on Windy's culinary street tour through Hanoi's Old Quarter began with Ms. Huyen, who struggles to raise and educate two children. She makes more than 1,000 spring rolls daily, which she sells for thirty cents each. Mixing bean sprouts, cilantro, basil, vermicelli, other fresh vegetables and pork, she wraps then flash-fries them before serving. Steaming hot and served with a chili dipping sauce, they are served in waxed paper. She is frequently asked to cater parties.

Dodging motorcycles, cars, and other pedestrians, we stopped next at Long VJ Durg. A green papaya and dried beef salad called Du Du was served chilled. Accompaniments included cilantro, basil, bean sprouts, vinegar and chili sauce.

After stirring the papaya with the jerky-like meat, the flavor was enhanced. Having spent two weeks in Asia without eating any salad, we devoured it eagerly. The Du Du was accompanied with grilled quail, including its head, cooked in a special moc mat seasoning.

In Vietnam and other Asian countries, it is a cultural tradition to eat half-hatched 14-day duck eggs. Since it takes 28 days to hatch an egg, the halfway point, according to the philosophy of yin and yang, is said to provide balanced energy. This tasting, half egg and half embryonic duck, might have overwhelmed Bizarre Foods' Andrew Zimmern. It was a course we couldn't stomach.

Grilled catfish was served on the second floor of a small restaurant, our first foray indoors. The fish was grilled tableside with a seasoning of galangal – similar to ginger – and turmeric. We added onion, dill, cilantro, and vermicelli in making our rice paper rolls.

The next stop was at one of Hanoi's most popular corner. Bia hoi, a freshly-brewed beer, is particularly beloved in the north (Vietnamese drink more than 3 billion liters of beer a year.) Our street side joint purportedly served Hanoi's best local draft beer. As we sat on small plastic stools, a light rain began to fall. We toasted one another with our mugs and ate freshly boiled shelled peanuts and rice crackers.

Pao Zi is similar to a Chinese bun. The light fluffy white dough is filled with pork, mushroom, glass noodles, onions, and a quail egg. Tummies full, we nibbled at the filling.

Our next stop was Hanoi's best eel vendor, where we ate a common dish of the Red River Delta.

After eating fresh fruit salad in coconut milk along the street, stuffed to the gills, we headed down a dark alley. Fortunately, Windy had a flashlight to help us navigate. Families lived along each side of the three-foot-wide passageway. Windy had done a personal census, and based on a massive tangle of electrical wires, he counted 120 families lived there. Combination bath and kitchens, were separated from living quarters, and shared by multiple families.

Had we not been stuffed, hot, and tired, Windy would have offered more tastings. We missed the French bread Vietnamese hamburger. Its ingredients include a fried egg with goose liver pate, roast pork, cilantro, and cucumber, all served with a spicy chili sauce.

The finale was weasel coffee. The animal eats coffee fruit (cacao) and the beans come out the other end, allegedly more potent. Expensive by Vietnamese standards, it is considered one of the world's strongest coffees.

Windy's culinary tour combines the flavors of fresh ingredients and the spices of Vietnamese, French and Chinese cultures. Try it, if you dare.

72. A Wok Around Vancouver's Chinatown

Sun Yat Sen Garden, Vancouver, Photo: Mary L Peachin

Bob Sung's tour is a labor of love, one in which this third-generation Vancouverite shares family roots blended with his Chinese cultural history.

During the frenetic days of the mid-1800s gold rush, Vancouver's Chinese population was confined to a restricted ghetto. Only in recent years has this City's Chinatown been identified by a colorful new Pender Street welcome entry gate. It is known for its classical gardens, historic landmarks, exotic and diverse foods, ethnic cookware, and exotic herbal medicine shops.

Sung's grandfather migrated to Vancouver in 1910. He was an English translator for the Chinese community and also participated in the Chinese Times Newspaper. In the same year, Dr. Sun Yat Sen came to Vancouver to initiate the fundraising campaign for the 1911 Chinese Revolution. After the revolution, China went from imperial rule to become a democratic country. Dr. Sun became the first president of the Republic of China. This historic background makes it appropriate that the tour begins in the garden named after Dr. Sun, who became a revered revolutionary and political leader in China.

Dr. Sun Yat-sen Classical Chinese Garden is a classical Suzhou garden that exemplifies the three Chinese Philosophical Traits of Taoist, Confucius, and Buddhist beliefs

Fifty-three artisans built the Classical Garden without the use of nails. A bracketing technique was used to join teak and camphor wood imported from China. The horizontal rooftop beam ends are pointed up "to prevent evil spirits from entering." The garden features elements of yin and yang. Symbolic plants include bamboo for strength and flexibility, and gingko trees for longevity. Visitors find solace, some taking time to meditate or gracefully perform a few of the hundred movements of tai chi. Bob explains philosophical interpretations seen in the different elements of architecture that many visitors would overlook.

After leaving the Garden, the tour heads to the nearby corner of Carrall and Pender Streets, both major Chinatown streets. The intersection is home to the Sam Kee Building. Built in 1913, this sliver, said to be the world's narrowest freestanding building, is registered with "Ripley's Believe It or Not" and the "Guinness Book of World Records".

A stop at Ming Wo Cookware gives Bob the opportunity to talk about the history and use of the Chinese wok. Forged of carbon steel, the wok needs to be cleaned and seasoned before use. Bob cautions never to cook using olive oil: "It burns quickly." Peanut oil is preferred!! After the wok is seasoned, garlic and ginger — is peeled then chopped — bringing the basic flavors for cooking most Chinese dishes. Most wok cooking is either by stir-frying or by steaming (medium amount of water in wok to steam the food in a covered ribbed bamboo basket)

Walking down Pender Street, we hear opera music from second-floor windows along with clicking mahjongg tiles from games being played at the Wing Sang, the oldest building in Chinatown. The owner, Mr. Yip Sang, was a prominent Chinatown merchant who built the building to make it his business and family compound.

During a stop at Newtown Bakery, grumbling tummies are given a treat of buttery, fresh-baked apple tarts. A thousand tarts are sold daily along with steamed buns, egg-custard tarts, and tapioca-and-rice cakes.

At Guo Hua Herbal Medicine store, Bob tells us about traditional Chinese remedies. The majority of these dried ingredients are consumed in soups or tea. Conpoy scallops are said to improve urinary tract or kidney function, gecko lizard is used for asthma or high fevers, shark's fin is considered a remedy for various cancers, and Asian cliff-dwelling swallows for birds' nests, made from bird saliva, is considered to improve libido, alleviate asthma, improve focus, and enhance the immune system. These items can sell in the hundreds of dollars for several ounces. As food and medicine are considered important aspects of Chinese culture, most ingredients are used for preparations of both.

Stopping to browse a store window filled with Chinese symbolic items, we see "joss" incense sticks and "hoong bow" red envelopes. The sticks are to be lit in temples to send acknowledgments and to show respect to ancestors. The red envelopes are used to gift money to young children and newlyweds as a sign of abundance and good fortune. There are also elaborate paper effigies of money, food and clothing which are burned at the temple as offerings to the ancestors

It is time for another snack as we watch Bob's friendly butcher slice chunks of barbecued pork. A few stores down, there are tanks of live seafood, followed by shops filled with fruits and vegetables. There is gai lan or Chinese broccoli, bok choy, soft and medium-firm tofu, ginger root, guava, mangoes, mangosteen, and oranges and kumquats, the latter two symbolic of wealth or abundance. The Chinese tradition of bearing gifts of oranges when visiting friends means bestowing abundance upon them.

Cured Chinese Sausage "Lup Cheung" and Soy-cured Pork Belly "Lap Yook," Photo: Mary L. Peachin

Finally, it is time for our highly anticipated dim sum lunch. It is great to have a large enough group, similar to those enjoyed by many Chinese families, to be able to taste so many delicacies. Fumbling with our chopsticks, we enjoyed "har gow" (shrimp dumplings), "eye gwa" (minced shrimp with Asian eggplant), and "ngoh my faun" (sticky rice wrapped in bamboo leaf). There is "foong jow" (braised chicken feet), "lo bahk goh" (steamed daikon or white radish cake), and "Suen joh guen" (tofu skin rolled with enoki mushrooms and black fungus). It is a feast.

The tour wouldn't be complete without a tea-full goodbye. At the Chinese Tea Shoppe, the Tea Master demonstrates the method of preparing green, oolong, pu-erh and black teas. He tells us, "Restorative ginseng tea is an expensive, acquired taste."

Inspired by an awareness of the public's ignorance about Chinatown, Bob Sung developed this cultural and culinary tour motivated by a proud century of local history. He realized that "these bustling Chinatown streets could be overwhelming to the uninformed." He's right, and we walk away satiated and better informed. As we say goodbye to Bob and Chinatown, we are grateful to him for helping us to better understand the significance of Chinese culture as well as its hustle and bustle.

73. Barcelona's Gràcia, the Trail of Pilgrims

Barcelona, on the Mediterranean coast of northeast Spain, has long been a popular destination, known for its scenic location, wonderful tapas and fresh seafood. It is the capital city of Catalonia, an "autonomous community" of the country.

Perhaps its most famous attraction is Basílica i Temple Expiatori de la Sagrada Família, commonly called Sagrada Família, or Holy Family. Designed by Catalan architect Antoni Gaudí

(1852–1926), the Roman Catholic church has yet to be completed. Visitors stand in line for hours to view this UNESCO World Heritage Site, which in 2010 Pope Benedict XVI consecrated and proclaimed a minor basilica.

Barcelona's other top tourist attraction is its tin-roofed public market, Mercat de Sant Josep de la Boqueria — simply referred to as La Boqueria — whose modest entrance faces La Rambla, a tree-lined pedestrian mall. The market dates to 1217, when meat products were sold from tables near the old city gate.

During a spring visit, we ventured off the tourist path with a Culinary Backstreets tour, meandering as we nibbled our way along the streets of Gràcia, a neighboring district of Barcelona.

Carmelite novitiates established a convent, Nostra Senyora de Gràcia, or Our Lady of Grace, in 1626. The independent municipality was annexed by Barcelona in 1897.

Six of us met up with Paula Mourenza, our guide, at a local bank for a five-hour walking tour along narrow, cobblestoned streets lined with interesting architecture and colorfully painted buildings. Following a path used several centuries ago as a pilgrimage route, we passed a colorful home known as the Calmata House. The builder was a follower of Gaudí's.

Our first stop was at Churreria. Open twenty-four hours, the narrow shop serves churros — fried dough dipped in sugar — using a recipe dating to the Middle Ages. Dough made of hard wheat flour is adjusted to account for ambient temperature and humidity. A close eye is kept on the temperature while the dough is fried in a combination of peanut, sunflower and olive oils, all of which have a high smoke point. It is alleged that churro dough was found in the tomb of Ramses II. Egyptian iron miners have been credited with first bringing churros to Spain.

By late morning we arrived at La Pubilla, built in 1912 as a traditional restaurant. Today it is considered a bistro and features a specialty of "breakfast with pork" served with beer or Cava (Spanish sparkling wine), and eggs with chorizo, paprika, rosemary, and honey.

Established in 1885, Graner Sala, one of the oldest shops in Barcelona, sells many varieties of nuts and vegetables. Along the way to Mercat de L'Abaceria we passed the central village square, Plaça de la Vila de Gràcia, noted for its beautiful clock tower.

Crème de Patisserie, an unrestored 19th century bakery, serves up pure dark chocolate-covered almonds and hazelnuts. Catalonia was the entryway for introducing chocolate into Europe.

Barcelona markets are filled with racks that hang Iberian hams, easily recognized by their black hoof, distinctive leg shape, and dark meat — a product of the black pig's acorn diet. The hams of this ancient breed require from twelve to as many as forty-eight months to cure, and there are several grades of quality.

Mercat de L'Abaceria shrimp and fresh fish, Photo: Mary L. Peachin

Mercat de L'Abaceria offered us the opportunity for a tasting frenzy. There were many kinds of both cow and goat cheeses and a variety of sausages. Olives were green and black; sweet, spicy, and briny. We learned about the process of making salt cod. Prior to refrigeration, the process was a necessity.

We were stuffed by the time we arrived at Cal Boter restaurant for lunch. Served family style, the meal included artichokes, marinated onions, and escargots. Snail tails are bitter, so we ate the heads, after dipping them in butter. The main course was a salt cod, rich with a mayonnaise and tomato sauce.

Before saying goodbye, we stopped at La Vermuteria del Tano for a vermouth tasting followed by a visit to La Bodega lo Pinyol, a tapas bar serving semi-seco (medium dry) cava.

It was a full day — one filled with history, many new tastes, and tired feet.

74. Oaxaca's Markets with Mucho Mole

Oaxaca fresh mole, Photo: Mary L Peachin

¡Proteínas! Oaxaca's cuisine is flavorful and unique. High on everyone's list for munchies are *chicatanas* and *chapulines*, crispy salty black ants and grasshoppers, addictive like potato chips. Oaxaca is even better known for its seven varieties of spicy to savory and chocolate-flavored mole sauces.

Suzanne Barbezet, owner of Oaxaca-Guides, led us on a four-hour street and market food tour. She buys only from personally tested vendors.

Oaxaca City's Mercado Sanchez Pascuas is home to Tamales Cande. Corn husks bulging with chicken, beans, and *salsa verde* are Cande's specialty.

A young boy outside the market is selling *nicuatole*. Indigenous to Oaxaca, this corn-based gelatinous dessert is frequently filled with chunks of fresh coconut.

La Cosecha (The Harvest) is considered an organic market. Sitting at a plastic checker-clothed table, we sipped *agua fresca*, a cool passionfruit drink. Our drinks were served with *memelitas*, blue tortillas with soft tops and crispy bottoms, filled with squash, peppers, and a delicious corn smut or fungus called *huitlacoche*.

Oaxaca crickets chapulinas, Photo: Mary L Peachin

Tortas La Hormiga serves the Mexican equivalent of a sandwich made with chorizo and cheese and many other fillings for tortas. Hormiga used to be a food cart at Conzatti Park, a well-manicured place where people picnic, get their shoes shined, or just relax on benches.

Mercado Benito Juárez, Oaxaca City's primary market, was our next stop. We sat at a crowded counter tasting a bowl of tejate. The refreshing drink's primary ingredient is cacao, which foams when stirred. It also includes corn, tea of mamey, a flower called *rosita de cac*ao, and *agua de chilacayota*. This nutritious, filling drink is also indigenous to Oaxaca.

20th of November Market (the date the 1910 Mexican Revolution began) offered *pan de yema* (a sweet bread made with eggs) and *pan de Casuelade Tlacolula*, baked with chocolate, raisins and cinnamon.

Sitting at a long table at Carnes Asadas Juquilita's, Suzanne selected a variety of thinly sliced beef, pork, and chorizo. As the meat grilled, we were serenaded by a guitar player. A frail, elderly woman was selling handmade toy tarantulas on a string. Purchasing one from her, I saw her cross herself. It was her first sale of the day.

Our final stop was Mayordomo La Casa del Chocolate, a chocolate store. Cacao, or chocolate, goes through two grinders with sugar typically added for mole or hot chocolate.

Muy llenos – quite full – we learned about Oaxacan food from an expert. Now David and I are craving mole.

75. Mexico City's Mercados La Merced and Jamaica

Among Mexico City's markets, La Merced and Jamaica are two of the most popular, the latter open 24 hours a day. Mingled between aisles of meat-carving butchers are merchants selling spice, vegetable-sellers, and lots of other items.

Everyone shares space with food vendors who hawk everything from tamales to tortas. You can't go wrong spending a few minutes ducking into any market you see, but La Merced, a commercial hub since the seventeenth century, and Jamaica attracts the most visitors.

No matter how much "se habla Español," it's worthwhile to join a Culinary Backstreets tour. They offer expert guides, easily navigate the twisting maze of narrow and confusing passageways, know the best vendors, which mole stand offers free samples, or simply provide names to unknown fruits, vegetables, and food stalls spread over acres in the market.

Dozens of packed booths can be found along the main food-stall drag, a place where market workers and shoppers gather at all hours to eat caldo de gallina (chicken stew), fresh tacos, pancita (a stew-like soup made from tripe found in the cow's stomach), or rich, pork posole soup.

Food vendors eventually give way to the meat section, where you can buy una vaca entera (a whole cow) for several thousand pesos or, for those less ambitious, a freshly hacked butcher's steak or chop as they show off their carving skills. If cow head is of interest stop by one of the vendors selling tacos de cabeza. The meat is sliced and steamed to order. Nothing goes to waste or is uneaten on any animal brought to a Mexico market.

Prickly pear cactus is a popular Mexican food item. Known as nopales, vendors spend hours scraping and removing its spines. Specialty vendors sell crisp-fried insects including crickets, grasshoppers, ants and escamoles (ant larvae) as well as tiny crayfish. Chicken intestines (cleaned, cured, and cooked) may look unsettlingly, but they taste like the richest, most savory bite of chicken you've ever eaten.

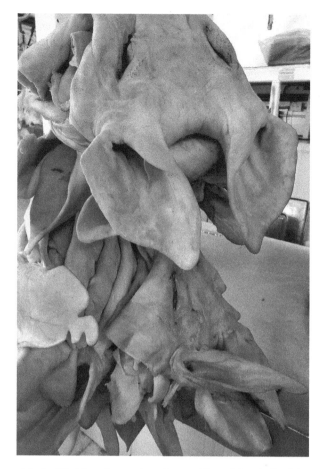

Mexico City's Jamaica market, pig ears, Photo: Mary L. Peachin

Hours can be spent watching mole made from scratch. Another option is visiting a market mole vendor, where rows of intensely flavored pastes are sold by the kilo.

Along the street outside the market, vendors sell sweets. A half-dozen stands attract customers to towering chunks of candied fruit attracting swarms of bees and flies.

While most of the market is dedicated to food and food-related products, there's a vast tianguis (open-air market) surrounding the official footprint of La Merced, that may as well be part of the market proper. There, you'll find everything from calendars to piñatas to cheap, made-in-China off-brand sneakers.

Francisco "Paco" de Santiago, a resident or "chilango" of Mexico City knows the area well. In addition to the markets, he points out historical places like the Señor de la Humildad Chapel, architectural landmarks, an historic cantina. He asks us to put away cameras, while taking a short cut down a street lined with hookers.

There is so much to see that days are required if you find yourself submerged in this interesting area of Mexico's past and present.

We were fortunate to have a taste of Mexico City's cuisine with cookbook author Christine Potters. Suzanna, our Oaxaca guide, introduced us. While Cristine didn't have any scheduled tours during our stay, we did enjoy dining with her in the outdoor patio of Azul Historico.

A colorful parakeet nibbled bird seed from the palm of my hand. When his tasty treat was finished, he hopped back to his cage platform to pick up a folded written fortune for me. Fortune-telling birds are a traditional part of Mexican restaurant dining. It was fun, and after the first fortune is read, the bird's handler might ask, "Want to see the rest of your fortune? Just give him whatever money you think is right, and the bird will eat more from you hand, then pull another fortune for you."

Rough-hewn wooden tables in a stone courtyard of a 17th-century palace were surrounded by a canopy of tall trees draped with lights. A native woman prepared handmade tortillas served warm in baskets.

We were being introduced to mezcal and other Mexican delicacies, which vary from the local Tucson Sonoran cuisine we eat. David, my husband, being a more adventurous eater drank his mezcal straight from a hand-carved gourd. I had a frozen mezcalita mixed with tamarindo that had a closer resemblance to a margarita.

Fortunate to have Christine Potters expertise, it was a jumping night with people still in costume from the day's celebration of Dia de Los Muertos. It was a great way to begin our five-day November culinary visit to Mexico City.

Part XV.

Falling in Love in Vancouver

Vancouver Royal Yacht Club in Stanley Park, Photo: Mary L. Peachin

Like many love affairs, this one was totally spontaneous. Escaping the summer heat of Tucson, David and I initially thought of Vancouver as our gateway to remote fly fishing. For three years we spent a few days in the city before heading to the wilderness. And in the process, we became "hooked"—not just on the fishing, but also smitten with Vancouver.

David and I fell hard, arriving at our feelings about Vancouver from different directions. Returning from one fishing trip, David and Jeffrey attended the 1986 World Expo. Staying in one of the few available nameless, unremarkable hotels, they were very expressed with Expo, and more so with Vancouver.

I was recruited by Canada Media Market and spent almost a decade fishing at upscale fishing camps to write stories for US publications. While traveling in and out of Vancouver, they put me up at the former Delta Pinnacle hotel where manager Philip Barnes always gave me a "room with a view." My "desk" overlooked the busy harbour.

Doormen Patrick Kosi (now the Head Doorman at Fairmont's Pacific Rim, and his associate, Raul parked my bike in the luggage closet, and they looked out for me. Vancouver was having a transit strike my first summer so my transportation was on two wheels. My regular dining spot, Cardero's, was about six blocks away. I found it comforting to know that if I didn't return by 9 pm, somebody would miss me.

One day, I looked down at the street and saw dirt. Checking out the sign, I called the number to ask, "What are you building?" The reply was condos, and my response "I want to buy one." Living with a CPA, I never made any real estate or other investments. David was cool with the idea. At that point, we had little to lose.

The condos wouldn't be for sale for six months, but they called as I requested. We looked over their web presentation, picked out the floor plan we liked, made a deposit, and were given six weeks to visit Vancouver to check it out in their now opened sales office.

The purchase turned out to be like winning a lottery. A prime spot in Coal Harbour, now one of Vancouver's most prestigious downtown neighborhoods.

During our three year wait, we rented a nearby apartment for a month for two summers to see if we liked city high-rise life.

When the building finally opened in 2001, the doormen, Patrick and Raul, hauled our clothes on hotel racks three blocks down Hastings street.

There was no infrastructure, a mail box, or any stores in the area. Today we have everything. Our anticipated tiny view of the harbour extends over Stanley Park and the marina.

Our Shanghai neighbor, Flora Wei, gave up her medical practice to give her son the finest education. Her husband commuted for visits. When we asked them what they were going when Tony graduated to attend Colombia, Jeffrey replied, "There is no place in the world like Coal Harbour." We agree with him.

Part XVI.

"Getting Old is Not for Sissies"

Bette Davis

76. My Orthopedic Surgeon "Fired" Me

"Moaning and groaning" are commonplace in senior social circles. The men in my husband David's ski group, now celebrating their 30th-plus annual trip, have established a time limit — a trip total of five minutes is all that's allowed to share stories about their aches and pains. Those conversations might include updates about Jim's new hip, Mark's upcoming knee replacement, or Ed's pending surgery and his need to borrow a walker.

Over the past 75-plus years, I have been fortunate to have had many great experiences, and a hell of a good time, wearing out my joints. I was Tucson's 25-yard Himmel Park freestyle-swim champion at the age of six. I swam for the YMCA at Davis-Monthan Air Force Base's pool, played USTA intercity tennis, spent snowy weekends swooshing — and tumbling — down Mt. Lemmon's ski slope, and enjoyed horseback riding at El Conquistador Hotel's stable, the site of present-day El Con Mall.

By the time my joints were approaching middle age, I was competing in international bill-fishing release tournaments and going scuba diving, and still do both. The latter is generally joint-friendly, but schlepping scuba gear and hauling myself out of the water as quickly as possible when nearby sharks are "shopping for takeout" is challenging.

Tennis elbow was my first joint issue. The second was deterioration of my right shoulder. Following a series of X-rays, I was shocked to learn I had no cartilage in ANY of my major joints.

Down the orthopedic path I crept, with a strong wind pushing me from behind. Under the care of an orthopedic surgeon in Tucson, I received cortisone injections and anti-inflammatory drugs, which relieved the pain for a while. During summers, I received physical therapy in Vancouver, B.C.

About 15 years ago, my Tucson surgeon gave me an ultimatum: "Don't come back to see me until you're ready to have *BOTH* shoulders replaced. No more cortisone or drugs." To be truthful, I've been thrown out of some nice places, but this toss was a bit scary, and I landed hard. Seeking a less-frightening path, I did some serious due diligence with references coming from Vancouver, Chicago, and Tucson. That led me to Rick Matsen, Head of Orthopedic Surgery at the University of Washington. He told me he could extend the life of my shoulder — to which I was personally attached — by doing a "clean and ream" of the troubled joint. Sounded like a reasonable solution so I flew to Seattle.

Dr. Matsen actually gave me seven years. My doctor in Vancouver — while giving me another cortisone shot — said, "Mary, you've been suffering with this shoulder for 10 years. Why don't you take care of it while you're in such good shape?"

It wasn't long before my University of Washington surgeon, Rick Matsen, made me the wide-eyed owner of a brand-new titanium right shoulder. (Gosh, I've surpassed my five minutes of moaning and groaning, and I haven't even complained about my deteriorating hips.)

When it was time for a new hip, Matsen referred me to another Seattle physician — his daughter — who had replaced his hip. Several weeks later, sedated with a spinal block and propofol, I was on Laura Matsen Ko's operating table being introduced to my new hip.

Six months later, when my other hip retired, I was given only a week's notice because Dr. Ko was preparing for her own new arrival — a baby. Before and after my hip surgeries, I worked hard in physical therapy — and still do — strengthening my core. It has paid off.

Two years ago, I came in third in the International Women's Billfish Tournament in Guatemala. I continue to work as a travel writer, and I'm writing this article while returning from Oaxaca, Mexico, where I ate *chapulines* (grasshoppers) and *chicatanas* (flying ants). Shortly, I'll be headed to Guerrero, Mexico, where I will roosterfish along the Zihuantanejo surf, then to Baja, Mexico, where I will snorkel with whale sharks and scuba dive.

My left shoulder, the cartilage gone forever, occasionally grates, but it remains basically painless. The shoulder might look awful on an X-ray, but it's still on the job. I hope the surgical part of my becoming bionic is over, but I continue to learn how to live with my replacement parts.

However, adjusting to my bionic body hasn't been without challenges. Anyone who has had a joint replaced probably has some lingering disability issues. I was mortified to have anyone see me using a walker or a wheelchair. I tossed the walker within a week of hip surgery, but initially, for about a month, a wheelchair was a necessity if I had to traverse any large airport. Hurray for our cozy Tucson International Airport, which I have always been able to navigate on my own. I'm not happy with the continual TSA pat-downs when my titanium and porcelain joints light up on their security screens, but I am happy that I recently was able to conquer conquered a 17-hour flight from Athens, and I am ready to tackle more travel challenges, glowing as I go through security.

My long-time friend, spinning buddy, and now retired physician Lori Mackstaller has always told me, "Mary, you have never been easy on your body so remember every time you hurt, how much fun you had wearing out your joints! It WAS worth it."

77. It's All About the Core

Since age six, I have competed in swimming, soon expanding my training with tennis competitions. Training was always part of my regular routine. When my children went to nursery school, I scheduled in nine holes of golf and an hour of tennis before they returned home.

Over the years, I participated in several rough-water swims in La Jolla, and a half-triathlon in Rosarito, Baja. Two of my friends flew in my airplane to San Diego, and we rode our bicycles to a nearby hotel. If I had to have a flat tire, it happened leaving the airport and not in the race. The three of us had arranged a driver to take us to the Mexican village.

79. My Tiny Pillow and Travel Tips

Luggage for two, packing light, Photo: Mary L Peachin

Men started the race first and I saw them run in, turn around, and walk out of the pounding surf. When my turn came, I found exiting the water more of a challenge. The 12-mile bike ride went fine, but the 2-mile run was a different story. I was never a runner. My two friends, and bystanders along the street, cheered as I made the two-hour qualification for a medal — barely.

My tennis team was great fun. One year my partner and I won the city doubles trophy. Another year, our team went to regionals in Phoenix in August. The court surface was so hot, at around 110 degrees, that our soles were melting. In high school, I played for Tucson High.

After graduation, I became a real "gym rat." I worked out in a different place every day with membership in only one club for a mere $16 a month. That's because I brought those gyms an entire spin class when my place closed.

For a decade I was an evening speaker on adventure travel for Canyon Ranch, one of the top spas in the country. They gave me the choice of a honorarium or a day at the spa. Using the latter, I found the latest in equipment and classes. I went from one class to another and ended the day with a massage. Then they discontinued the evening speaking program. Their guests were exhausted from their daylong workout.

I would like to think I was responsible for getting two of the staff to open a spin studio, an addictive aerobic bicycle class. It became so popular that many of the gyms offered it. I also had my own personal trainer.

Whoever said, "Getting old is not for sissies" nailed it. Aches and pains and getting up slowly in the morning have replaced hopping out of bed. I continue to train privately in Pilates and gyrotonics and feel every cent is well spent.

John White, formerly head of Pilates at Canyon Ranch, is the greatest. He has worked around my fragile joints and replacements, strengthening my core beyond my surgeon's belief. A strong core allows your joints to move more efficiently, relieving some of the stress of repetitive action.

Sam Prouty has done the same using gyrotonics, a more-stretching and strengthening of the core muscles. Philip Seth has done the same for me in Vancouver. Both have offered online instruction during the pandemic. All are master instructors.

Keeping fit is key to staying healthy, and I for one, am keen on staying that way.

There are many places that actually ask your preference on the type of pillow you want. That's not an issue with me. My pillow, like me, has been around the world.

It's a small airline-size, actually Japan Airlines, that lives in my small suitcase. When I return home, I wash the case, and back it goes in the top of my suitcase, ready for the next trip.

These days, there is nothing consistent about commercial airplanes. While currently empty due to the coronavirus, they are usually packed full, routes are less direct, airfares are higher, and fees for checked luggage are on the rise. Let's face it—travel has become less fun and more of an ordeal. But there are ways to minimize the hassle and the cost. Some are common sense; others are less obvious.

Ticket cost is often the deciding factor when making airline reservations, but there are other flight criteria to consider when calculating value and travel experience: the type of aircraft, the flight times, services provided, and the flight's on-time service record. Most of that information can be found on an airline's website as you peruse the flight options. But be sure to bring your patience to the search, because finding the information isn't always easy to find.

Although online travel search engines, like Kayak, and some airlines still package roundtrip flight options, it has been a number of years since I booked a roundtrip ticket. I opt for one-way flights so I can pick and choose the times and connections that are most convenient for me. Often the least expensive roundtrip packages include a red-eye or late-night flight or a long layover, which is why they are less expensive. These days, there is seldom a discount offered solely for booking a roundtrip ticket.

On a route I routinely fly—San Francisco to Vancouver, British Columbia—Air Canada and United codeshare a flight. Both airlines offer a flight that departs San Francisco from the same gate, time, date and arrives in Vancouver at the same time. How can that be?

Code sharing, or codeshare, is an agreement between airlines to fly one aircraft on a route but market it separately under each airline's own designator and flight number. The codeshare is often revealed on an airline's published schedule, with the words "operated by" and the name of the code sharing airline written beneath the flight number.

For example, if you purchase a ticket from United for travel on a United/Air Canada code sharing flight, your ticket will have a United flight number, but the aircraft on that route might be operated by Air Canada. These travel arrangements can have benefits and drawbacks. They can make it easier to book a trip on a single airline and to handle baggage transfers. But they can also prevent you from earning frequent-flyer miles for the flight, enjoying other frequent-flyer perks, and making connections. Do your research. Details vary by airline.

Recently, I ran into trouble with code-sharers United and Turkish Air when I was booking a trip from Tucson to Istanbul for my husband and myself. United was routing me from Tucson to Newark, New Jersey, to Istanbul. A route from Tucson to Houston and then connecting with the nonstop Turkish Air flight from Houston to Istanbul would have been a much better option for us. So, I booked a United round-trip Tucson/Houston flight and then a separate roundtrip Houston/Istanbul ticket on Turkish Air. United brusquely informed me that it wouldn't transfer my luggage from the United flight to the Turkish Air flight in Houston. Our response? We booked the flight schedule we preferred and carried on our luggage. The key is to *travel light*.

There can be other concerns when booking your trip from point A to point B on two different airlines, as we did to Istanbul. The airlines will not have a record of your connecting flight, and if arrival and/or departure times change, it could prevent you from successfully making a connection. If you miss a connection and are stranded midway through your route, you will be responsible for rebooking and purchasing another ticket to get you to your destination.

Several programs are available to help you navigate security systems and expedite screening. Speedy screening can make the difference between making or missing a connection and can save frequent travelers hours of waiting in security lines. Become familiar with U.S. Customs and Border Protection Trusted Traveler programs: Global Entry, NEXUS, SENTRI, and TSA Precheck.

Global Entry expedites the screening and entry of pre-approved, low-risk international travelers coming into the United States through select airports. NEXUS allows prescreened travelers expedited processing when entering the United States and Canada. SENTRI (Secure Electronic Network for Travelers Rapid Inspection) is a program similar to NEXUS but applies to entry into the United States from Mexico along U.S./Mexico border ports.

TSA Precheck is an expedited security screening program for U.S. citizens. Air passengers considered low-risk who qualify for the program can receive expedited screening either as a member of the program or another specific trusted traveler group.

There is some overlap between programs. All require pre-approval for membership and a nonrefundable fee. Applicants undergo a background check, a personal interview, fingerprinting or iris scanning, and photographing.

The weight and rolling ability of your suitcase could be critical to saving big bucks by allowing you to carry on your luggage and also avoiding overweight-baggage charges. Bags that roll easily and are lightweight and soft sided are easier to maneuver down the narrow aisles of an airplane and fit into overhead compartments.

Colorful bags are easily identified among the hundreds of black bags on the baggage carousel. Black bags can be personalized with bright-colored tape, ribbons, tags, and similar identifying features to help them stand out.

Pack clothes that can be easily washed and dried and do not require ironing. I travel with only a wheeled bag, a backpack, and my lunch bag. I pack only sample/travel-size creams and liquids that are 3.4 ounces or less and meet flight travel restrictions.

If you see me in an airport and I look as if I may be headed to the Arctic, it is because I am boarding a long flight and wearing two to three layers of clothes: the first layer is something comfy for sleeping, the second is a fleece top to keep me warm during the flight, and the third includes my heaviest coat, which I'll put in the overhead compartment. I'm also wearing the heaviest shoes I'll need for the trip.

If it's an outbound flight, I'm also likely to be lugging emergency snacks: I never travel without hard-boiled eggs, unsalted individually packed almonds, a protein bar or two, and dried fruit.

If I'm traveling with what appears to be a feast, possibly last night's dinner leftovers, you can be sure that I am not checking any luggage and need to make a quick connection. Airlines have never given me any grief over a carry on with food which covers more clothes, shoes that didn't fit into suitcase.

Yes, it's all a hassle but worth the trouble so I can keep on traveling.

78. Marrying an Adrenaline Junkie

On my way to the building laundry room, I ran into Mary in the garage. What an unlikely place to meet "the woman of my life." We had moved into adjacent apartment buildings on Chicago's Near North Side. Her roommate Patricia, a high school friend of mine, introduced us. We had several dates, then I went into an 18-month seclusion to study for the CPA exam.

It was a December afternoon when we had this fortuitous garage run-in.

I asked her for a date on New Year's Eve. The next two months the relationship became more serious, and we had lots of fun.

We took in a young Barbra Streisand at Mr. Kelly's, saw the original Temptations sing at a Southside Baptist church, cheered for the Chicago Cubs and Blackhawks. Water skiing on Wisconsin's Lake Geneva was a great weekend getaway, while catching smelt at Foster Avenue Beach was party time. We loved going to the Whitehall for a martini, Caesar salad, and hot fudge sundae — skip the entrée. Going dancing whenever we could, we headed to the lofty Pump Room bar in the Ambassador Hotel. Sliding up to the bar, Mary typically was offered a drink by an admiring gentleman, only to have him discover there were two of us. There was no cover charge to dance to the big band if you were sitting at the bar.

David releasing ocean run cutthroat on Atha River, Photo: Mary L Peachin

Mary told me in late February, 1965 that her dad was coming to town. Was he coming to check me out? Leon was awesome, impeccably dressed, a towering six-foot-four, handsome and charismatic man. I offered to take him to the airport when he left to return to Tucson. I was hoping that his head wouldn't hit the roof. We were in the same Volkswagen Beetle where, several weeks later, I asked Mary to marry me. Happily, when she said yes, I didn't drive off the expressway.

My parents were curious or skeptical or both. The next week we were flying to Tucson to introduce our families. Mary's parents didn't own a dry goods store, it was Levy's of Tucson. Her grandparents were not grocers. They owned Simon Brothers, a wholesale grocer with clients like Notre Dame and Sara Lee.

Not only was everyone happy with one another, Mary's maternal grandparents and mine became close friends and took vacation cruises until the tragic death of Mary's grandparents in Tucson's 1970 Pioneer Hotel fire, which killed 29 people.

Married June 1, 1965, we were parents a year later. Moving to a north shore Glencoe apartment for Suzie's birth, three years later, we bought our first home in Highland Park for Jeffrey's arrival.

When my parents retired to Florida, in 1970, we began thinking about warmer, sunny winters. Leon got wind of our thoughts of leaving Chicago. The next week I was offered the position of chief financial officer of Farmer's Investment Company, the largest farmer in Arizona. They owned the pecan orchards between Tucson and Green Valley.

I assume full responsibility for Mary taking flight, literally. I also bought her an 18-speed bicycle. We took one 45-mile downhill ride in Taos, New Mexico. The next thing I knew, that fall of 1983, she was riding 500 miles across Arizona.

While staying at my business partner's home in San Carlos, Mexico, Mary spent two entire days snorkeling. I signed her up for dive lessons and bought her all the gear. During tax season, when I was working every day of the week, she began her quest to dive the world. I didn't know in advance about her shark diving, but when I found out, I was proud of her.

A book offer brought her a new platform, as a travel writer and photographer. After 55 years, our family is still tight. Fly fishing is our "family sport." Throughout the years, I have traveled the world with her, all seven continents, but mostly above the ocean's surface, and usually not when she's on assignment.

Can I really describe this remarkable wife, mother, and grandmother, who gets high on adrenaline, whose middle name is "Fun?" I'll welcome your suggestions.

David F. Peachin

CPSIA information can be obtained
at www.ICGtesting.com
Printed in the USA
LVHW071510010423
743232LV00020B/1303